ON THE SEMANTICS OF SYNTAX

CROOM HELM LINGUISTICS SERIES
edited by Roger Lass

COREPRESENTATION OF GRAMMATICAL STRUCTURE
Michael B. Kac

ON CASE GRAMMAR
Prolegomena to a Theory of Grammatical Relations
John M. Anderson

DEFINITENESS AND INDEFINITENESS
A Study in Reference and Grammaticality Prediction
John A. Hawkins

ON THE SEMANTICS OF SYNTAX

MOOD AND CONDITION IN ENGLISH

EIRIAN C. DAVIES

CROOM HELM LONDON

HUMANITIES PRESS
Atlantic Highlands, N.J.

British Library Cataloguing in Publication Data

Davies, Eirian
    On the semantics of syntax.
    1. English language – Semantics
    I. Title
    422   PE1585

    ISBN 0–85664–642–3

First published in the USA 1979 by
Humanities Press, Atlantic Highlands, N.J.

Library of Congress Cataloging in Publication Data

Davies, Eirian.
    On the semantics of syntax.

    (Croom Helm linguistics series)
    A revision of the author's thesis, London, 1976.
    Bibliography: p.
    Includes index.
    1. English language – Mood. 2. English language
    – Semantics. 3. English language – Syntax.
    I. Title.
    PE1290.D3 1979   425   78–11943
    ISBN 0–391–00936–2

Printed and bound in Great Britain

CONTENTS

Preface

Symbols and Notational Conventions

1. Introduction   15
2. On Literal Meaning and 'Significance'   19
3. A Framework of Semantic Analysis   43
4. Decision   81
5. Telling   105
6. Knowledge   123
7. Performance   139
8. Condition and Reason   146
9. Conclusion   177

Appendix I   179
Appendix II   189
Bibliography   195
Index   202

FOR MY PARENTS

PREFACE

This book is a revised version of a PhD dissertation (University of London, 1976), which was begun in 1967. The kernel of the notions in Chapters 3, 4, 6 and 8 was presented in a paper 'On modal verbs and conditions in English' given at the Linguistics Association conference at York, April 1972. Much of the material on imperatives and interrogatives in Chapters 4 and 6 and Appendix I has been used in lectures which I gave as a member of the Department of English at the University of Wales Institute of Science and Technology at Cardiff (1967-72) and I am grateful to D.J. Young, my colleague there, for his encouragement, and also to the students who tested it out with me. The basis of Chapter 5 was given as a lecture in the Department of Language at York University in November 1973.

I am grateful to M.A.K. Halliday, who was my supervisor from 1964-7 and subsequently read earlier drafts of Chapters 3, 4 and 8 when I had no further claim on his time. My thanks are due to my colleague at Bedford, J.A.W. Kamp, who read and commented on the dissertation version of parts of Chapter 8, and to R. Lass of Edinburgh University for the many helpful comments he has made on the entire dissertation. My debt to Vivian Salmon, who was my first teacher in linguistics when I was her student at Bedford College, has been a continuing one since those days, and is very considerable. Finally, I have to thank Gwenna Howard who typed the manuscript and ensured that I finished it.

<table>
<tr><td>Bedford College,
University of London.

March 1978</td><td style="text-align:right; vertical-align:top">E.C.D.</td></tr>
</table>

SYMBOLS AND NOTATIONAL CONVENTIONS

Introduction

The dialect discussed in the book is southern standard British English (abbreviated 'SSBE'). In cases where this dialect differs sharply from other dialects of English, in particular in some of the modal verbs, the restriction is occasionally stressed. I use, throughout, the description of intonation in this dialect given in M.A.K. Halliday (1967a) *Intonation and Grammar in British English*, and the notational conventions which I use are his.

Table of Symbols and Notational Conventions

1. Abbreviations and Conventions Introduced in this Book

SU	'situation of utterance'
CSU	'current situation of utterance' } Chapter 5
OSU	'original situation of utterance'
SP	'situation of performance'
Sθ	'situation of thesis' (Chapters 6, 7) } used interchangeably
LMM	'literal mood meaning'
FOS	'first order significance'
SGS	'surface grammar specification'
LMMS	'literal mood meaning specification'
Ov	'occurrence value' (of an event)
Ov +/−	'positive/negative occurrence value'
DS(v)	'description sign (value)'
DS +/−	'positive/negative description sign'
Dr	'decider'
Kr	'knower' } 'secondary' roles
Pr	'performer'
Tr	'teller'
S	'speaker'
A	'addressee' } 'primary' (speech) roles
3	'third party'
Dr$^+$	'authoritative decider'
TO	'original teller' } Chapter 5
TC	'current teller'
OS	'operation sign' §§154-5
D	'deciding'/'decision operation'

D^+	'decision operation, positive sign' (implemented decision/'decided')
D^-	'decision operation, negative sign' (unimplemented decision/'undecided')

and so, for:

K +/−	'knowing operation'
P +/−	'performing operation'
T +/−	'telling operation'
Tc	'telling in its construction aspect'
Tp	'telling in its presentation aspect'
[ ]	square brackets enclose (i) a statement of role combinations (ii) a statement of relevant operations marked for sign
{ }	brace brackets are used to enclose the full LMMS (consisting of (i) and (ii))
:	'the secondary role to the left of this symbol is occupied by the primary role player specified to the right'
( )	parentheses (i) enclose an occupancy statement of this last type (ii) enclose two primary roles where joint occupancy is stated
(S + A)	'both speaker and addressee': joint/multiple occupancy
=	'the secondary role to the left of the equals sign is occupied by the same individual(s) as the secondary role to the right of the sign'
≠	'not equal'; 'the secondary roles on either side of this symbol are occupied by different individuals'
↘	'operates on'
→	'yields'

cf. §§ 154-5

2. Conventions of Phonological Notation
(cf. Halliday, 1967a: 53)

Tone (pitch movement on tonic)

1	fall
2	high rise
3	low rise
4	fall-rise
5	rise-fall
//	tone group boundary
_____	word containing tonic syllable is underlined

Symbols and Notational Conventions

Tone is shown by an Arabic figure placed immediately after the initial tone group boundary marker.

3. Logical Notation

⊃	'implies' (sign of material implication)
~	negation sign
≡	equivalence sign
V	disjunction: 'either or both'
/	disjunction: 'either or neither'
&	conjunction
A ⊂ B	'set A is included in set B'
x ∈ Y	'x is a member of set Y'
x ∉ Y	'x is not a member of set Y'
A ∪ B	'the union of sets A and B'
[ ]	square brackets, used to enclose members of a set
O	deontic modal logic operator: 'obligatory'
P	deontic modal logic operator: 'permitted'
	Chapter 4 (cf. Von Wright, 1951)
df	definition

Symbols introduced here:

W	operator in a modal logic of probability: 'inevitable'
M	operator in a modal logic of probability: 'non-inevitable'
K	used as an operator in an 'epistemic modal logic': 'known'

4. Other Conventions

*	before a sentence: 'unacceptable'
(?)	before a sentence: 'dubiously/marginally acceptable'
V-ed	past participle of lexical verb

(Some further notational conventions (for surface grammar specifications) are used in Appendix I, but are defined there.)

1 INTRODUCTION

§1.   I take there to be two forms of meaning realised in linguistic form, which I shall call (i) Interpretational meaning and (ii) Interactional meaning.

§2.   Interpretational meaning includes sense and reference (Frege, 1952) and covers roughly the area of Austin's (1962) 'locutionary meaning'. The areas of linguistic form concerned include features of case (Fillmore, 1968; Anderson, 1971), transitivity relations (Halliday, 1967b and 1968), number, and the denotation of lexical items.

§3.   Interactional meaning is the area of Frege's 'force' (cf. Dummett, 1973: 295-363; and Hare, 1971: 22-4) and of Austin's (1962) 'illocutionary force' (cf. Searle, 1969). It includes the area of Bühler's (1934) 'Appel' (conation) function of language, and some elements in his 'Ausdruck' (expression) function (cf. the discussion in Isačenko, 1964). Stenius (1972: 182-202) discusses aspects of this area of meaning under 'Mood'. The areas of linguistic form concerned are: forms of the lexical verb traditionally taken to indicate mood (Sweet, 1891; Kruisinga, 1932; Poutsma, 1928; Jespersen, 1924; Curme, 1931), modal auxiliary verbs, word order and intonation;[1] some explicit performative verbs; and forms of address, honorific titles and so on.

§4.   These two kinds of meaning correspond with the two main functions of language: (i) interpretation of the world; (ii) the establishment and embodiment of social relations and interactions. Under (ii) I include the manipulation of social reality. Through this, changes in physical reality may be achieved (through commands which are obeyed, through verbally organised teamwork which succeeds, etc.) cf. Halliday (1970b, 1973) on functions of language and 'macrofunctions'.

§5.   Both types of linguistic meaning need to be taken into account.

Neglect of interpretational meaning leads, in lexis, to a view of the vocabulary which does not account for denotation (e.g. Firth, 1962:1-32; criticised on these grounds in Lyons, 1966): and, in grammar, to a view of meaning too much governed by the contextual features of particular occasions.

Neglect of interactional meaning fails to account for different modes of referring (cf. Searle, 1969: 122-3, for a discussion of this area).

It would constitute a serious problem in any attempt to elucidate 'communicative competence' (Hymes, 1972). See Strawson (1971: 170-89) for a valuable discussion of approaches weighted in favour of interpretational meaning (as expounded by Chomsky amongst others) and interactional meaning (as expounded by Grice and others) (cf. Chomsky, 1976: 36-77, which includes a reply to Strawson).

§6.   I distinguish 'lexical' from 'grammatical' meaning: the denotations of names from relations established among names. The distinction applies within both interpretational and interactional meaning. The question of whether one of these factors governs the other, and if so, which, and to what extent, I shall leave to one side, as far as it concerns interpretational meaning which I do not discuss as such. With respect to interactional meaning, my concern is with grammatical meaning, and I shall argue for some semantic categories in this area which are not directly realisable in lexis; hence in Austin's terms, for primary performatives which have no explicit performative counterparts. I do not approach the problems involved within the framework of generative semantics as has been done in some recent work (e.g. Ross, 1970; Lakoff, 1972; Gordon & Lakoff, 1975; Sadock, 1974). Austin's (1962) work on illocutionary force I take to depend largely on distinctions of lexical meaning (cf. discussion in §51 below).

§7.   Forms of address, honorific titles, etc. give lexical realisation of features of interactional meaning. Such terms name social relationships which are confirmed, and sometimes established (for the purposes of a given situation) by their use; that is, to use them is to recognise individuals as the holders of (chiefly) institutional roles (cf. §63 below). Austin's lists of explicit performatives relate principally to institutional roles (e.g. I *acquit* to that of a judge) but also to socio-linguistic roles which I term 'secondary' (cf. §§ 76-7 below).

§8.   The grammatical aspect of interpretational meaning is the semantics of mood: the level of semantic organisation realised grammatically by distinctions between Imperative/Indicative/ Subjunctive; between declarative/interrogative; and by different modal verbs.

§9.   I shall call this aspect of meaning 'mood meaning' and abbreviate 'MM'.

§10.   More strictly, mood in English realises the interpenetration of features of interactional and interpretational meaning. It is the area of the grammar which realises different fashions in which they combine.

§11.   I follow Sweet (1891: 293) in regarding mood as 'expressing different relations between subject and predicate', among other things. Bolinger's (1967) discussion of links between the imperative and infinitive is relevant here.

§12.   I take declarative, interrogative and imperative as categories of grammatical form (not to be equated with the speech function categories of statement, question and command) (cf. Sweet, 1891: 507-9; Halliday, 1970a: 40; 1970c).

§13.   MM involves at least:

(i)   The speaker's attitude to the content of what he says. (Cf. Jespersen, 1924: 313, who gives 'fact-mood', 'thought-mood' and 'will-mood' on this dimension. Poutsma (1926: 161-2) refers to predications of certainty, conviction, uncertainty and rejection.)

(ii)   The 'mode of referring' (Searle, 1969: 122-3) and subject-predicate relations.

(iii)   The speaker's attitude towards (an)other(s) in the speech situation.

(iv)   The socio-linguistic roles taken up by participants in the verbal interactions, and the 'linguistic moves' made towards one another.

The notion in (iv) develops a suggestion I made in a previous article (Davies, 1967: 30-1) that 'features in the deep grammar of . . . English clauses are systematically related to factors in the situation of the process of their production'. For 'deep grammar' I would now substitute 'surface grammar'.

§14.   I postulate that certain situational factors are the main elements in a system of semantic distinctions underlying surface distinctions of mood in English. Chief amongst these are certain socio-linguistic roles and associated operations, together with different relations of overlap/separation between the situation of utterance and that in which the event being spoken about occurs. These notions are developed in Chapter 3 below.

§15.   Connections between mood of the verb and types of conditional sentences are generally accepted, although difficult to state systematically. I suggest that the framework of semantic analysis sketched above is relevant to an understanding of different kinds of conditional sentences, and also to some of cause, reason and purpose (Chapter 8).

§16.   One of the greatest difficulties in the semantic analysis of mood is caused by the apparent many-to-many relation between categories of form and those of meaning. Generally more of the latter have been distinguished than of the former. See the discussion in Jespersen (1924: 319-21) of 'notional' approaches to mood; and cf. Poutsma's comment (1926: 11-12) on a mood system built on 'an emotional basis': 'the number of conceivable psychical dispositions being endless, this system would lead to the distinction of a practically countless number of moods. Thus there would be a mood of fear, hope, scorn, expectation, positiveness, doubt, hesitation, etc., etc.'

Austin (1962: 149) estimates the number of explicit performative verbs (each presumably representing a distinct shade of illocutionary force) at between 1,000 and 9,999. There are probably fewer than twenty grammatical categories of mood.

§17.   In what follows I propose a small number of semantic primes (as in §14), different combinations of which give a larger, but still relatively small, number of semantic categories of MM.

§18.   In so doing I distinguish between 'literal MM' and 'significance'. Literal MM is context independent. Categories of significance are derived from the combination of categories of literal MM and contextual features. One category of MM in combination with different sets of contextual features yields different categories of significance. There are many more categories of significance than of literal MM (LMM).

§19.   In this way a notion of 'stages' is introduced, mediating between a small number of meaningfully distinct grammatical categories and the very wide range of different significance which each may ultimately have in use.

Notes

1. I use the analysis of intonation in British English given in Halliday (1967a), and adopt his notational conventions throughout (cf. the Table of Conventions).

§20.   Austin's point that primary performatives are ambiguous with
respect to illocutionary force (1962: 32-3) may be looked at from
another angle. Accepting that, for example, the imperative may be
used as an order, a purported order, advice, entreaty, and so on, one
may ask: 'Is there a common element of meaning, attributable to
the imperative construction as such, which is found in all these uses,
and which is an essential element in the final effect achieved in each
case?' The answer I believe is 'yes'; or, rather, there is a complex
common element, which consists of a particular combination of
features. Let us take this, in the first instance, as a list of semantic
features constituting a somewhat rearranged version of Searle's
propositional content and preparatory rules for the non-defective
performance of the illocutionary act of Request (1969: 54-71).[1]

(i)   The one envisaged as carrying out the action is the
addressee.
(ii)   There are grounds for assuming that the addressee will not
carry out the action without being at least encouraged to do so.
(I shall call this an assumption of 'negative inertia'.)
(iii)   Following from (ii): there are grounds for assuming that
the action concerned is not being, and has not been, carried out at
the time of utterance.
(iv)   There are grounds for assuming that the addressee is
capable of carrying out the action: that it is possible for him to do
so in the given circumstances.

These features are common to all the uses of the imperative
mentioned by Austin, including 'entreaty'.

§21   Assumptions (i)–(iv) above are proposed as elements in the
meaning of the imperative construction which governs the effects
its use will have in different contexts. That is, when one or more
of these assumptions is broken by contextual features in a particular
instance, it is not the case that the imperative construction 'means'
something else in terms of literal mood-meaning; rather it is just
because it retains its constant LMM that its use produces different
effects and potentially different reactions in the addressee, according

to the contextual variation.

§22.   If this is the case one would expect the different speech acts which may be performed by using an imperative, all to be defective in the same ways according to which of the assumptions (i)–(iv) is broken in context. Let us examine this prediction.

§23.   Suppose that (i) is broken. If I turn to you and say *Go away*, but it is clear from other features in the situation that it cannot possibly be *you* whom I envisage as 'going away', then you might conclude one of a number of things: that 'you' were not the addressee (and so that (i) was not broken); for example you might think that a look which seemed to be directed at you was in fact travelling over your left shoulder to someone behind you, or that I was merely 'quoting at you' a remark which I lacked the courage to address openly to the person I had in mind (a form of behaviour particularly liable to cause misunderstandings); or that I had suddenly lost contact with reality, or was issuing a 'coded' message (for example, if we both knew that I wanted someone else to hear me say that to you, but did not envisage that you would do it); or simply, that I had become momentarily confused or unhinged in some way. This would be true whether the imperative concerned had the illocutionary force of order, command, advice, entreaty or permission. All would be defective in the same way. And in all these cases, the conclusion drawn would not be that the LMM of the imperative had changed; but, rather, just because it would be assumed to remain constant, on that basis one would conclude that there is something odd about who the addressee is (not the apparent one, not 'you'), or about the way I say it ('play-acting' in some sense), or about my mental condition.

§24.   Comparable points may be made about cases in which (ii) is broken. Suppose you show every sign of being about to change the bulb on a lamp which doesn't work, and I say to you *Change the bulb*. This would be equally odd (and probably irritating) whether it was perceived as a command, or as advice or entreaty. In all these cases its use reveals my assumption that you are not going to do so without some urging on my part (when it ought to be clear to me that you are on the point of doing it of your own accord). If the illocutionary force involved is that of giving permission (you are not normally allowed to touch my precious possessions) then, for the same reason, the effect of my using the imperative here may convey some shade of reproof. That is, use of the imperative conveys the speaker's assessment that (ii) obtains. Where it does not obtain in practice, the addressee may conclude that the speaker has not noticed this, or that he refuses to recognise it, or that he feels it should obtain, and is implying this by behaving as if it did, in issuing his imperative. To say *Have a drink* to a guest who is clearly on the point of helping himself, may in this way be felt to convey some hint of reproach (even when not intended to do so). That is, the speaker's assumption (conveyed by his use of the imperative) that the addressee is not going to carry out a particular action without some encouragement from him, when clearly unjustified in a given context, may sometimes be slighting because it conveys lack of recognition of commendable intentions, and at other times reproachful because it implies perception and rejection of less acceptable intentions.

§25.   Cases in which (iii) is confounded in context are similar to those in which (ii) does not obtain: the effects produced are simply rather more marked. For example, to shout *Kick the ball* at a player who is doing so conveys that one does not recognise his efforts in that direction as worthy of the name. Where the addressee already has carried out the action in question, use of an imperative either reveals the speaker's ignorance of this fact, or conveys that he thinks it was not adequately performed. To say to me, *Look it up in the dictionary*, when you are in a position to know that I have already done so without success, indicates that you feel that I did not look carefully enough on that occasion. This is the case whatever the illocutionary force carried by the imperative.

§26.   Again, where (iv) does not obtain in a given context, any illocutionary act for which the imperative is used, will be defective in the same way. It is equally odd to request, order, advise, entreat, command or permit me to *Catch the ball*, if it is clear to both of us that I am not going to be able to do so. Even so, imperatives used in circumstances where it is not absolutely clear to the addressee that he is unable to perform the action concerned may act as encouragement, for they convey the speaker's assumption that he is capable of doing so.

§27.   Features (i)–(iv) are common to all imperatives. But a further feature in the LMM of the imperative (contained in Searle's additional preparatory rule for order and command (1969: 66) should be added here: namely, the assumption that:

(v)   the speaker has the right to decide whether or not the addressee carries out the action.

§28.   This feature appears at first sight to separate imperatives used in order, command and permission, for example, from those in request, entreaty and advice, and so on.

§29.   I would want to meet this objection to the inclusion of (v) in the LMM of the imperative, by saying that imperatives used in request or entreaty generally carry a surface marker of the reduced authority of the speaker in terms of (v). That is, they assume his right to wish rather than to decide. This 'marking' has the form, either of the presence of *do* (in the positive), or of initial adverbial modification, such as *please/for heaven's sake*, or of marked intonation: some element of rising tone, generally a rise-fall (tone 4); or some combination of these features (cf. Appendix I). That is, I would argue that such imperatives may be distinguished in terms both of surface form and LMM, and that they constitute a different sub-type.

§30.   Where (v) in its strong version is broken, the use of an unmodified imperative is usually ineffective, and may involve the speaker in uncomfortable consequences, because his own assessment of his authority to decide another's actions which it conveys is not shared. The result is a defective order, command or permission, but not a request. That is, disparity between the speaker's assessment and the facts of the case as perceived by others does not lead to a reinterpretation by them of the LMM of the imperative form, but to a reaction based on its having an LMM with the strong form of (v). Someone to whom an unmodified imperative is addressed by another whose authority to direct his actions he would not be conventionally expected to recognise, does not normally reason with himself that as the circumstances invalidate the usual meaning of that form, the form must mean something else which would be more appropriate (e.g. a request). On the contrary, he would accept it as conveying the speaker's assumption of the strong version of (v) and conclude something unfavourable about him, or judge his behaviour as comic perhaps. (Children using the unmodified imperative to adults are generally taught to change the form (add modification: *please*) rather than accepted as having intended to make a request.)

§31.   I distinguish between (v) and a closely related element in the LMM of imperatives, namely the assumption that:

(vi)   the speaker has the right to tell the addressee his decision or wish concerning the latter's action. ((vi) is also covered by

Searle's additional preparatory rule for order and command.)

This may fail to apply on a variety of formal occasions, or where there is great disparity in relative status between a (low-ranking) speaker and a (high-ranking) addressee. But it may also fail on more ordinary occasions where the status of speaker and addressee is similar, for example, one child to another, even where the speaker is not giving his own decision but merely relaying that of a more authoritative individual (cf. §§186, 236). Use of the imperative may be challenged on the basis of the speaker's lack of authority not only to decide, or wish, but also on the grounds of: 'Who are you to tell me/Who are you to express your wishes to me (in these circumstances)'. Conversely, it is on the basis of (vi) that imperatives can be used to give advice in cases where there is some indication that someone wishes to be told another's decision or wish.

§32.   I would argue on these grounds that all imperatives share features (i)–(iv) and (vi) as elements in the LMM of the construction, irrespective of its illocutionary force in use; but that two sub-types of imperative may be distinguished according to the version of (v) which applies, and that this distinction is reflected in surface form.

In this view, Searle's propositional content and preparatory rules for request (and order and command) (to which (i)–(vi) are roughly equivalent), seem appropriate to the specification of requirements for the non-defective performance of those illocutionary acts only in so far as such performance is dependent on the use of the imperative construction. At least this is so unless it can be shown that a different grammatical construction contains these same elements in its LMM.

§33.   This conclusion holds as long as one remains within language. But a beckoning gesture could satisfy all Searle's rules for the non-defective performance of an order, including his essential rule 'Counts as an attempt to get Hearer to do Act'. This is one result of his admitting primary illocutionary acts without specifying their linguistic characteristics. The relation of Searle's theory to any linguistic account of illocutionary force is that of the general theory to a special theory.

§34.   If (i)–(vi) are elements in the LMM of the imperative construction, and, so, part of the specification of its grammatical meaning, it is clear that grammatical meaning, seen in this light, is not the same thing as deep grammar. Its elements are situational factors, not grammatical entities such as 'deep/logical subject' and so on.

I am far from suggesting an imperative morpheme in an underlying PS tree. I would claim that there is an area of semantic organisation underlying surface syntax, rather than either deep structure, as in 'classical' transformational grammar (Chomsky, 1965) or a 'semantic syntax' as in the generative semantics approach (cf. McCawley, 1968; Ross, 1970; Lakoff, 1972; Sadock, 1974; and papers in Seuren, 1974), which in some ways provides a 'deep lexis'.

For the most part I believe that one-to-one relations can be established between categories of surface grammar mood and specifications of situational factors in LMM. But allowance for asymmetries here is parallel to allowing for them between deep and surface grammar. It is in principle no more, and no less, a difficulty to account for ambiguous surface constructions, and for 'deep'/ semantic specifications with more than one surface representation, on this approach than on the others just mentioned.

§35.   So far we have looked at six situational features proposed as part of the constant LMM of the imperative. I now propose that there are other such features which are relevant to the effect of that construction in use, but are not elements in its LMM. These include the wishes of the addressee with respect to, (a) carrying out the action concerned, and (b) being told what to do. Differences here vary systematically with differences in the illocutionary force which the imperative has in use.

There are two relevant questions, both of which concern features mainly in the situation of utterance (SU).

(a)   Is there some indication that the addressee wishes to do x?

(b)   Is there some indication that the addressee wishes to be told the speaker's decision/wish?

Where the answer to both (a) and (b) is 'no', use of the imperative X constitutes a command. Where it is 'yes', use of the same construction constitutes the giving of permission. In the case where, although there is no indication that the addressee wishes to do x, it would conventionally be assumed that he wishes to do y, of which doing x is a necessary or sufficient condition, and where the answer to (b) is 'yes', use of the imperative constitutes an instruction. For example, notes on how to use a kitchen gadget: *Set the browning control knob* (in order to get the sort of toast you like).

Where the answer to (b) is 'yes', use of the imperative gives advice, irrespective of the answer to (a). In the paradigm case of (b) being fulfilled, where Q says 'What shall I do?', R may reply X, where x is an action which it is quite clear that Q does not want to do (e.g. *Give in to him/Resign*). Here Q cannot reasonably object to being told to do x, only to the fact that it is x rather than y that he is being told to do.

Clearly the picture could be refined further, for example by distinguishing for both (a) and (b) where the answer is 'no', between a definite 'wish-that-not' and mere neutrality on the addressee's part. This would yield different types of command according to the assumed degree of 'addressee-resistance'.

Use of the modified imperative form will also have different force according to these assumptions concerning addressee's wishes. For example, where the answer to (a) and (b) is 'yes', use of that construction constitutes an offer (or invitation); where the answer to both is 'no' it gives a request. (*Please take one* could have either force accordingly.)

I shall not attempt a full account of the ways in which the imperative may be used.

§36.   What happens when things 'go wrong' in the cases just sketched? That is, when the speaker's assessment that the addressee wants to do x is mistaken, and is not shared by anyone else present? Use of the imperative has the illocutionary force of command in that context, irrespective of the speaker's intention to give permission. That is, in contrast with the cases considered in §§23-32 above, the conclusion drawn is not that something has gone wrong, but that a different illocutionary act has been (non-defectively) performed. That is, the result of the mistaken assumption in this case would be a well-formed command, not a defective permission. If it was perceived that the speaker had made a mistaken assumption, 'correction' would take the form not of advice to change the construction type (contra §30) but of contextual information, 'I don't think he wants to' (so do you really want to make that command?).

§37.   Why should it be that a mistaken assessment of (a) and (b) need not be perceived as a mistake, whereas one with (i)–(vi) would be? The answer is that the latter affect literal meaning, the former only affect use.

§38.   The LMM of a construction governs the range of illocutionary forces which it may have in use (one cannot use an imperative to state a report of a past event, for example), but does not account for any of such forces in itself. Types of illocutionary force are derived from the combination of the LMM of a construction with certain features in the situations in which it is used on different occasions. Illocutionary force is a category of non-literal meaning. I shall say that it belongs to the level of 'first-order significance' (FOS).

§39.   There are several different illocutionary forces potentially associated with the imperative in a systematic way, as above. This applies in a parallel fashion to indicative declaratives and inter-rogatives, and to other classes of sentences distinguished in surface grammar under mood.

§40.   The approach to illocutionary force given in §38, accommodates not only the one-to-many relation between construction type and force in §39, but its converse: the fact that one illocutionary force may be carried by more than one construction type.

§41.   In considering this, a difference between various illocutionary forces is immediately striking: some are much more flexible in this respect than others. Take, for example, 'warning' as opposed to 'question'.

There is no particular grammatical construction type which is more associated with conveying the force of warning than any other. Warning may be conveyed by any construction whatever. For example, each of the following might have this force in appropriate circumstances: (a) //1 <u>Hi</u>//, (b) //1 Mr Jones is <u>here</u>//, (c) //1 I'd give you two minutes in that <u>atmosphere</u>//, (d) //4 <u>Mickie</u>//, (e) //1 What are you <u>doing</u>//, (f) //1 <u>Run</u>//, (g) //1 Trespassers will be <u>prosecuted</u>//, (h) //1 If you do that <u>again</u>//1 I don't rate your chances of survival very <u>highly</u>//, (i) //1 You can't expect me to agree to <u>that</u>//, (j) //1 How <u>difficult</u> you can be//, (k) //2 Do you <u>mean</u> that//, (l) *Live wires.*

Part of the reason for the length of this list (which could, in principle, be extended indefinitely) is that we lack a clear defini-tion of what a 'warning' is. If it is taken as an indication that some-thing which is dangerous to the addressee is about to happen, we have the sort of open-ended list of constructions just given, for the non-defective performance of this act will depend crucially on the addressee's perception of what is dangerous to him and what is not. This may easily be different from the speaker's view of the matter. If a wife says to her husband //1 Mr Jones is <u>here</u>// this may be intended simply as an announcement; but if the husband knows that the only reason for Mr Jones to come would be to serve him with a writ, her remark would have the force of a warning to him. Even the sound of someone's voice, irrespective of what he is saying, will serve as a warning if one is afraid of being seen by him. A speaker may easily warn someone of a danger approaching him without being aware of doing so.

//1 <u>Hi</u>// generally has the force of a greeting, //1 Mr Jones is <u>here</u>// the force of a statement. Neither would lose this unmarked force in circumstances in which they served as warnings.

If one utterance may have two different illocutionary forces simultaneously, this argues for more than one level of non-literal meaning. That is, warning must be a different kind of force from greeting or statement. I shall say it is a category of 'higher-order' significance.

'Question' on the other hand is more closely associated with (non-modal) interrogatives than with other classes of constructions; and where a non-interrogative construction type conveys the illocutionary force of question it generally differs in some formal surface feature (such as rising as opposed to falling tone) from others of its class. Let us accept (e) and (k) above as interrogatives carrying the illocutionary force of question in context. These could be used to alert the addressee that something unpleasant (such as the speaker's anger) threatens him: that is, as warnings. If so, question and warning are also categories at different levels of significance.

§42. Catergories of first-order significance include question, statement, command and permission, among others. All such categories may be carried by more than one grammatical construction type (with its associated LMM), but it is characteristic of them that the range of such types is limited in each case.

Given a category of first-order significance and the construction (+ LMM) used to convey it, one can deduce certain contextual features which must (or could not) have been operative. For example, given that an utterance had the significance of permission, and that its grammatical form was imperative, one can deduce that there must have been some contextual grounds for assuming that the addressee wished to carry out the action in question. But it is the claim implicit in foregoing sections that, given the construction + LMM and particular contextual features, one can deduce first-order significance, which is more interesting.

§43. I propose for the moment that first-order significance is a value of an 'expression'. The expression has the form 'X + C', where X is a variable whose values, '$\alpha, \beta, \ldots, \nu$' , represent different combinations of surface grammar construction type and LMM, and C is a variable whose values, 'a, b, . . . , n', represent different contextual features of the type discussed in §35. 'X + C = V' states a first-order significance, V, whose value may be worked out where the values of X and C are known. It follows from this approach that, where the value of V is known, the value of either X or C may be worked out, as long as that of the other is known. That is, given the first-order significance, one should be able not only to deduce contextual features, where construction type + LMM is known, but also to deduce the construction type + LMM used where the contextual features are known.

§44.   This last claim raises various difficulties, two of the most serious being that (i) if a category of first-order significance is equivalent to an illocutionary act, it may be conveyed without using any linguistic construction at all (cf. §33), and (ii) it is characteristic of such categories that they may be conveyed by more than one construction type (cf. §§40-2). We can neutralise the first objection by defining first-order significance as attaching to linguistic constructions in use, but the second requires further discussion.

§45.   Let us take 'invitation' (cf. §35) as a category of first-order significance which, when the context gives grounds for assuming the addressee's wish to carry out the action, may be conveyed by at least two different grammatical construction types:

(a)   The modified (+ *please*) imperative, e.g. *Please come in*; and
(b)   A polar-interrogative containing the volitional modal verb *will*, often also modified by *please*, e.g. *Will you come in please*.

The LMM for (a) has been given above as features (i)–(vi) (§§20, 29, 31). One proposal for that of (b) might be as follows:

1. The one envisaged as carrying out the action is the subject of the sentence: the 'performer'.
5. The speaker has the right to wish with respect to the carrying out of the action.
5'. The addressee has the right to decide whether or not the action is carried out.
6. The speaker has the right to tell the addressee his wish concerning the latter's action.
6'. The addressee is expected to indicate his decision, but there is no requirement or expectation that this should be done verbally.

Features 2–4 are the same as (ii)–(iv) for the imperative. Sentences of the type of (b), as opposed to those such as (a), allow a third person subject: the addressee need not be the one envisaged as carrying out the action, as in *Will Jim come in now please* addressed to Jim's mother. Where this is so, the addressee is still formally presented as the one to take the decision. Features 5′ and 6′ could be added to the LMM of the modified imperative.

Differences in the LMMs for (a) and (b) are slight, centring on the question of whether or not the addressee is obligatorily the one envisaged as carrying out the action. Differences between the grammatical constructions might also be thought slight, since the imperative may take a tag containing *will*, as in *Please come in, will you* which links it with the modal interrogative form.

In this case, then, the two constructions used to convey the one first-order significance are closely related in terms of LMM and also capable of being linked in surface grammar. A comparable analysis may be obtained, showing a close relation between the (unmodified) imperative and the declarative construction with modal *will*, used as command (e.g. *Eat that porridge/You will eat that porridge*), where the imperative has the strong form of (v) and the modal declarative has speaker-, as opposed to addressee-, decision. Here also, the non-imperative allows a third person subject.

§46.   Should one say, then, that constructions capable of conveying the same category of first-order significance always have much in common, both in LMM and surface grammar terms? The answer, I believe, is 'partly yes and partly no' with respect to primary performatives. (It is uniformly 'yes' in an uninteresting way with respect to explicit performatives, which are all declaratives, and, where a single first-order significance is concerned, would have the same type of introductory verb.)

On the basis of the notions outlined in §43, one would predict that if the construction-type + LMM varied, then the contextual features must also vary, if the significance value were to remain constant. This, I believe, is very much what happens. If one thinks of a set of rules giving necessary and sufficient conditions for the non-defective performance of an illocutionary act of a certain type (that is, if one specifies one category of first-order significance in my terms), the outcome is a list of situational factors, some of which are conveyed by using a given construction type (that is, they are elements in its LMM) and others of which are supplied by the context in which the construction is used. What appears to matter for the non-defective performance of the act is that all these conditions are satisfied, but there is no rigid restriction as to which factors should be present in the LMM of the construction, and which in the context (although aspects of the total effect such as 'degree of formality' may vary accordingly).

In this way, the first-order significance of permission may be conveyed by a declarative modal with *can/may*, where the assumption that 'the addressee wishes to carry out the action' is part of the LMM of the construction, or by an imperative, where this assumption is derived from context and is not part of the LMM.[2] Use of the declarative modal in circumstances where it was clear that the addressee did not want to do the action might well give the impression of a 'high-handed' speaker who either had not noticed this fact, or was acting on a strong assumption that the addressee ought to want to do it and therefore felt justified in ignoring the indications that he did not want to. Effects vary in degree, according to content and relationships between speaker and addressee. *You can wash up now*, when I am reading the newspaper in front of the fire and show every sign of having forgotten about it, may be annoying or may produce guilt (according to my view about whether or not I ought to want to); *You can wait*, said to someone, especially a stranger, who is clearly anxious to do something now, would often be considered insulting.[3] Such 'misuse' would have these effects precisely because the feature 'addressee wants to' is part of the LMM of the construction.

On the other hand, use of the imperative in similar circumstances would give a command, which might well seem less high-handed than the inappropriate permission given in the declarative modal.

This discussion illustrates the quite common case where a given situational factor may form part of the LMM of one type of construction, but constitutes a relevant feature of context only, in an FOS rule for another. This affects the range of FOS possibilities of each, and the contextual features needed to establish them.

§47.   I have attempted to distinguish LMM from significance, and have also suggested (§41) that there are probably different levels of significance: at least first-order, as opposed to higher-order, levels.

§48.   Categories of higher-order significance would include warning and perhaps others such as commendation and congratulation. Such categories would usually be carried by a wide, perhaps unlimited, range of different grammatical construction types. I would expect no particular correspondence between such categories and features of the surface grammar of mood, but see them as produced by the combination of a category of first-order significance with further contextual features which would often have to do with one participant's knowledge of an event or state of affairs not mentioned in the construction used. At this level, something might fairly easily be understood in a way in which it was not intended to be taken. Conventions governing usage in this area tend to vary more between different groups in a speech community than do those relating to first-order significance, both with respect to what forms count as capable of conveying such significances, and also with respect to the circumstances in which they are used. For example, *You'll do* would count as a high commendation among some speakers of British English, but not for others. The study of such conventions leads into the area of socio-linguistics.

§49.   There may well be one (or more) intermediate level between categories of first-order significance and those of the higher level just suggested. For example, advice shares characteristics both with categories of first-order significance (cf. §35) and with warning (in that it may be carried by a wide range of construction types). Further, it may combine both with a first-order category such as command and with a higher-order one. For example, suppose, in response to some indication that you want suggestions about taking your car to Scotland I say, *Don't trust those tyres too far*; I am simultaneously issuing a command, advising and giving a warning. Where two or more illocutionary forces may combine on one utterance there is prima facie evidence that they are not at the same level of significance.

§50.   In considering warnings the notion arises of different types, as well as different levels, of significance. That is, why should an utterance such as Austin's example (1962: 33) *There is a bull in the field* be capable of counting as a warning? The answer must lie chiefly in its content, in its interpretational meaning, and neither in its LMM, nor in its first-order significance, as I have used the term so far. The categories of first-order significance discussed above are categories of interactional significance, the product of LMM and contextual features to do with attitudes and reactions. But I would not want to exclude the notion of categories of first-order interpretational significance, seen as the product of literal interpretational meaning and contextual features to do, perhaps, with reference. Certainly the final significance of any utterance contains elements of both aspects of meaning, and both types of significance. In the example above, its significance as a warning would derive largely from the choice of proposition, in combination with the contextual feature that speaker and addressee (or perhaps only the addressee) hold the view that 'all bulls are dangerous' together with an assumption to do either with the possibility of the bull getting out of the field or the addressee going into it. These are principally matters of interpretational meaning and significance, but they combine with the first-order interactional significance of statement. *Is there a bull in the field?* would not constitute a warning in the same way (although there are cases where a question may convey a warning, cf. § 41).

Warning, then, seems to be a category of 'mixed significance' combining both interpretational and interactional elements. This is probably the case also with other categories of higher-order significance, such as commendation, which function as verbal social moves towards another, and so are interactionally meaningful, but rely partly on features of interpretational meaning and significance to achieve their effect.

§51.   Interactional significance may combine with interpretational significance, or it may be derived from interpretational meaning. Austin's explicit performative constructions seem to me to involve mainly the latter process. The interactional significance of *I order you to go* derives chiefly from the lexical interpretational meaning of the item *order*, although clearly there is combination also, in the sense that the first-order interactional significance of statement is a necessary element. (*Do I order you to go* would not have the same status.) However, Austin's classes of these constructions (1962: 147-63) are established chiefly on the grounds of the denotation of the introductory verbs.[4] Explicit performatives give lexical specification of the significance which they are intended by the speaker to have. In this sense they represent the rather artificial case where intended significance is made context-free. Most of them do not often occur in spontaneous speech, because contextual features supply what is needed to establish significance, and because they introduce unwished-for inflexibility. We learn something of an addressee's predispositions and assumptions from his reaction to the use of a construction which may have more than one significance; and sometimes our intention in using it is to test which of its possible significances he will select. This gives useful information about his frame of mind, which may condition our next move in the interaction. For example, if I say to someone, *Come here*, and he simply comes immediately, I can expect to base my future moves towards him on the assumption that he recognises me to have authority over him and will do as he is told. If, though, he chooses to treat this as a request and responds by saying something such as, *Would love to some other time but can't manage it now*, I will know that he regards us as equals and does not feel that I have any right to direct his actions.

If the accompanying circumstances are such that I do have a right to direct his actions in that instance, the second type of reply would be clear insubordination and would, for example, be punished in a school or in the army. Deliberate misinterpretation of clear significance is an effective form of insult, and insult would be the higher-level significance of the second type of reply in such circumstances.

The relationship of intention to significance is not, therefore, one to one, if it is possible for us to intend the addressee to choose between two equally possible significances on a given occasion as a guide to us understanding his disposition. Where there is only one significance possible the speaker's intention is perhaps more directly related to it (but cf. §53).

§52.   There is another aspect of significance which derives from co-text, rather than context. This is the area of, for example, agreement/ contradiction and challenge/acceptance. One may postulate interactional discourse units consisting, in the simplest case, of an initiating move and a rejoinder (cf. Sinclair and Coulthard (1975) for a model of discourse analysis along such lines, applied to the classroom situation).

Agreement and contradiction may derive either from LMM or from literal interpretational meaning. That is, one may contradict another either by denying the same proposition which he has affirmed (a matter of LMM in my terms, cf. Chapters 5 and 6) or by affirming a proposition which is a contrary (or contradictory) of that which he has affirmed. For example, A: 'Jane is in London.' B: 'She isn't.' as opposed to, A: 'Jane is in London this week.' B: 'She left Heathrow half an hour ago with Bill on a flight to New York.' This applies equally to denying a proposition which is a contrary (or contradictory) of that which the other has denied, as in, A: 'The building is not well-heated.' B: 'It isn't cold there.'

Similarly, agreement may be achieved in parallel ways in both cases: by affirming the same proposition which another affirms, or denying what he denies; or by affirming another proposition which implies that which he affirms, or denying another proposition which is implied by that which he denies. For example, A: 'The building is cold.' B: 'It's like a refrigerator.' A: 'John hasn't come.' B: 'There isn't any sign of him.' The commonest form, though, is probably the adverbial marker of 'consonant' affirmation or denial followed by an additional affirmation/denial which is in an 'and' relation with the original one. For example, A: 'The building is cold.' B: 'Yes, and draughty.' A: 'There isn't any central heating.' B: 'No, and no electric fires either.'

Challenge may be achieved in various ways, including that of replying to one question with another, as in A: 'Are you going tonight?' B: 'Are you?'. 'Truncated' forms (both declarative and interrogative, e.g. *It is(n't)/is(n't) it*) are essentially rejoinders; the declaratives being used in agreement/contradiction, the interrogatives in challenge/acceptance (an area discussed in more detail in Chapter 5 below).

There seems to be a case for postulating a discourse unit with two elements of structure: 'initiative' and 'reply', and for using the terms 'contradiction', 'challenge', etc. to refer to the 'combinatory' or *discourse* interactional significance of the construction at the second place. ('Answer' might then be reserved for the statement in a 'neutral' (question + statement) combination.)

A category such as 'contradiction' is derived from the combination of the mixed first-order significance (FOSs) of two constructions. Its relation to the LMM of the construction which conveys it is, therefore, to be seen in terms of stages and is not one-to-one; but neither is it random. Further, it might be proposed that features relating to 'combinatory potential' should be seen as part of the LMM of the 'truncated' constructions, in that LMM has been seen as governing the significance(s) which a construction type may have in use, and these constructions are restricted to 'reply significance' in the suggested interactional discourse units.

§53.   Apart from some mention in connection with explicit performatives, we have come so far with little reference to the concept of utterer's intention (Grice, 1957, 1968, 1969, 1972) except to imply in passing, by allowing for 'accidental' commands and warnings (§§36, 41), that, far from this determining the significance of the use of a construction, the two may even be in conflict.

I take the literal meaning of a linguistic form to be attributable to that form *per se*, independent of context, and would regard utterer's intention as an element in context, and, further, as one which does not contribute to first-order significance as I have outlined it.

It seems to be that intention, like illocutionary force and significance, must be seen as 'many-levelled'. There are, after all, many quite different kinds of intention. In uttering U, where U is a (non-modal) declarative sentence, and where it has the FOS of statement, I may intend you to know or believe the proposition expressed in it, or I may intend merely to show that I know it to be the case and be entirely uninterested in what you believe (cf. Chomsky, 1976: 61-3), an objection which I believe survives Grice's adaptation of his formulation of the role of intention in utterer's meaning (1969: 174-7). I may intend both to affect your knowledge/belief, and to show you my own; and, I may simultaneously intend a number of things, such as that you should accept my authoritative pronouncement as the final word on the matter and stop arguing with me, and/or that you should alter your plans in the light of the information I have given you, or that you should admire my perspicacity, or sympathise with my predicament as I have described it to you, or feel guilty in view of some new light I have shed on someone else's behaviour, and so on, indefinitely.

Now, one could argue that I could not reasonably have any of the intentions in this last list if I did not also have the intention that you should believe what I was saying (the intention of affecting your propositional attitude), (although I might perhaps have the intention that you should accept my pronouncement as authoritative and final in an argument, without having the intention that you should know or believe the proposition concerned, just as long as your acceptance showed in your behaviour, (a) by your ceasing to argue, and (b) by other subsequent behaviour in line with the assumption that what I said was the case). The general point here is that, in uttering U, I can simultaneously have different sorts of intentions: to affect your propositional attitude (e.g. make you believe x); to affect your next move in the verbal interaction (e.g. make you stop talking/encourage you to go on, etc.)); and, in addition, others: to make you feel important/'small'; to wound, insult or flatter you; to make you 'hang' yourself by giving you enough 'rope'; to make you angry or pleased; and so on. The possibilities are as open as the endless subtleties of human relationships and interactions. In saying something with as simple a literal meaning as *Sam came home on Wednesday* I may intend that (i) you should believe that proposition, (ii) to show you that I know, (iii) to stop you speculating about whether or not he would ever reappear, and

(iv) to cause you to express pleasure at the ending of my anxiety about his whereabouts. Finally, (v) I might also intend to assert myself at your expense in saying what I do, if you are the local Jeremiah and take an inordinate pleasure in other people's misfortunes. The reasonableness of my having the third and fourth intentions would depend on contextual features: my knowledge of your propensities/expectation of your probable behaviour, in the case of the third, awareness of social conventions of politeness (a 'regulatory rule' in Searle's terms, 1969: 33-42) in the case of the fourth. So also would that of my having the final intention of 'putting you down'. The notion that context may influence which intentions I have in uttering U potentially adds an interesting complication to any account of meaning based on intentions.

As with illocutionary forces (§41), I would argue that the possibility of having several intentions simultaneously, with respect to making one utterance, constitutes prima facie evidence for the existence of different levels of intention.

In this example, my utterance of U would generally have the effects wished for in the third and fourth intentions, whether or not I intended them. That wished for in my fifth intention would depend partly on whether or not I had correctly assessed the contextual features of your character and intentions, and partly on whether or not you recognised my intention. If I were wrong, and you also did not recognise my intention, the effect I intended would not come about: you would be pleased for me. If I were right but you did not recognise my intention the effect I intended would probably come about: you might feel slightly deflated. If I were wrong, but you did recognise my intention, you would probably feel wounded, insulted, angry, because of the estimate of your character which my having that intention implied; and this total effect would not be that which I initially intended. If I were right, and you recognised my intention you would probably be even more angry, insulted, etc.

One has here, potentially, a case where the addressee's recognition of a speaker's intention, instead of being a necessary element in the fulfilment of that intention, works to produce an unintended result. Speaker's intention here is related to, but cannot on its own govern, significance, in which the attitude of the addressee is a necessary element.

Clearly, language use is intentional activity. This has the status of a general principle, much on a level with Lewis's convention of truthfulness (1969: 148-52) and Grice's co-operative principle

(1975: 45). But the relation between utterer's intentions and the meaning of linguistic form seems to be a much more debatable matter. Higher-level intentions, such as the fifth one above, have little direct relation to it. They involve a series of implications, many of which are contextually derived. To an important extent they are a matter of what is not said, rather than of what is, and so are well outside the scope of our investigation, which is principally into the literal meaning of grammatical construction types.

The view that 'lower-level' intentions, principally those of affecting the propositional attitude of the addressee, are related to linguistic form is less open to objection. It might be argued that this sort of 'speaker's intention' should be seen as part of the LMM of construction types, so that they would convey it in use whether a particular speaker on a given occasion actually had this intention or not (cf. Searle's approach to 'insincere promises', 1969: 62).

To some extent my notion (§247) that one element in the LMM of the non-modal declarative is the feature: 'speaker presents himself as knowing whether or not x is the case' could be re-phrased as 'speaker intends to show that he knows that x is the case'. This does not involve an intention to alter the views of the addressee; but if 'rhetorical question' is allowed as a category of FOS, the speaker's intention, or wish, to persuade the addressee might be seen as a contextual feature entering into the establishment of categories at this level of significance.

There is some connection between distinctions I suggest below under 'telling' (Chapters 3, 5) and points covered by Grice (1975) in discussing conversational implicature.

§54.   I take the interactional significance of a construction type in use to involve several different levels, but the relationship between one level and the next to be the same in principle. Starting with a construction type together with its associated LMM, the first-order level of significance is 'reached' by combining this with contextual features, chiefly at this stage, assumptions concerning propositional attitudes held by the addressee (his wishes or beliefs concerning x). This may be expressed as a constitutive rule in Searle's terms (1969: 33-42) of the form: 'X counts as Y in context C', where 'X' is the construction type + LMM, and 'Y' is a category of FOS, e.g. 'Imperative counts as command in context where addressee shows no inclination to perform the action'. A second level of significance might then be reached by combining a category of FOS with further contextual features, perhaps at this stage to do with the addressee's attitude towards the speaker telling him something (his 'verbal social move attitude'). If so, 'advice' might be a category of second-order significance. The same rule would account for this: 'X counts as Y in context C' but 'X' would be a category of FOS, 'Y' a category of second-order significance, and the features relevant in specifying 'C' would differ in type, e.g. 'Command counts as advice in context where addressee indicates that he wishes to be told what to do'.

It is clear from this example that one category of second-order significance would relate to more than one FOS; and the converse would also apply.

Second-order categories might combine with further contextual features of a yet different type to give categories of a third level; and so on.

This rather simple model ignores complications to do with the stages and ways in which interactional significance combines with its interpretational equivalent, and also fails to allow for 'discourse significance'. But it raises one point of interest: namely, how many levels of significance could be seen as 'obligatory'? There is a strong case for saying that all sentences will have FOS. (In fact this might be used to define what a sentence is. Constituent clauses within a sentence cannot have FOS unless they are paratactically linked main clauses and perhaps not always then.) There may be a case for suggesting that second-order significance is also obligatory: 'all free-standing utterances count as verbal social moves'. But it seems clear that higher-order levels of significance, such as 'warning', are optional. Not only the nature, but the number, of levels of significance above two, attaching to the use of a construction type, is probably entirely determined by context. A division between obligatory and optional levels of significance might mark a line at which the meaningfulness of an utterance becomes a matter outside the scope of linguistics as such. (It would mark a genuine meeting point with literary criticism in the study of texts involving dialogue, and in an interesting way, where contextual features have to be supplied by surrounding narrative.)

§55.   The rest of this book deals principally with LMM, although questions of FOS sometimes intrude. I take the characteristics of LMM to include the following:

(i)   It is context-independent. LMM attaches to a construction type irrespective of particular circumstances (including those of the speaker's actual intentions) on any given occasion of its use. It is a semantic specification which a construction type has, *per se* (cf. Searle, 1969: 42-3 on 'having meaning').

(ii)   The LMM of a construction governs the range of different FOSs which that construction may have in use. Any given FOS which the construction has in use will be the product of its LMM and features in the context of utterance.

(iii)   LMM is a level of semantic organisation in which the primes are situational factors of certain types. The next chapter discusses their nature. These are the basis of a grammatically oriented semantics (as opposed to a semantically oriented grammar).

(iv)   The relation between LMM and surface grammar is such that, in principle, one specification in terms of the former will attach to one specification in terms of the latter, and conversely. That is, I postulate a correspondence between the two types of specifications. This is a strong claim, and to some extent is a matter of faith. It becomes more possible to substantiate, however, given the proposed distinction between LMM and FOS.

§56.   I state LMM as bundles of (situational) semantic features, and refer to construction types in the grammar by names which label bundles of surface grammar features. These surface grammar specifications (SGSs) are equivalent to labels for different 'paths' through a 'system network' (cf. Halliday, 1967b, 1967c, 1968). I use a 'systemic' approach only for surface grammar. For Halliday (1966a) system networks constitute the organisation of deep grammar.

I do not attempt to give a full system network description of the surface grammar of mood, but one proposal for a fragment is included as Appendix I.

§57.   In this way, I take the relation between LMM and SG specifications to be one between the intensions of sets rather than between their extensions (despite earlier references to 'categories of LMM' and 'classes of constructions').

§58.   Terms such as 'imperative', 'interrogative', 'declarative', 'subjunctive', 'indicative', I take to label a combination of one LMM specification (LMMs) with one SGS.

§59.   The relation between semantic features and those of surface grammar could be expressed as a rule of the form: 'x stands for y' where 'x' is an SGS, and 'y' an LMMS.

§60.   The content and form of LMM specifications is the topic of the next chapter. I do not write them as rules but prefer to regard them as bundles of features.

Assumptions (i)–(vi) in §§20, 27, 31, were closely related in

form and content to Searle's rules for the non-defective performance of the illocutionary act of ordering. But I have allowed for
LMM and FOS to be distinguished. A statement of LMM then need
not specify sufficient conditions for the non-defective performance
of an illocutionary act, although the use of a construction with a
given LMM may, in some cases, itself be a necessary condition of
such a performance of a given act. LMM is simply the literal interactional meaning of surface grammar features, specified in terms of
a situational semantics.

I shall express the equivalent of (i)–(vi), and other comparable
sets of features, in terms which, I believe, allow more easily for
generalisations to be shown, and for more concise statement. I take
the sociological concept of *role* (cf. Chapter 3) and state some LMM
features in terms of combinations, or 'occupancy', of roles, others
as attributes of roles. I also make use of a notion of activity
characteristically associated with each role chosen, and state further
LMM features in terms of such 'operations' and attributes of operations. As a rough, illustrative comparison, (i)–(vi) relate to the
proposed form of statement as follows (taking the 'strong' version of
(v)):

(i)	(Addressee : Performer)	(role combination)
(ii)	Performance operation$^{-\text{probable}}$	(operation attribute)
(iii)	Performance operation$^{-\text{achieved}}$	(operation attribute)
(iv)	Performer$^{+\text{capable}}$	(role attribute)
(v)	(Decider:Speaker)	(role combination)
(vi)	(Teller:Speaker)	(role combination)

which could be more concisely expressed as:

$$\left\{ \begin{array}{l} [((Tr = Dr^{+}) : S) \neq (Pr^{+} : A)] \\ \left[\begin{array}{l} Decision^{+} \\ \quad Performance^{-} \\ \qquad Inertia^{-} \end{array} \right] \end{array} \right\}$$

giving an LMMS which would combine with the appropriate SGS
to yield 'imperative'.[5]

§61.   I take there to be more than one aspect of LMM. For example,
features of decision or wish play a part in the meaning of some
constructions, but not in that of others, and the same applies to
features of 'knowing'. I suggested (§52) that some 'truncated'
constructions might include features to do with their 'reply' status

in two-place discourse units as part of their LMM. This is an area
in which LMM is linked to aspects of the meaning of features of
text grammar.

Finally, there is the description of an extra-linguistic event
presented in a sentence. I take the manner of describing this event
in certain respects, for example, as 'achieved/unachieved', to fall
under LMM. This is an area in which the latter interlocks with
literal interpretational meaning.

Notes

1. I arrived at an analysis similar to Searle's independently from a starting
point in interactionist role theory (cf. Chapter 3). See §§ 60, 167 for a
formulation in those terms.

2. *Do* imperatives realise an LMM feature of 'speaker's wish' (weak (v)).
For this reason they may be used in polite permission (addressee's assumed
wish voiced by speaker as if it were his own). Otherwise entreaty/request
(cf. Appendix I).

3. Use of a declarative *can* construction would have a different significance
here according to whether it was clear in context that the addressee 'wanted
not to wait', or whether it was merely a case of the absence of grounds for
assuming that he did want to.

4. In his later approach to constatives (1962: XI–XII) Austin suggests
that they also carry some illocutionary force, and are not, therefore, completely distinct from explicit performatives in this respect. This raises the
difficulty that there is no formal distinction between a sentence such as,
There is a bull in the field as a constative, and as a primary performative used
with the illocutionary force of 'warning'. Further, he treats the related construction type with *state,* e.g. *I state that there is a bull in the field* as an
(expositive) explicit performative, thereby appearing to allow for a different
proportion to exist between *There is a bull in the field* used as a warning, and
I warn that there is a bull in the field, from that between *There is a bull in the
field* used as a constative, and *I state that there is a bull in the field*. He does
not apply the primary/explicit distinction to constatives, claiming (1962:
134) that 'to say "I state that he did not" is to make the very same statement
as to say "He did not": it is not to make a different statement about what "I"
state (except in exceptional cases . . .).'

It is because Austin relies chiefly on the denotative meaning of the explicit
performative verb to establish types of illocutionary force that he arrives at
categories of primary performative such as 'warning' which do not correspond
with any linguistic feature (cf. §41 above).

From the point of view of linguistic analysis, explicit performatives are
more usefully distinguished into classes according to their grammatical
characteristics, such as their capacity to take an 'accusative + infinitive'
construction (cf. *I order you to go* v. **I apologise you to step on your toe*),
than in terms of referential meaning. The two do not always coincide. For
example, both *agree* (**I agree you to go*) and *promise* (*I promise you to go*)
are classed as commissives (1962: 156). Grammatical distinctions of this
kind realise different 'role configurations' (cf. Chapter 3); e.g. in *I order you
to go*, the one who 'tells' the construction is not the one (envisaged as)

performing the action, whereas in *I apologise for stepping on your toe* these 'roles' are occupied by the same individual. There are further more complex distinctions, which I do not pursue here. But I would claim that explicit and primary performatives can be systematically related in terms of the model proposed in this book, the former being 'less direct' ('realising more operations', cf. §153).

The use of explicit performatives in legal language results from the requirement for pronouncements to be unambiguous in every respect.

5. '+/−' following an operation name indicates 'implemented' (positive operation sign)/'unimplemented' (negative operation sign), cf. Chapter 3, §§ 120, 124-8. '+/−' following a secondary role indicates 'authoritative'/ 'non-authoritative'. ('Authoritative' in the case of the performer role gives 'capable of carrying out the action'.) 'Inertia' represents an assumed probability of occurrence of the event in the absence of the decision being made and told. '+/−' as a superscript here indicates that expected occurrence value.

':' indicates that the secondary role to the left of this symbol is occupied by the primary role-player (s) stated to its right.

'Dr', 'Kr', 'Tr', 'Pr' are introduced as abbreviations for 'Decider', 'Knower', 'Teller' and 'Performer' respectively. 'S' is used for 'Speaker', 'A' for 'Addressee', '3' for 'Third Party'.

3   A FRAMEWORK OF SEMANTIC ANALYSIS

§62.   Language is one form of social action, whatever relationship to mind it may also have. This being so, one would expect a model applicable to social interactions in general to apply to language as a special case.[1] Role theory, as developed in symbolic interactionist social psychology, provides one such framework of explanation (cf. Mead, 1934, 1936, 1938, 1964; Lindesmith & Strauss, 1968; Rose, 1962).

§63.   Role theory in general provides a model for interpreting certain kinds of predictable behaviour patterns in individuals by linking them to the social structure and to relationships with others.

The former involves the concept of 'institutional roles', the status of the individual within the institutional power structure of a society, and the aspects of his predictable behaviour which are derived from this. Examples of such roles would include: teacher, student, judge, clergyman, policeman, Member of Parliament, etc. Individuals playing such roles derive an important part of their social identity from the institutions to which they belong, and of their authority (where this is relevant) from the part which these play in the structure of society (cf. Turner, in Rose, 1962: 20-40; Kelvin, 1970: 139-67). Hence, many of the patterns of behaviour of such individuals, and the reactions of others to them, may be explained in terms of their social roles, rather than of their individual personalities. The actions of a policeman directing traffic are authoritative and admit of no argument, but the individual playing this role may be rather mild and indecisive by temperament in private life. The reactions of others to him in his official role will be based on that role, and the authority of the civil power which attaches to it, and not on any guesses about his individual disposition. Hence the concept of institutional roles can be used to explain a type of social interaction which would remain puzzling if viewed only in terms of the individual personalities involved.

Role theory in relation to less public social interactions has been applied chiefly in the area of family relationships (cf. Burgess & Locke, 1953; Rose, 1962; Stryker, 1962: 41-62; Farber, 1962: 285-306). Here also important generalisations concerning the behaviour of individuals, and the reactions of others to it, may be captured in terms of a roles model, which states expectations attached to the occupation of a particular status within the family structure. For example, certain general assumptions about behaviour patterns associated with the status of *mother* are generally current in society, and particular individuals may attempt to adapt their own personalities to match them.[2] Again, reactions of others towards the behaviour of an individual may be illumined by role theory. A child may be more likely to accept his elder sister's authority if she has taken on the role of mother in that family in the absence of an adult to fulfil it.

In both types of role, the question of predictable reactions in others towards behaviour associated with the role is part of its definition. That is, it is part of the definition of the role of police- man that someone playing that role is conventionally agreed to be able to expect motorists to obey his signals, show him their licence if asked to, and so on. An individual who takes on the role of mother will be expected to perform caring and control functions in the family, and will be responded to accordingly both by those within the family and outsiders. Taking on a given role involves accepting that others' expectations of one will vary accordingly. Role analysis, especially as treated in symbolic interactionist theory, involves patterns of reaction, rather than patterns of behaviour seen exclusively in terms of the one from whom they originate.

§64.   There are two elements of role theory, common to both areas of application, which are key points for my purposes here:

(i)   A given individual may occupy several different roles (of both types). A man may be a teacher during the day, and a student in evening classes. He may be father, husband and son simultaneous- ly at the same breakfast table.

(ii)   A given role is simultaneously occupied by a wide range of different individuals who may vary considerably in personality. There are many policemen, teachers and students in society; there are millions of individuals occupying a family role as father, mother or child.

Roles and individuals vary independently. Roles are not tied to individuals; and individuals are not tied exclusively to particular roles.

§65.   Role theory provides a framework in terms of which to study the standard types of social interaction which make life in society sufficiently regular and predictable to be manageable. It offers a model to account for characteristics of behaviour held roughly in common by large numbers of people; and it indicates one respect in which the organisation of society is a structure which is more than, and in some ways independent of, the sum of individual human beings who, taken together at any one time, compose it.

§66.   I would claim that role theory is relevant to the interpretation of language as social activity in a strictly comparable fashion. It provides a model for the explanation of those standard types of linguistic social interaction which make patterns of communication in society sufficiently regular and predictable to be interpretable; and which are 'codified' in linguistic form. That is, I claim that role theory is the appropriate model in terms of which to analyse the interactional aspect of the meaning of linguistic form.[3] I believe it is necessary to an understanding of the social aspect of linguistic meaningfulness, which is an essential element in the semantics of natural languages.

§67.   It is a central idea in Mead's thought that social interaction involves the individual in taking on the role of the other with whom he interacts. This includes 'responding to one's self as another responds to it, taking part in one's own conversation with others, being aware of what one is saying and using that awareness of what one is saying to determine what one is going to say thereafter' (Mead, 1964: 205). This view of role-taking underlies the selection of situational factors as input to the semantics of mood made below. Factors such as whether or not the speaker presents the addressee as knowing something which he himself does not, or as sharing his own knowledge, are to do with the process of taking on — taking into account — the role of the other in a conversation as part of a process of directing one's own present and future participation in it. I take factors of this kind, parts of such a process, to be realised in syntactic form.

§68.   Certain roles have traditionally been associated with linguistic description: those of *speaker* and *addressee*. Here the independence of role and individual is particularly pronounced: it is of the essence of successful conversation that there should be a regular exchange of these roles between the individuals taking part.

§69.   The role of *speaker* is essential in any linguistic act, and is the least abstract of all the roles we shall consider. It could be defined as that of one who emits linguistically meaningful sound waves; and the individual fulfilling it in a given instance could be identified by means of a scientific instrument. I shall use it in a rather more abstract sense to refer to one who produces or issues linguistic forms, whether spoken or written.

§70.   The role of *addressee* is less mechanical. It has several aspects, all of them deriving to some degree from the verbal interaction, rather than from physical activity (such as being the 'receptor of linguistically significant sound waves'). One may in fact 'address' someone physically absent. 'Addressee' may be seen as the role of the one(s) to whom the speaker directs his remarks. In this way it is a role imposed on another by the speaker, potentially without permission. Seen in this light, it is a potentially 'passive' role, one which is assigned rather than voluntarily taken on by the individual concerned, although in practice (in the ordinary case where the addressee is present) some indication of his acceptance of that role is generally necessary for the satisfactory progress of the inter-action, and the speaker will usually demand one if not spontan-eously given: 'Are you listening?'/'I'm talking to you', etc. The role of addressee is potentially distinct from that of 'one who hears', or 'one who listens', and does not relate to any attribute *per se* of the one on whom it is imposed.

§71.   There is another member of the set of traditionally accepted 'speech roles': namely, 'third party'. This role can be negatively defined in terms of the other two as that of 'one who is neither speaker nor addressee with respect to a given utterance'. These three roles derive from the function of language as a mode of social interaction. I group them together as 'primary roles'.

§72.   I shall say that an individual playing a primary role 'occupies' that role. More than one individual may jointly occupy the one primary role. Role-occupying individuals may be explicitly named (e.g. in vocatives).

Within primary roles, I distinguish between 'participant' and 'non-participant', according to whether or not a role is obligatorily occupied in the situation of utterance. 'Speaker' is a participant role, third-party non-participant. 'Addressee' presents more problems. I shall say that it is obligatorily occupied, but not always in the situation of utterance. In the case of soliloquies, the occupant of the addressee role could be said to be either the same individual who occupies the speaker role, or some unspecified (absent) 'other'. There are no devices in English grammar which realise an LMM feature 'without addressee': mood does not distinguish 'soliloquy only' forms (but cf. §§238 and 227 for discussion of the realisa-tion of 'unspecified, absent addressee').

Although the role of third party is non-participant, it does not follow that an individual playing this role at one point in a conversation may not play a participant role at another. His role may switch even within one utterance, as in *John plays tennis, don't you*, which can be used where *John* and *you* refer to the same currently present individual, and the speaker changes his addressee from someone else to John between main clause and tag. On the other hand, the individual(s) occupying the third-party role may be altogether outside the situation of utterance. Distinctions between a present and absent third-party role-player are not realised in pronominal person.

§73.   Where a role is occupied by more than one individual I call this 'multiple occupancy'. It is realised by plural number in nouns and some pronouns, or by listed paratactic nominal groups. Multiple/single occupancy of the addressee role is not distinguished in the pronoun, except by qualification, *you two, you all*, or by linked nominal groups, *you and Mary*.

Primary roles may combine, but different combinations are not distinguished in surface pronominal form. Speaker may combine with addressee as in *We can tell him later*, or with a third party as in *We came to see you*, or with both as in *We all need food to live*. Number distinctions in pronouns reflect role occupancy rather than primary role combinations.

§74.   Primary roles are occupied by individuals. But sometimes an individual may speak for someone else, or for the community at large rather than, or as well as, for himself. This notion of a 'mouthpiece' speaker enters into the LMM of some constructions (cf. Davies, 1967: 24-5), underlying examples such as *We can go now*, where the speaker is not the one giving permission (discussed under 'relayed speech': cf. §§186, 236 below), and certain constructions of obligation such as *Parents should teach their children kerb drill*.

§75.   The primary roles are not, however, adequate for the explanation of LMM. To adapt Bloomfield's example (1935: 22-7), if Jack says to Jill, 'That's an apple', he is the speaker, she the addressee; but this is also the case if he says to her, 'Is that an apple?' The two utterances represent different verbal social moves towards another. I shall say that they have different LMMs and that this is realised in syntactic form. But the distinction cannot be shown in terms of the roles of speaker and addressee on their own.

§76.   I suggest the introduction of a further kind of role to account for this distinction: 'secondary roles'. Secondary roles involve patterns of behaviour typically entered into in speech interactions which are not restricted to the mechanics of speaking and listening. They involve modes of behaving towards the other, fashions of presenting oneself, and the expression of attitudes, not only towards oneself and the other, but towards the content of what is said, and the occurrence of non-verbal events.

§77.   I propose four secondary roles, and define them as follows:

(i)   *Teller:* 'The role of one who dominates the conversation at any given point, and holds and uses the conversational initiative.' The role of teller derives from the dynamics of the social interaction. That of speaker derives from the mechanics of speech production, and there are cases where the two roles may be played by different individuals. There are several different aspects to the activity associated with the role of teller, which included selection of what to talk about. (See below, §§115-18.)

(ii)   *Knower:* 'The role of one in a position to know the truth, or otherwise, of a given description of an event or state of affairs; one who can vouch for whether or not something is the case.' The knower is assumed to be able to show that his knowledge is correct.

(iii)   *Decider:* 'The role of one in a position of authority to decide whether or not a particular event shall take place.'

(iv)   *Performer:* Principally, 'the role of one envisaged as carrying out an action in the "real" world'. That is, the actor/agent/initiator in Halliday's terms (1967b, 1967c, 1968). However, I shall use it more inclusively to refer to the grammatical subject (whether explicitly realised or not), thereby also including the existential subject and Halliday's attribuant ('one to whom a quality is attributed'). This may not be a very satisfactory usage in some respects, but it allows certain generalisations to be made which are otherwise more awkward. My concern is with the 'mood subject' and not with distinctions of transitivity relations or of case. The role of performer is a link between the interactional and interpretational aspects of grammatical meaning.[4]

Secondary roles as a group are less tied to the situation of utterance than the primary roles. I suggest below that they may be assigned to individuals who are absent from that situation in which the constructions in whose LMM they feature are used. As with primary roles, secondary roles are only transiently played by given individuals, and are exchanged during the progress of a conversation.

§78.   Secondary roles differ from each other in the degree to which
they are specifically restricted to a linguistic mode of social action.
There are non-linguistic patterns of behaviour associated with the
roles of both knower and decider. Someone may 'look knowing'
or point to something in response to a question, or otherwise
indicate that he knows something which others do not, without
actually saying anything. Similarly, one may indicate a decision
about whether or not something is to happen non-verbally, for
example, by gesture. In both cases the point at issue here is that
there are also verbal devices available: the non-verbal devices for
manifesting role-playing are not relevant to this analysis.

It should be stressed that the reality of the knower's knowledge
or the decider's authority to direct whether or not something
should happen is not at issue in connection with linguistic form.
It is the question of who (in terms of primary roles) is assigned
such a role, or presented as holding it, which matters. The possibility of inappropriate assignment always remains open (and may
be exploited with sarcastic intent).

The role of performer is potentially entirely non-linguistic, in
so far as the activity associated with it involves action in the 'real'
world which may have nothing to do with language (for example,
running, laughing, kicking, etc.). It may, of course, be language
activity (saying, asking, etc.), or it may be activity obligatorily
mediated by language, for example, acquitting, condemning, etc.
(many explicit performative verbs feature here). But the interesting point is that the role of performer is obligatorily 'linguistic'
in quite a different sense: that in which it constitutes the result of
an analysis within interpretational meaning. That is, even taken
loosely as another term for the grammatical subject, and therefore
as a cover term for several different types of 'actor' (and none),
the role of performer involves categories for the analysis of 'reality'
which are established within the interpretational semantics of a
language, and do not exist independently as *a priori* categories in
reality imposing themselves on linguistic form.[5]

The role of teller is exclusively linguistic: only verbal activity
is associated with it.

§79.   The role of teller primarily relates to the situation of utterance.
The role of performer is 'anchored' in the 'situation of performance', that situation in the 'real world' in which the event/state of
affairs takes place. The roles of decider and knower can be thought
of as 'mediating' roles, in the sense that they relate the activity

of telling, in the one situation type, to that of performing, in the other. That is, they involve the relation of the verbal social move to the (mainly-non-verbal) activity or state of affairs which it is 'about'.

§80.   Secondary roles are played by primary role-players. That is, I shall describe the 'occupation' of secondary roles in terms of primary roles rather than in terms of individuals. A given individual may play roles of both types simultaneously, but it is his status in primary role terms as a secondary role occupant which is realised in surface grammar.

§81.   Different occupation of the secondary role of performer[6] is realised in surface grammar by prenominal person (':' signifies 'is occupied by'):

  (Performer : Speaker)   first person
  (Performer : Addressee) second person
  (Performer : Third party) third person

It is also, more interestingly for our purposes, one feature realised in distinctions of mood, e.g.

  [(Performer : Addressee) . . .] ; jussive imperatives
              (e.g. *Come here*)
  [(Performer : Third party) . . .] ; optative subjunctives
           (e.g. *God save the Queen*)

In relation to occupancy of the performer role, combinations of primary roles are grammatically realised:

  [(Performer : (Speaker + Addressee)) . . .] ; inclusive ('joint')
            imperative (e.g. *Let's go*)

§82.   The occupancy of both primary and secondary roles is 'assigned' by the speaker. That is, one individual who selects himself as speaker (whether in response to another's expectations/demands or independently) casts another (or others) in the role of addressee, thereby establishing remaining others as third party. He simultaneously assigns secondary roles to himself, the addressee and/or to third parties. In using the construction which he does, he establishes the occupancy of both primary and secondary roles. Assignment of secondary roles may be done in various ways and sometimes a speaker may reinforce an assignment made by a previous speaker. Questions of manner of assignment are discussed in Chapter 5 below. Realisation is mainly phonological (different tones) rather than syntactic.

§83. The teller role is peculiar with respect to assignment. I shall say that it is shown as 'transferred' in polar interrogatives such as //2 Is it raining//, where the speaker acts as teller in choosing the proposition to be talked about, but also, in addition to casting the addressee as knower, assigns to him the role of subsequent teller in so far as the speaker's use of this construction incorporates a demand for reply. This demand element can be accounted for by the notion of 'teller role transference'. As with other matters of role assignment, one is here in a borderland between LMM and those elements of context which combine with it to yield first-order significance. Polar interrogatives need not have the FOS of 'question', and differences in their 'value' here are often realised by tone.

§84. In some cases where the current speaker reinforces a role assignment made by the previous speaker, this may involve his agreeing in the assignment of the teller role to that previous speaker. This occurs only where a single proposition is involved as in, A: //1 It's raining; B: //1 Is it// ('I see, I didn't know before you told me. I accept that you are legitimately in the conversationally dominant role of "telling me how it is" and choosing what to talk about.') B's utterance is one instance where the roles of speaker and teller are occupied by different individuals and provides some support for wishing to distinguish them.

§85. No one particular secondary role is obligatorily occupied in all construction types, although I shall say that the role of teller is 'relevant' even in constructions such as dependent and embedded clauses, which I take to have derived telling (cf. Chapter 5). Nevertheless, no construction type is neutral to secondary roles; one or other (or more than one) of them always features as 'occupied' in LMM. Where LMM involves only one such role, this will be the teller, as in *Hello/Blast!* Where it involves two, one will always be the performer, as in '*John having arrived* (they started out)', where I take the dependent clause to have performer and knower in its LMM.[7] Where there are three roles, two will always be teller and performer, the third either decider, as in *Come here*, or knower, as in *It's raining*. Some constructions involve all four roles, as in *He should have taken more care*, where the role of one who knows (that he didn't) is occupied, as well as the role of one who 'decides'.

§86.   This approach involves the notion that certain roles are not relevant in the analysis of certain construction types. Different types of LMM can be distinguished according to the criterion of which secondary roles are involved or 'relevant'. LMM types established on this basis are linked to traditionally recognised divisions within surface grammar. For example, the LMM type where the roles of teller, performer and decider are relevant, but that of knower is not relevant, is linked to imperative mood, and to hortatory and optative subjunctives; the LMM type where teller, performer and knower are relevant but decider is not, is linked to indicative mood and subjunctives of 'imagination' or possibility. I shall refer to such LMM linked divisions of surface grammar below as 'areas' of the grammar.

§87.   Where a given secondary role is not relevant to the LMM of a construction type, I shall say that the latter is 'neutral' to the activity associated with that role. For example, imperatives are 'neutral to knowledge'. Some verbless constructions, such as *Hello*, are neutral to knowledge, decision and performance. This statement would apply to the traditional category of interjection in general.

§88.   Secondary roles may combine with each other. That is, one primary role player may occupy more than one secondary role simultaneously, as in (non-modal) declaratives, where the speaker occupies the roles both of teller and knower. Constructions having the same secondary roles in LMM are distinguished principally by variations in their combinations and occupancy. For example, both (non-modal) declaratives and polar-interrogatives involve the roles of performer, knower and teller, but differ in these terms:

Declarative: [(Knower = $\overrightarrow{\text{Teller}}$) : Speaker]
Interrogative: [(Teller : Speaker) ≠ (Knower : Addressee)]

(where '→' above *Teller* signifies that this role is transferred; '≠' signifies 'occupied by different individuals').

Occupancy of the performer role in both types of construction is realised by person, and is not relevant to mood distinctions between them. Imperatives and optative subjunctives also involve the same secondary roles as each other, but differ in terms of their occupation and combinations.

e.g. Jussive imperative : [((Tr = Dr) : S) ≠ (Pr : A)]

Opatative subjective: $[(Tr : S) \neq (Pr : 3_1) ; (Dr : 3_2)]$

(The grammar does not distinguish different types of subjunctive according to whether the third-party performer is also decider, or whether a second third party occupies that role. *God save the Queen* (Performer = Decider) and *Long live the Queen* (Performer $\neq$ Decider) are not grammatically distinct, except in terms of word order. They both take the same 'periphrastic subjunctive' paraphrase: 'May God save the Queen'/'May the Queen live long'.)

Further types of imperatives and subjunctives can be distin-. guished in terms of this approach (cf. Chapter 4 below).

§89. Neither the primary nor the secondary roles on their own are sufficient to provide a framework for the analysis of the semantics of grammatical mood and categories of speech function. It is their combinations, among themselves and, through primary role occupancy of secondary roles, with each other, which are realised in surface grammar.

§90. What I shall call 'the principle of asymmetry', whereby one primary role player may simultaneously occupy more than one secondary role (§88), applies conversely where two primary role-players jointly occupy a secondary role. I analyse 'joint' imperatives, such as *Let's go* (cf. §81) in this way:

$$[((Dr = Pr) : (S + A)); (Tr : S)] .$$

I shall say that the decider and performer roles here each have 'multiple occupancy', and that each is equally 'shared' between speaker and addressee. The greater initiative associated with the speaker is accounted for by the fact that, on his own, he also occupies the teller role.

Non-modal tag declaratives also involve multiple occupancy of a secondary role by speaker and addressee, in this case that of knower. Here, too, the sharing is equal, but where there is rising tone on the tag, this may indicate two instances of the knower role with respect to the one proposition rather than multiple occupancy of the one role.

§91. The notion of multiple occupancy and sharing a secondary role depends on there being only one activity associated with playing that role which both occupants jointly engage in: one decision and one performance in the case of *Let's go*, one act of knowing in the case of a tag declarative such as //1 John takes <u>sugar</u>//1 <u>doesn't</u> he//.

Some constructions involve two such activities, and two instances of the role, each with single occupancy. The test for this is whether the possibility of opposition is explicitly allowed for, as in //1 <u>Let's go</u>//2 <u>shall we</u>//, where I would want to postulate two instances of the decider role rather than the sharing of one (although the performer role would remain shared), on the basis that the construction does not assume a joint decision but specifically allows for a negative decision by the addressee. Similarly with //1 John takes sugar// 2 <u>doesn't</u> he// where allowance is specifically made for the addressee to know 'that not-x' in opposition to the speaker knowing 'that x'.

In both these cases the distinction between multiple occupancy of one role and single occupancy of two is carried intonationally, by rising tone on the tag. In both examples, the repeated activity of deciding or knowing applies to the same event or state of affairs. The addressee's potentially opposite decision is still about 'our going'; his potentially opposite knowledge concerns the same topic of 'John's taking sugar'. I shall say that constructions of this type, which have two potentially opposed varieties of the same activity associated with the one type of secondary role, realise 'multiple occurrence' of that secondary role (and different occupancy in each 'occurrence').

§92.   There are types of construction with two instances of a secondary role in which the activity associated with the 'second' occurrence of the role does not apply to the same topic as the first. For example in, *You needn't come to the lecture* the performer is shown as having some choice about whether or not to do so, as a result of the teller's decision. The performer's decision relates to whether or not to carry out the performance of going to the lecture; the teller's decision applies to constraints on the performer's freedom of choice. There are here two decisions taken by two different secondary role players about two different (but related) matters. The case for postulating two separate decider roles is strong. I shall say that, where the role in question has different occupancy in terms of secondary as well as primary roles, the construction realises 'role separation'.

§93.   I use the term 'operation' for a typical activity associated with a given role, and distinguish four: telling, knowing, deciding and performance. These are defined below (§114). For the moment, let us take 'performance' as that activity (or state of affairs) in the real world which is described in a clause. Examples such as, *Having finished his breakfast, John went out* illustrate a case where there are two performances both carried out by the one performer, and two clauses, but only one surface grammar subject. That is, there is secondary role, with single (third-party) occupancy, with which two distinct operations are associated. I shall say that the performer role here is 'spread' over two operations.

§94.   One operation may be 'split' between two role players in cases where each is presented as carrying out part of it. Non-polar interrogatives give an illustration of this, although not in its 'pure' form (which applies chiefly to two-speaker discourse units; cf. §52, and Chapter 6, §254 below). For example, in //1 When did John <u>come</u>//, the speaker presents himself as knowing that 'John came at some time', and the addressee as knowing not only this but also 'at which time'. Here the speaker knows part of the description of an event, the addressee knows with respect to all of it. There is inequality of knowledge, and to this extent the knower role can be said to be split in such instances. More genuine 'splitting' applies in the case of the teller role here, in the sense that the speaker tells part only of the complete description, and transfers the role of teller to the addressee only with respect to the remaining part (the lexical specification of *when*, e.g. *yesterday*). That is, the demand made in using a non-polar interrogative is not for a telling operation on a complete description, but only on one (or more) grammatically specified element(s) within one.

§95.   I suggest the notion of 'double operation' to account for example examples such as, *John's a fine player, he really is*, where one speaker, occupying the roles of both knower and teller, repeats his operations of knowing and telling with respect to a single description. (This would apply if he repeated only one operation in this way.)

§96.   The foregoing distinctions can be summarised in Table 3.1.

§97.   Both institutional and family roles may be authoritative (e.g. judge, teacher, parent), or non-authoritative (e.g. 'accused', student, child). This applies also to interactional secondary roles in LMM. Those so far proposed are all authoritative; but each of them could be matched with a non-authoritative counterpart. One might distinguish: the role of one who does not dominate the conversation in his utterance, but suggests rather than tells; the role of one who thinks that he knows, but cannot substantiate his opinion; the role of one who decides what he wants, but lacks the power to ensure that it happens; and a performer whose capacity to carry out an activity is doubtful.

The notion of 'role separation' (§92) represents one alternative

Table 3.1

No. of 'occurrences' of roles	Multiple/ single occupancy	No. of operations	No. of 'topics'	
1	Single	1	1	Unmarked
1	Multiple	1	1	Sharing
2	Single in each occurrence	2: 1 actual + 1 potential	1	Multiple occurrence
2	Single in each occurrence	2: 1 actual + 1 potential	2	Separation
1	Single	2	2	Spreading
2	Single in each occurrence	1	1, but divided	Splitting
2	*Same* single occupant in both occurrences	2	1	Double operation

to this proliferation of secondary roles, although it is not altogether satisfactory. While it may account for the element of performer-choice in modal constructions used in permission, it does not do so for those conveying obligation, such as *John should feed his dog raw meat* or *Children should brush their teeth regularly*. In such constructions both the speaker's expressed wish (or opinion that something is desirable) and a final decision by someone else are indicated. The assumption that the desired event is not currently taking place, and some expectation that it is not likely to, are also conveyed. The one envisaged as taking the authoritative decision is perhaps seen as the occupant of the performer role in the first example, and as some other unspecified (non-performer) third party in the second. Both 'decisions' relate to the same event in each example ('John's feeding his dog raw meat'/'children brushing their teeth regularly') and in each the speaker's is potentially opposed to that of the performer/third party. In these respects, such constructions could be said to realise multiple occurrence of the decider role; but, as the speaker is the occupant of the teller role in each case, the two occurrences of the decider role in the first example are occupied by different secondary role-players (teller, performer) which I have treated as a feature of role separation. In the second example, where the 'second' occurrence of decider is not occupied by a secondary role-player, it is easier to argue for multiple occurrence, if the speaker's occupancy of the teller role is discounted (Occurrence$_1$: (Speaker = Decider); Occurrence$_2$:(Third party = Decider)). Neither example, however, carries rising tone, which I have treated as characteristic of multiple occurrence.

The position seems to be intermediate between multiple occurrence and role separation, and, especially bearing in mind differences between the two examples, the picture remains unclear (but cf. §§183, 194, Chapter 4 below).

However, it does seem that this construction type realises an LMM feature of a teller who does not have the power to decide, in the sense of having the authority to see his decision implemented.

I shall attempt to deal with this by postulating the notion of 'attributes on roles'. That is, all four secondary roles will be marked for '+/− authority' in both instances where they have multiple occurrence or separation. This is not the only area in which 'authority marking' is of use (cf. §60 for the notion of a '+ capable' (i.e. '+ authority') performer).

§98.   I have used, without exploring, a distinction between two types of situations in considering the different secondary roles (cf. §78). This distinction is intimately bound up with the differing characteristics of these roles, and of the activities associated with each. The two types of situation can be seen as the 'locations' in which secondary role-players typically carry out their 'operations', and I hope to show that the feature of 'placement' in these terms is realised in surface grammar.

§99.   I distinguish between the situation in which an utterance is produced, the 'situation of utterance' ('SU'), and that in which the event to which it refers takes place: the 'situation of performance' ('SP'). (For the latter cf. Ellis, 1966, who uses the term 'situation of thesis'.) In these terms, Halliday's work on transitivity roles (1967b, 1967c, 1968), Fillmore's on roles and case (1968) and Anderson's treatment of case (1971) involve the analysis of features in SP. My notion of the (cover-all) performer role provides a device for linking whichever set of SP roles is chosen, as a group, with the primary and (other) secondary roles of LMM analysis (cf. Ross, 1970; Fillmore, 1972; for a different view of connections here).

§100.   Two features of situation types are relevant to this analysis:

(i)   The degree of overlap, or the separation, of SU and SP.

(ii)   The 'placing' of the occupants of secondary roles, and the operations which they carry out, in SU or SP.

Both are elements in LMM.

§101.   I define SU in terms of participants, rather than co-ordinates of time and place. Place may vary, as when two people talk while walking, and time may extend over variable periods, some of them quite long, within what I would see as one SU. Conversely, one participant in a conversation might leave, and a new individual join in, within a short space of time, and in the same place. Here I would distinguish two SUs. Topic of discourse is not a deciding factor. The SU may be discontinuous; if, for example, two participants in a speech event are interrupted by a third who then leaves and they resume their conversation, one SU would be discontinuous and 'enclose' the other. SU is a social situation, described in terms of the number and identity of participants and their relationships with each other, including the degree and type of their common knowledge and shared attitudes.

Taking Firth's (1962: 9-10) outline of a framework of analysis for the 'context of situation', one corollary of this last point is that the 'relevant objects' in SU are determined by the participants, at least as much as by their physical environment at the time of speaking. Degree and type of common knowledge governs possibilities of exophoric reference (Halliday & Hasan, 1976: Chapter 2), and this need not be dependent on shared surroundings. In fact, although shared surroundings at the time of speaking may contribute the identification of a referent, they do not often do so unaided. It is frequently the addressee's knowledge of what interests the speaker, what he is likely to notice, which enables him to identify correctly the referent of an exophoric pronoun in their common environment.

Where there is a high degree of common knowledge and shared attitudes, and also of knowledge of one another, between speaker and addressee (for example between members of one family),

exophoric reference may be unambiguously made to objects
altogether outside the physical environment of the utterance.
For example, a wife might begin a conversation with her husband
by saying, *Did he say anything about it?* The husband may well
correctly identify the individual referred to by *he* and the object
referred to by *it* on the basis of his knowledge that, for example,
the household boiler has broken down, that this is the only currently
urgent topic of conversation to his wife, and that Mr Jones, as the
only person capable of mending it, must be the referent of *he*.
I shall call such features of common knowledge 'item assumptions'
when they are exploited by a speaker to supply referent specification for exophoric pronouns. The form of this question also
assumes that the addressee had been able to hear *him* speak since he
last saw the speaker, and implies that what *he* had to say about *it* is
of interest to both speaker and addressee. If her question had been
What did he say about it? the further assumption is made that *he*
did 'say something about it'. The last, which I shall call a 'statement
assumption', is a feature of LMM. The first is implied by casting the
addressee in the role of knower; the second follows from Grice's
co-operative principle, and is a matter of significance.

The intelligibility of utterances making item assumptions, as
illustrated, depends heavily on the addressee sharing the speaker's
knowledge and attitudes/interests, and on his knowledge of what is
likely to be on the speaker's mind. Questions such as those above
would be unintelligible to a detached third party (and are sometimes
used for this reason).

Statement assumptions do not depend on common knowledge.
Non-polar interrogatives regularly realise assumed joint knowledge of
a proposition containing one (or more) indefinite quantifiers, in the
way illustrated above, whatever the relationship between speaker
and addressee (cf. §94).

The SU is that situation from which factors concerning the
participants, including their shared assumptions and common knowledge, their attitudes, relationships and interactions (both verbal and
non-verbal) feed in to the linguistic form of the ongoing verbal
interaction (together with whatever physical objects and features
of time and space the participants select as relevant).

§102.   I define SP as that situation in which the event or state of affairs
under discussion takes place: that is, in which the 'performance
operation' is carried out, or its result obtains. Different SPs, and
types of SPs, may also be established in terms of participants

(transitivity roles in Halliday's terms (e.g. 1970), in his ideational component). It is a major function of transitivity or case analysis to show just which of all the features in a given SP are selected within linguistic form (*la langue*) as elements of literal interpretational meaning.

§103.   SU and SP may entirely coincide, be completely separate, or overlap with one another to varying degrees.

§104.   Bloomfield's (1935) category of 'displaced speech' covers cases in which they do not coincide. It is here, in particular, that human language is more highly developed than any animal communication system, in its capacity for use in predictions about the future, hypotheses, contingency planning and reports of past events: the formulation of knowledge and speculation about 'the not-now-and-not-here' (cf. Hockett, 1958: 574-80; 1966: 11, 16-18; Linden, 1976: 49-76, 136-67).

Constructions of reasoning, both inductive and deductive, rest on a basis of displacement: it is this feature of human language which makes them possible, and it is the separation of SU and SP in reality which makes them necessary.

The capacity of human language to be displaced is central to its role in cultural transmission (Hockett, 1958: 579-80; cf. Linden, 1976: 142-4, 151-2).[8]

§105.   Different relations between SU and SP are among the factors realised in distinctions of mood and tense. Indicative mood typically realises cases where SU and SP do not coincide, ranging from complete separation, as in *John ate it* (shown as 'not-now' and not shown as 'here') to considerable (but not complete) overlap, as in *John is eating it*, which, even when it means 'here and now', does not preclude the possibility that he began to do so before the beginning of the conversation: 'SP may begin before SU begins.' This possibility is excluded in imperatives (cf. §§20, 25). Jussive imperatives (when not otherwise adverbially specified) potentially realise complete overlap of SU and SP: there is one situation in which both the performance and the telling operation take place. *Eat it*, on its own, generally means 'do it here-and-now'.

§106.   Tense realises distinctions of SU–SP overlap on the dimension of time both in the indicative and subjunctive moods. Only rough distinctions of time are realised grammatically in the form of the full verb in English. The considerable complexity and sophistication of time reference which is possible in the language depends principally on lexical selection in the adverbial, on verb form + adverbial combinations (cf. Crystal, 1966; Quirk *et al.*, 1972: 84-93, 482-505), and on the use of auxiliary verbs.

§107.   The distinction between the two inflectional full verb tenses ('plain' past and present) in the indicative can be largely accounted for in terms of whether SP ends before or after SU begins. Where SP ends before SU begins, this is realised by past tense. *John was happy* says nothing of how John may be feeling at the time of our conversation or thereafter; *John ran home* means that this activity is presented as being over before the point at which I am telling you about it, and nothing is suggested about what he may do in the future. This applies also to the past with progressive aspect (cf. Quirk *et al.*, 1972: 92-3) as in *John was enjoying himself.* Where past progressive realises an event in an SP within which the SP of another event is included, both end before SU begins, as in *John was gazing at the night sky when he saw the comet.*

§108.   Present tense realises cases where SP ends after SU begins. This is about as much as one can say of the present tense, for it does not realise any more specifically delimited area of time. The 'plain' present may even exclude the time during which SU takes place, as in *I walk to work* (which one would probably not say while in the process of doing so). One may note here the stative sense which verbs used dynamically elsewhere have in the plain present, as in *I come from London*: 'I am a Londoner'/*Joan sings*: 'Joan is a singer'. Here the SU is included in an SP which extends in time both before and after it: the performance is presented as characteristically attributable to that particular performer at any time. Present tense here realises a universal quantifier of time, 'at all times', 'on every occasion', with respect to the performance of an individual. It is closely related to the 'universal present' in examples such as *Whales are mammals* where there is, in addition, a universal quantifier governing the subject, 'All members of the set of whales . . .'. Here the predicate 'performance' applies at all times to all members of the set named in the subject.

The plain present may often be used to refer to future time when limited by adverbial specification, as in *Joan sings tonight/ I fly from Heathrow this evening.* In both these cases progressive aspect is perhaps more likely, because that form realises 'performance on one particular occasion'. Its relation to the plain present is 'limited:unlimited' in this respect. The progressive present comes closest of all the indicative tenses to realising complete SU–SP overlap, for the one particular occasion is often largely the same as

SU. But, as in, *I'm flying from Heathrow this evening*, it does not exclude a time after that at which the SU has ended; nor (cf. §105) does it exclude an earlier beginning for SP than for SU.

Both the plain present and the progressive may be used to refer to an event in an SP which either completely overlaps with, or is included in, SU, but in such cases either adverbial specification or contextual features are needed to make this unambiguous. For example, *Laker bowls/is bowling from the pavilion end*, occurring in a running commentary would realise such total overlap or inclusion, as would, *The lights are going out all over London as I write.*[9] But it is not an element of the meaning of the present tense in itself. The one feature of meaning which is common to all uses of the present tense is simply that the time of SP does not end before that of SU begins. It does not necessarily realise any overlap between the times of the two situations.

§109.   I have treated tense in terms of the time of ending of the situation in which a performance takes place in relation to the time of the beginning of the situation in which talking about it occurs. Features of the beginning and ending of activities have traditionally been taken to fall under aspect rather than tense (e.g. Poutsma, 1926: 291-301). But, if such features are realised in the 'plain' tenses, there is reason to treat other realisations of them under tense also, rather than aspect. I shall, therefore, take *to have* + V-ed combinations, sometimes treated as perfective aspect (e.g. Quirk *et al.*, 1972: 90-2), as (periphrastic) tenses, using the terms perfect (*have/has . . .*) and pluperfect (*had . . .*). (Cf. Jespersen, 1931: 3, 47-84.)

§110.   Both perfect and pluperfect realise the feature, 'SP begins before SU begins'. They differ with respect to whether a third situation is indicated, but neither form realises a feature of definite ending of the performance in SP in relation to another situation.

The perfect realises not only cases where SP overlaps with SU, ending after the latter begins, as in *John has lived in Paris for ten years* (and still does), which gives no indication about probable ending, but also cases where SP and SU may be 'contiguous' but have minimal, if any, overlap (SP ends just as SU begins) as in, *I've just finished* or *John's mended that fuse now*. In further examples, such as, *I've read that book again and again*, there may be a gap between the ending of the SP of the last occurrence of this performance and the beginning of SU.

The pluperfect realises the relation between the SP of its own event and that of another event which takes place before the on-going SU begins. This intervening situation may either be a second SP or a second SU. I shall take it as SP_2 for the moment. SP_1 may be shown to end before SP_2 begins, as in *When John had finished his breakfast, he went out*, or *He felt happy because he had finally found the answer*; but it may also indicate some overlap, as in the dependent clause of an 'open' conditional sentence, such as '*If John had caught the bus*, Jane would have seen him' (so let's ask her if she did), where the SP of 'Jane's seeing him' would either be at the same time as that of 'John's catching the bus' or subsequent to it, and possibly separated by an interval (she saw him when she got on at the next stop).

Both perfect and pluperfect are in themselves indeterminate with respect to the SP ending. However, there is a fairly strong tendency for the perfect (with present tense *has/have*) to realise 'SP ends after SU begins', unless this is over-ridden by adverbial specification to the contrary, and for the pluperfect (with past tense *had*) to realise SP_1 ends before SP_2 begins (as well as before SU begins) unless this is countered by features in the syntactic co-text.

Indicative past tense also realises, by implication, the feature, 'SP begins before SU begins'. This is implied by 'SP ends before SU begins', since an 'end' assumes an earlier beginning. We may now summarise a four-way set of distinctions of time in terms of relative ends and beginnings of situations, as follows:

(i)   'SP ends after SU begins' : Present
(ii)   'SP begins before, and ends as or after, SU begins' : Perfect
(iii) 'SP (begins and) ends before SU begins': Past
(iv) 'SP_1 (begins and) ends before SP_2 begins (SP_2 begins and ends before SU begins)' : Pluperfect

Since the same dimensions are involved throughout, it seems reasonable to treat all four together as different tenses.

§111.   The question of whether or not a secondary role is assigned to a participant role-player in SU — and, if so, to which one — enters into the LMM of constructions. For example, the role of decider is obligatorily assigned to a participant role-player, either the speaker or a present addressee (or to both jointly in inclusive *Let's* con-structions) in imperatives, and assigned to a third party (the non-participant role, cf. §79) in optative subjunctives. This is one major distinction between the two sets of construction types. Here the

question of whether the decider 'operates' in SU or SP underlies
a distinction of mood. In terms of SU–SP overlap, imperatives of all
kinds realise the feature 'SP begins after SU begins'; and optative
subjunctives realise 'SP ends after SU ends'.

§112.   With respect to literal interpretational meaning I distinguish
between a 'description' and a 'proposition'. This relates to the
question of which element(s) in the event or state of affairs in SP
are selected for linguistic presentation. 'Description' is the general
term, and covers any linguistic realisation of 'real-world' features:
it need not involve predication. For example, I shall say that both
the utterances *Hello!* and *John came home yesterday* present descriptions. 'Proposition' I use as a special term to refer to a 'complete
description'. All propositions are descriptions, but not all descriptions are propositions; for example, *Hello!* presents a description,
but not a proposition.

By a 'complete description' I mean one in which there is an
'established subject–predicate bond'. Imperatives do not present a
complete description, but non-modal indicative clauses do, even
when non-finite and/or embedded (as in '*John's coming home
frequently* was a mistake'). By a 'subject–predicate bond' I mean a
relation between a subject and verb, both explicitly present in
surface structure which could in some circumstances be marked for
concord. The description presented in an imperative is not complete in this sense; neither is that in a subjunctive construction, nor
that in one containing a modal verb (since the modals are not capable of inflecting for number of person). However, *John's coming
home* as a non-finite embedded clause relates to the non-embedded
finite forms, *John is coming/comes/has come*, all of which are
marked for concord.

§113.   A description is not susceptible to analysis in terms of LMM;
but there are different types of description in terms of transitivity
or case relations. I would include a proper name on its own as one
type of description. This suggestion relates to Frege's view
(discussed in Dummett, 1973) that a sentence, minus force-indicating devices, is a complex name. That is, I take a description to be
that aspect of the sentence which has no LMM, but does have
literal interpretational meaning, and allow for it to be either
'simple', when it realises no transitivity or case relations (and
has only lexical interpretational meaning), or 'complex', when it
does realise such relations (and therefore also has grammatical
interpretational meaning). Nominalisations such as the gerundive

nominal 'His doing x', are, for me, descriptions to which no force-indicating devices are attached; and to term them 'complex names' seems apposite. I shall, below, phrase the description element in a sentence in this form to clarify its outline when stripped of the force-indicating devices which, in combination with it, confer 'sentencehood' on the whole.

Descriptions do not vary, as such, according to what is 'done to' them in terms of the addition of force-indicating devices. The description presented as known and told in the sentence *John comes home frequently* is exactly the same, per description, when presented as known but told only derivatively and realised as a non-finite embedded clause at subject in '*John's coming home frequently* was a mistake'. On this view, finiteness and tense do not realise features of the description, but of 'force' (LMM).

§114.   In §93 I introduced the term 'operation' for a 'typical activity' associated with a particular secondary role, and distinguished four, according to the roles. I now define them as follows:

(i)   Telling: constructing a linguistic description and presenting it to another (or others) in a speech interaction. (Telling constitutes a verbal social move.)

(ii)   Knowing: taking cognizance of the relation between a description and the 'reality' to which it refers so as to assign it a known occurrence value (a 'knowledge value': 'KV') and relate it to SU in terms of relative sequence in time.

(iii)   Deciding: making a judgement about which occurrence value shall attach to an event.

(iv)   Performing: carrying out an activity or entering into/ being in a relationship or state (including 'existing') in the 'real world'. The activity, etc. concerned is often extra-linguistic, but it may involve language, as in verbs of *saying, telling, asking*, etc., or operations associated with the mediating secondary roles, as in verbs of *knowing/thinking/believing*, or of *deciding/wishing/wanting*, etc.

§115.   The telling operation has two aspects:

(i)   construction of the description;

(ii)   presentation of the description (associated with conversational dominance, cf. §77).

They are closely connected in that, when a participant takes to himself the right to choose what to talk about, this is an important aspect of dominating a conversation. This remains true even where the teller role is transferred and the addressee assigned the role of knower in polar interrogatives. It is for this reason that, for example, a policeman interviewing a suspect could remain highly dominant in the verbal interaction while using only interrogative constructions; and an examiner using them does not lose the initiative to the candidate.

§116.   I use the term 'construction' of the description to denote an activity roughly comparable to Austin's idea of the 'locutionary act' (1962: 94-107). Chomsky's remarks on the creative nature of language, and the native speaker's capacity to produce and understand a potentially infinite number of different sentences (1965: 6, 57-8) apply to the construction of descriptions of all types, but particularly to that of propositions.

'Choosing what to talk about' and 'constructing a description' are different aspects of the same activity. The latter in one sense depends on the former; for to construct any description involves not constructing its complementary, and this is what is involved in choice of topic.

§117.   The choice of which description to construct and present contributes to higher order levels of significance and affects the structure of discourse. Grice's example (1975: 54) of the remark 'The weather has been quite delightful this summer, hasn't it?' in response to another speaker's comment that 'Mrs X is an old bag' is a good illustration of significance, deriving mainly from choice of description. It is this 'choice' element in the teller's operation which is related to questions of common knowledge, shared assumptions (concerning both facts and social norms) and presuppositions in general.

The choice of description is a major element in the verbal social move which the teller makes towards his addressee in presenting it; and the significance of this choice is interpretable not only in terms of the 'Co-operative Principle' and its underlying maxims which Grice outlines (1975: 45-56), but also in terms of the dynamics of discourse. For example, a teller may choose to present a proposition on which he knows the addressee holds strong views, and his making this choice may be interpreted as signifying that he wants the addressee to talk at length and to extend the conversation (? 'discourse significance') or that he is challenging or encouraging the addressee (high level interactional significance).

§118.   In constructing the description which he uses in making his verbal social move, the teller selects elements in extra-linguistic reality and organises them within the rules governing categories of literal interpretational meaning and their realisation. These include rules governing the organisation of information in terms of relative prominence of different elements (cf. Halliday, 1967c, 1967d, 1968, for a discussion of this area under 'Theme').

§119.   The teller presents the description. This aspect of the telling operation is realised grammatically on the one hand in the main clause/dependent or embedded clause distinction and, on the other, by mood. Dependency realises 'spread' telling in the sense that there is one teller and one full telling operation for more than one description, so that the dependent clause is told only derivatively, in as far as it presents a modification of, or element in (when embedded) the main clause which is fully told. If one takes all dependent clauses as realising elements within the structure of a super-ordinate clause, then embedding realises an LMM feature of derivative telling, in which a description is not told in its own right but only in as far as it forms part of another description.

Tone realises features of the dynamic aspect of the telling operation, principally teller role transference of different types (giving, claiming, accepting and returning, etc.). Such features contribute to the establishment of interactional discourse units (cf. §52, and Chapter 5 below).

§120.   I use the term 'sign' for the semantic distinction between positive and negative when grammatically realised either with respect to a description or an operation. There are two basic types of sign accordingly.

§121.   I use the term 'occurrence value' ('Ov') to refer to the happening of an event (/state of affairs) in extra-linguistic reality. One or other Ov (positive/negative) is built into every description which involves a predication (either actual, as in non-modal declaratives, or potential, as in imperatives). I shall say that selection of an Ov is part of what is involved in the construction of (most) descriptions, and that it is one aspect of 'choosing what to talk about': that is, part of the telling operation. I shall call description sign 'DS'.

The Ov selected for presentation in the description need not be 'actual': the event may be presented as not yet having begun to take place, as in jussive imperatives. DS is neutral to the question of whether or not the performance operation is shown as 'achieved', as witness not only imperatives but also the fact that the description in the dependent clause of an open conditional sentence is marked for DS: '*If it rains/doesn't rain*, we'll leave early.' In counterfactual conditionals DS, as realised in surface polarity, is the opposite of the Ov known actually to have occurred, as in '*If they'd invaded* they would have won', where the teller assumes common knowledge of the fact that 'they didn't invade' (and that 'they didn't win') (cf. §307).

§122.   Not all descriptions have sign. Some simple, incomplete descriptions such as *Hello/John* are neutral to the positive/negative distinction. Sign in the sense in which I am using the term depends on there being at least a potential subject—predicate bond; the description must be about a performance, rather than being a name or constituting a performance in itself without describing one, as with *Hello*.

§123.   In exclamative constructions the description has an obligatory sign value: non-choice positive, as in *What a beauty (that is)!/How well he rides!* There are no parallel negative constructions, **What a beauty that isn't!/*How well he doesn't ride.* The contrary of the description in such a construction is not realised grammatically but lexically (by an autonym where one exists), e.g. *How badly he rides! What a beauty* does not appear to have an autonymic variant: **What an unbeauty/*(?) What an ugliness.*

Polarity in some negative interrogatives with falling intonation, such as *Isn't that nice!* does not realise description sign. Here too the description is non-choice positive, and the construction does not paraphrase as, 'Is that not-nice'. The notion 'exclamatory force' derives from that of non-choice sign. In cases where this is not realised syntactically, as in 'rhetorical' questions (which are syntactically identical to open questions) context supplies the information that sign is non-choice. Rhetorical questions have the FOS of 'exclamation', but this is not their LMM. I shall use the term 'exclamative' for the LMM feature, realised in syntactic form, and 'exclamation' for the category of FOS which may result from the combination of the contextually supplied feature 'only one Ov possible in these circumstances', with a number of different construction types. (This approach excludes utterances such as *ouch* from the category of exclamations. I would class them as ejaculations.) Exclamatives realise the feature non-choice DS. Non-choice DS as an LMM feature of exclamatives is always positive.

§124.   'Operation sign' applies not to the description, but to what is done to it or with it. I relate this to the implementation of operations. 'Implementation' is a feature of an operation as 'authority' is a feature of a role. Because they do not always coincide both notions are needed.

§125.   Certain constructions are neutral to particular operations. For example, imperatives are neutral to knowing, and knowing is irrelevant to imperatives. An operation may be relevant and yet not implemented. For example knowing is relevant to constructions such as *John may like chess*, even though neither speaker nor addressee is shown to occupy the role of knower. Here I shall say that the knowing operation is unimplemented (and that decision is irrelevant). In a comparable manner, decision in optative subjunctives such as *God save the Queen* is relevant but unimplemented; the role of decider is occupied by a third party, and the outcome of the decision operation is uncertain (the construction is neutral to knowing/knowing is irrelevant).

There is some connection between third-party occupancy of the knower or decider role and lack of implementation of the associated operation. This is not true of performing and telling which may be relevant but unimplemented, even with speaker occupancy.

§126.   I shall use the terms 'achieved'/'unachieved' for implemented/unimplemented performance. An achieved performance is one which is presented as actually taking/having taken place.

§127.   Telling in its construction of description aspect is everywhere implemented, and in its presentation aspect everywhere relevant. It may, in the latter respect, sometimes be unimplemented.

There are two dimensions in terms of which telling may be assessed for implementation:

(i)   full/derived (cf. §119);
(ii)   immediate/distanced.

Unimplemented telling relates not only to the occupancy of the teller role, but also to the 'placement' of the telling operation. Telling shown to take place outside the ongoing SU I shall say is 'distanced', and unimplemented even where there is speaker occupancy of the role, as in *I wanted to see the black pair in the window please*, used as a polite form of request, with *wanted* referring to present time (SU). Here the teller is '− authority'.

§128.   Where an operation is implemented, the secondary role concerned is always '+ authority' (cf. §97). This may also be so in some cases where the operation is unimplemented, as in jussive imperatives with (performer$^+$).

§129.   The operand for the operations of knowing and deciding is description sign: this is what is known or decided on. Sign also applies to these two operations. I shall say that, when implemented, they have positive, and when unimplemented, negative, sign. Knowing/deciding sign and description sign are independent variables. This is clearly so where the former is positive: *John went/ didn't go*; *Go/don't go*, but one may also have 'unknown' (negative knowing sign) attached to either a positive or negative description, as in *John may like chess/John may not like chess*; and, similarly for 'undecided' (negative deciding sign).

§130.   Implementation refers to the carrying through of an operation within or (for those other than telling) before the SU. An implemented operation is one presented as complete with reference to SU; an unimplemented operation is incomplete in the sense of not being brought to a conclusion before SU ends. Implemented operations are actual, unimplemented operations non-actual, but possible. Both are relevant. All relevant operations are marked in the semantics for +/− implementation; e.g. 'decision$^+$' indicates an implemented decision operation, 'knowing$^-$', indicates an unimplemented knowing operation.

§131.   Distanced telling involves the displacement of the telling operation to a situation outside SU, with or without the additional feature of non-(current-) speaker occupancy of the teller role (as in past tense reported clauses).

§132.   Description sign represents the selection of an Ov as the topic. The notion of Ov relates to the performance operation in extra linguistic reality. The Ov selected for discussion may be the opposite of that assumed to be known to have actually occurred in extra linguistic reality. What seems to be involved here is distanced telling of a particular kind, one involving 'non-presentation'.

§133.   'Non-presentation' involves just that: the Ov known or decided on is not what is presented as the topic for discussion. This is the area of 'imaginative tenses' (cf. Jespersen, 1940). I shall say that constructions such as *If only I'd known . . ./If I were you . . ./Had they invaded . . .* realise presentation of the Ov which is accepted as known not to have actually happened. The Ov selected for discussion (DS) is the opposite of that which is accepted as known. Constructions of this type have distanced telling ('I do not say it here and now'); but not all distanced telling involves this sign reversal element, DS ≠ Ov.

§134.   I shall say that the distinction between immediate/distanced presentation constitutes (positive/negative) telling sign, which is distinct from description sign. There are four kinds of 'operation sign' which combine to give a 'force sign' – those of telling (presentation), knowing and decision and performance. All these types of operation sign are elements in LMM, which is the semantics of force-indicating devices.

Operation sign is realised in surface grammar by features of mood; partly, although not systematically, by the modal/non-modal verb distinction (cf. Chapters 6 and 7). I take the indicative/subjunctive distinction to relate principally to telling sign, although there are problems with that view.

Clearly this partial summary represents a considerable over-simplification. Subsequent chapters attempt to substantiate these claims adding some necessary qualifications. But I believe that the outline is in essence correct.

Description sign is what is realised in surface polarity (with some exceptions among modal verbs). But it is important to note two major features of description sign:

(i)   It is potentially opposite to the occurrence value in extra-linguistic reality, and is, in principle, a different concept.

(ii)   Its relation to Ov is determined partly by operation sign.

§135.   The area of English grammar in which description sign is the opposite of what is known/assumed/expected includes not only imaginative tenses but also modal verb constructions (which are unknown/undecided) and optative subjunctives (which are also undecided).

For example in *The train may have been late* which is 'unknown' but has positive description sign, the construction simultaneously tells us the possibility that 'it was late' and suggests the greater possibility that 'it wasn't'. The suggestion element emerges more clearly with the negative; *The train may not have been late* conveys the implication that there is a strong possibility that it was late. One would not use the negative construction where trains habitually ran on time.

§136.   It is possible to say, as a rough generalisation, that negative knowing or telling operation sign determines a relation of opposi-tion between description sign and occurrence value (where Ov is extended to cover what is/was expected to happen, in addition to what is known to (have) occur(red)).

This covers cases of 'unknown', of distanced telling where this applies to knowing, and of 'undecided' where knowing is also relevant. However, with decision constructions in general the position is more complicated, in that they all assume an opposition between inertia and decision. That is, the standard case in decision is, 'DS $\neq$ (probable) Ov'.

§137.   The decision operation is about reversing inertia, i.e. it involves countermanding the expected Ov. Decision positive operation sign is more strongly reversative in this respect than negative operation sign (the 'undecided' option). This is the opposite state of affairs to that obtaining with respect to the knowing operation. The 'undecided' constructions always involve two decision operations; that of the teller is decided, that of the performer is generally undecided.

Surface polarity realises the sign of the teller's decision (even if non-authoritative), which is told, as opposed to that of the performer's decision which, when made, is non-presented (e.g. *You shouldn't have gone*), and when unmade may be open and neutral to telling. In the latter case there is some implication either that the two will probably be in harmony (permission), or in conflict (compulsion/prohibition): *You can come in now/You must go.*

§138.   Imperatives are basically neutral to performer's decision. He is not presented as having any choice (except perhaps in optatives, such as *Let John come*, where it would be generally conveyed that he wants to). Where two decisions are involved one belongs to the teller, the other to the addressee.

Subjunctives present the speaker-teller's wish, but divide between those where knowledge of the actual state of affairs is unpresented (and opposed to this wish) and others in which this is left open, as in *God save the Queen.* There are problems concerning the status of *wish* in terms of this framework: the notion of 'undecided' in this connection is open to objection, for it is not lack of decisiveness which is involved, but that of lack of power to implement the decision. Optative subjunctives have told wish (the teller's wish is what they present), and this wish is not necessarily opposed to what is the case. If one uses the notion of 'undecided' for wish, for the time being, they represent a case where, contrary to the normal position for decision constructions, there is not an opposition between description sign and occurrence value. If so, operation sign here ('lack of decision') has the standard effect of reversing the typical relation between description sign and Ov (here from opposition to harmony).

§139.　　As a general rule, it is description sign which is realised in surface polarity; operation sign is realised in distinctions of mood. Cases, principally *can't* and *needn't*, which are generally treated as realising 'modal negation', present interesting exceptions, and will be discussed further in the relevant sections of Chapters 4, 6 and 8. Negation in certain interrogatives, such as, *Isn't that nice!* which, similarly, does not realise description sign, may be linked with them.

§140.　　I suggest that the following partial outline in Table 3.2, may be drawn (where telling is full and immediate). ('Pb' = 'probable'/ 'expected'):

Table 3.2 Operation Sign

A	Knowledge	Positive: (known)	$DS = Ov$	*John went/ didn't go*
		Negative: (unknown)	$DS \neq (Pb)\, Ov$	*The train may/ may not be late*
B	Decision	Positive: (decided)	$DS \neq Pb\, Ov$	*Go/don't go away*
		Negative: (undecided)	$DS = Pb\, Ov$	*Must I go?*

§141.　　Where telling is distanced, the following, again partial, picture emerges for knowledge:

Table 3.3

Operation sign		
Positive: (known)	$DS \neq Ov$	*If only he'd come . . ./If I were you . . ./ If they'd invaded . . .*
Negative: (unknown)	$DS = Ov$	*If he'd been there he would have seen them (so let's ask him if he did)*

§142.   The full picture, as explored to some extent in subsequent chapters, is a great deal more complicated than these rather selective fragments would suggest. But perhaps enough is shown to indicate some usefulness in distinguishing DS from Ov, and to suggest the possibility that mood selection may govern the meaning of surface polarity in some cases. It would be crucial to the substantiation of such a claim that mood could be shown to correlate with operation sign. I shall offer further arguments in support of this notion below. Here a brief survey of the surface grammar of modality, the subjunctive and modal verbs seems in order.

§143.   I distinguish between an inflected and periphrastic subjunctive. All inflected present subjunctives of knowledge have a periphrastic equivalent with *should* + V base (as do indicatives in conditional clauses); subjunctives with past inflection have a periphrastic equivalent with *did* + V base. Pluperfect subjunctives have the form *had* + V-ed (which is identical to that of the pluperfect indicative).

§144.   *Should* in the periphrastic subjunctive is distinct from *should* functioning as a full modal verb. Compare: *If John should come*, 'If it should be the case that John *does* come', with *John should come*; (i) 'It is desirable that John *should* come' and (ii) 'It is likely that John *will* come' (i.e. periphrastic subjunctive *should* applies to the complete description). Modal verb *should* applies only to the predicate. Compare also: *John should come*: 'It is the case that he is likely to' with *If he should*: implying 'It may be the case that he does/will' (which has unimplemented telling in the dependent clause).

Subjunctive *should* realises operation modality, modal verb *should* realises 'description modality' (an incomplete description in my terms with a non-established subject—predicate bond). This might be compared with the *de dicto/de re* distinctions within alethic modalities (cf. Von Wright, 1951: 1).

§145.   Main clause subjunctives all realise decision. These do not have a *should* paraphrase. Where present, they have a *may* + V base equivalent; where 'past', they commute with the *to* infinitive, which has almost entirely superceded them in contemporary English. (*Oh that I were in England*)/*Oh to be in England.*
Compare:

God save the Queen/May God save the Queen:

> *God should save the Queen.*
> ('*I wish/hope that God does/will . . .*' *'*It is the case that God
>   ought to . . .*').

Constructions with (performer: addressee) demand *may* to disambiguate them from imperatives: *May you succeed.* This also applies generally for the third person performer, e.g. *May he prosper* (cf. (?) *John come*, where *may* can perhaps be omitted, but **he prosper* where it cannot).

§146.   Periphrastic subjunctives in dependent clauses following a main verb of wishing, etc. generally have *would* (or *could*) but not *should*; e.g. *I wish he would come more often* (as a variant of *I wish he came more often*). Compare, however, *I demand that he (should) go* and *I wish that he (should) be summoned.* Here a distinction between [Dr = Pr] and [Dr = Tr] with respect to the performance in the complement clause is realised grammatically by the choice of modal verb in that clause. The last pair of examples realise [(teller = decider) : speaker].

§147.   The differences between periphrastic subjunctives with *should* and *may* can be summarised as:

(i)   *Should* applies to the description as a whole, *may* to the subject—predicate bond;
(ii)   *May* realises wish and *should* does not.

Main clause subjunctives all realise decision: where present, they realise unachieved performance in the sense of it not yet being completed; where past they realise lack of performance: it is excluded from SU and not the case 'now'. The former do not realise DS ≠ Ov; and they are neutral to the question of whether the performance has yet begun. The latter do realise DS ≠ Ov; performance is shown as definitely not yet in progress in SU.

§148.   The inflected subjunctive with past form does not have a modal equivalent. Where it refers to present time, as in, *I wanted to see the ones in the window*, the marking for an unreal, 'extra' degree of 'pastness' realises the distancing of telling, rather than performance, from SU. Where it has future time reference, as in '*If it rained* (the match would be cancelled)', there is a paraphrase with *were to* + V base, 'If it were to rain . . .'. This can be interpreted as: marking for one degree of extra (unreal) pastness, plus marking for 'unachieved' (the infinitive). This gives distanced telling of present occurrence together with 'unachieved', which in this case has the stronger sense of 'unbegun'; 'unbegun now' = 'future occurrence'. In both cases the past subjunctive realises DS = (Pb)Ov.

§149.   The pluperfect subjunctive also realises an extra degree of marking for pastness in some cases, although in others it cannot, for standard English is only able to express two degrees of pastness. Compare: *If only I had known!*, where an extra degree of pastness (realising distanced telling) seems probable, with *If she had seen him* (she would have telephoned before we set out) where the 'double degree of pastness' is accountable for in terms of performance alone. Non-standard English can indicate a third degree: *If she'd have seen him . . .*

§150.   I have now illustrated the notion that more than one different operation may be realised in a construction. To this I have, in references to performer- and teller-decision, added the idea that the one type of operation may 'occur' more than once. This parallels the notions in §91 concerning multiple occurrence of roles.

§151.   The notion of recursive applications of one operation is most obviously relevant where such re-application is lexically realised as in, 'I know that you know that I know', etc.

Some explicit performatives involve two (or more) operations of different types. Compare *I order you to go* with *I apologise*. These are quite different construction types, both semantically and grammatically.

(i)   There is a distinction between the lexical realisation of force attached to the performance in the description as opposed to the non-lexical realisation of force attached to a description which is of a 'force performance', i.e. 'apology' is a verbal social move, but *going* is not.

(ii)   Opinions differ as to whether the *I order . . .* type is simultaneously a present report (of simultaneous action) and therefore always involves knowledge (of decision), as well as the decision itself, or not. Lewis (1972: 211-2) suggests that such constructions are ambiguous as to force (command/report); I would prefer to say that they realise both.

§152.   I introduce the term 'plane' to refer to an area of grammatical semantics within which distinctions to do with one of the four operations are systematised. There are four planes, one for each of the four operations. A 'plane' does not correspond directly with classes of surface grammar constructions, for most of the latter realise features from more than one plane. The usefulness of the notion of planes lies within the semantics. Often a semantic feature within one plane is only grammatically realised when combined with another in a different plane.

The main area in which intra-plane distinctions are realised directly in surface grammar is that of telling. The following chapters are organised in terms of planes. That is, although the constructions discussed all involve the realisation of features in at least two, usually three, different planes, they are grouped together and discussed chiefly from the point of view of one plane at a time. I shall treat syntactic devices realising elements within one plane as constituting an 'area' of the grammar.

§153. Levels of Directness

Immediacy in terms of SU is an important factor in relation to all four operations and the occupancy of all four roles.

Constructions may be rated as more or less direct according to the following factors:

(i)   Number of operations
      (a) different operations
      (b) repetitions of the same operation.

(ii)   Distancing of any operation from SU.
(iii)   Number and authority of secondary roles involved.
(iv)   Sign of operation(s). (This is partially derivable from (ii) and (iii).
(v)   Degree of SU/SP overlap.

The following chapters subdivide constructions into 'direct' and 'indirect' according principally to the occupancy of secondary roles and the placement of the operations under focus within/outside their typical location.

§154.   Summary of Framework of LMM Analysis So Far Proposed

I Primes

(a)   Roles: primary/secondary.
(b)   Operations: activities associated with secondary roles.
(c)   Planes: areas of semantic organisation each relating to one role and its associated operation.

II Attributes on Primes

(a)   Attributes on roles: +/− authority.

(b)   Attributes on operations: +/− implementation, i.e. 'Operation sign'.

III Attributes Relate to:

(i)   Occupancy of secondary roles in terms of primary roles. Third-party occupancy often correlates with: '−authority' role.

(ii)   Placement of operations: Displacement correlates with: '− implemented'.

IV 'Stages'

(Each operand contains any 'previous' one(s).)

(i)   Features in extra-linguistic reality, including occurrence value.

(ii)   Description + Description sign.

(iii)   Operation sign + (Description + DS): semantic 'clause type'.

(iv)   Full force indicator as vehicle for description: semantic 'sentence type'.

Telling in its construction aspect operates on (i) to yield (ii).

Telling (Presentation)/Knowing/Deciding operate on (ii) to yield (iii).

Where either Knowing or Deciding or both operate on (ii) Telling (Presentation) also operates on the product of either or each to yield (iv).

Where Telling (Presentation) alone operates on (ii) this yields (iv) directly.

The notion of 'stages' should not be taken to have a temporal or logical status. For example, the relation between DS and Ov may be governed by Knowing/Deciding sign at a 'later' stage. I do not suggest a simple 'progression' between stages in any literal sense. The notion is a convenient abstraction.

V Operands

The operand in each case except the 'first' (extra linguistic reality) is the relevant sign. Even at the first stage, occurrence value may be thought of as the sign of the event/state of affairs; and this is operated on to yield description sign. One may summarise as follows:

where

'↘'		indicates 'operates on'
'→'		indicates 'yields'
'Tc'	=	'Telling (construction)'
'Tp'	=	'Telling (presentation)'
'K'	=	'Knowing'
'D'	=	'Deciding'
'OS'	=	'Operation sign'
'DS'	=	'Description sign'.

then:

(i) $Tc ↘ (Ov) → DS$

(ii) $K/D ↘ (DS) → OS(DS)$

(iii) $Tp ↘ (OS(DS)) →$ 'Full force indicator'.

Tp/K/D may each have positive/negative operation sign. This feature
of operations is partly determined by authority occupancy and
combinations of roles, partly by the 'placement' of the operation
(itself largely corresponding with participant/non-participant occupancy of roles).

The 'full-force indicator' is a bundle of semantic features underlying the complex of syntactic features of mood and polarity for
which a construction is marked.

§155.   The notion of operands, operations and stages provides a framework comparable to that postulated for levels of first order
significance (cf. Chapter 2).

Rules for the LMM of a sentence can be postulated in comparable terms, e.g.: '$A ↘ (B) → E$', where 'A' is the name of an operation,
'B' names an operand, and 'E' is either an operand at a different
stage, or else a semantic 'sentence' type (which is itself one element
in 'X' in a FOS rule of the form 'X counts as Y in C'), cf. §54.

Notes

1. Austin (1962), Searle (1969) and Grice (1968, 1969) all make this
assumption. I take the statement that 'language is (amongst other things) one
form of social behaviour/action' as a basic premiss, which is given.

2. As family roles are not always biologically determined they may be
viewed as institutional to some extent, although 'private' rather than 'public'.
They are social, interactional roles. (Cf. in this connection the use of family
role names to designate priests and members of religious orders, 'father',
'brother', 'mother', 'sister'.)

3. Very roughly, one can associate institutional roles more closely with lexical interactional meaning, and non-institutional roles (cf. §§ 76-7 below) with grammatical interactional meaning (LMM).

4. Problems with this approach arise in some decision constructions, particularly the imperative. I would see the decider role there as a 'putative causer' where there is unimplemented performance, roughly comparable to 'ergative' (or 'initiator') in a construction realising implemented performance; and the performer as 'actor' (or 'goal' in a passive, such as *Let every man be given food*). The identification of 'performer' as realised by mood subject breaks down in this area to the extent that I postulate a performer in the LMM of constructions with no subject element, such as *Come here*.

I take 'mood subject' in imperatives to be the subject (where present) of the first verb in the construction (cf. Appendix I). This means that, in optatives the mood subject realises the occupant of the decider role (the addressee), as in *You let John come*, although in jussives it realises that of the performer (again the addressee), as in *You come here*. In optatives, then, there is a case where the performer is not mood subject, but subject of an embedded clause. This analysis applies, similarly, in *I order you to go* and other constructions in which a decision operation is lexically realised. Optative *let* can be thought of as the imperative of a verb of allowing, and the decider of the event in the embedded clause can be seen as also the performer of an 'allowing action'. In this sense there are two performances (of different types) in such constructions.

In first person interrogative *will* constructions, in my dialect, the mood subject cannot realise 'actor' in terms of transitivity: *Will I go?* is unacceptable, *Will I be admitted?* is acceptable. If performer is equated with mood subject, this means that there is a restriction on its transitivity status in this case. With *shall I* the opposite restriction applies. Here the mood subject cannot realise 'goal', but has to be 'actor'; e.g. *Shall I get a copy?* means 'Would you like me to fetch one?' and not 'Am I going to receive one?'.

5. That is, I take the view, now generally accepted among linguists, of Saussure (1916: 156), Hjelmslev (1961: 50-1) and others. Cf. Chomsky (1976: Chapter 2).

6. An occupant of a secondary role may be named, through naming of the primary role-player. This applies mainly to the role of performer, when occupied by a third party, but is possible also for speaker and addressee occupants of that role: '*I, John Smith*, undertake . . .'/'*You, Mary Jones*, shall be responsible'. In reported speech where the performance in the 'outer' (reporting) clause is verbal, naming of this performer simultaneously names the speaker of the 'inner' (reported) clause, and so, the occupant of the knower and teller roles in that other situation of utterance, as in '*John* said Jane was coming'.

Vocatives attached to (jussive) imperatives in naming the addressee also name the performer; attached to optatives they name the decider. Vocatives attached to indicative declaratives/interrogatives may, but need not, name the performer.

7. The dependent clause here has 'derived', as opposed to 'full' telling (cf. §§127, 227). The role of teller is, however, relevant.

8. Displacement is essential to written language. In as far as human language is displaced, gesture becomes less a possible alternative.

9. The limitation to 'performance on one particular occasion' realised in the present progressive explains the unacceptability of that construction in cases of 'statement of origin', e.g. **I am coming from Geneva* used to describe the speaker's home town. *I come from Geneva* is similar in some respects to *I walk to work*.

4 DECISION

§156.   The decision plane is that area of the semantics in which distinctions to do with the occupancy, occurrences and combinations of
the decider role, and the application of the decision operation, are
systematised. Such features are realised mainly in constructions
of non-indicative mood: imperatives, modal verb constructions and
optative/hortatory subjunctives. I suggest that explicit performatives
such as *I order you to go* are 'reported' forms in the first instance,
and that this is realised by the indicative mood of the verb in the
matrix sentence. The decision features which some exercitives
convey are lexically realised in this main verb, and grammatically
realised in features of the complement clause (cf. §146).

§157.   It is characteristic of all constructions realising decision factors
in LMM, that they involve an assumption about a probable
occurrence value of the event selected for presentation. I shall call
this the 'inertia' or 'inertial value' of the event. This is either
assumed to be opposite to description sign, or not assumed to be
the same. There are no cases where the assumption is that it is the
same. In this respect decision constructions are the reverse of constructions involving full knowledge. Description sign in decision
constructions is the opposite of probable Ov and the same as that
Ov which is decided on or wished for. Description sign is realised
in surface polarity. This amounts to saying that surface polarity
realises the Ov which is decided on or wished for as opposed to that
which is presented as otherwise likely to occur. But neither of these
opposed Ovs is presented as achieved or actual (except where the
lexical verb is marked for perfect tense: should *have gone*).

§158.   Decision constructions typically realise incomplete descriptions,
except where knowledge is also relevant, as in, *You should have
written/You might have helped* (we both know that you didn't).
The 'knowledge that not' underlying such positive constructions is
not presented and contrasts with the description sign.

§157.   The typical role configuration in decision constructions is:
[Decider ≠ Performer] . There are exceptions, principally in uses of
will and *shall*, but, as a rough generalisation, it is not unreasonable
to say that decision semantics is chiefly about the attempted
imposition of the teller's will on that of the performer: the influence

of verbal activity on extra-linguistic, non-verbal activity. Of course the picture is muzzy: there are constructions which convey that the teller knows he hasn't got the power to enforce his wish on the performer but thinks it may be worth trying to influence a more powerful intermediary, and so on (e.g. grandmother to mother: *Should John eat sweets between meals?*). But as a general rule, some attempt to influence what happens in extra-linguistic reality, whether direct or indirect, is involved in telling a decision or wish, even though it may be simultaneously conveyed that the performer is his own man and has the upper hand.

§ 160.   Decision constructions realise assumptions about another's wishes, likely behaviour and 'status' relative to the speaker (cf. Chapter 2). Constructions of direct decision, in particular, may be seen as constituting 'pieces' in a 'game' of verbal social interaction. To utter an imperative, for example, is to make a move in such a game. The assumptions and expectations concerning another, which are elements in the LMM of this construction, are such that, in using it, a speaker declares his assessment of what *is* and of what has gone before, as well as attempting to influence what happens subsequently (cf. Lewis, 1969; Wunderlich, 1974). I see such situational factors as 'input' to the grammatical semantics of mood.

§ 161.   Constructions realising decision can be usefully divided into: (i) those where only the teller's decision is presented (e.g. jussive imperatives); and (ii) those where both the teller's and the performer's decision are at issue. The latter subdivide into those where the teller's decision is presented as dominant (e.g. modal verb 'prohibition' constructions such as *You can't come*) and those where the power to decide is shown to belong principally to a third party, who may, but needn't be the performer, as in *Latecomers should wait until the first interval/Long live the King*, which simultaneously realise the teller's wish. The teller role may be occupied either by the speaker alone, or transferred to the addressee.

§ 162.   Decision constructions also divide according to the placement of the decision operation (which is related to, but not determined by, the occupancy of the decider role). Placement of decision within/outside SU is one dimension of contrast; and within/outside SP is the other. In both cases, a construction may be neutral to the distinction, so that decision may be 'unplaced' with respect to SU or SP or both.

§ 163.   I divide the following discussion, in the first instance, between constructions realising dominant decision within SU ('direct decision'), and outside it ('indirect decision').

§164.   Constructions of direct decision include the different types of imperative, and constructions containing the following modal verbs used in a non-epistemic sense, together with their corresponding negatives: *may/can, must, might, could, shall, will*; and *needn't*.

§165.   Constructions of indirect decision include both types of volitional subjunctive (optative and hortatory) and modal verb constructions containing *should(n't), ought(n't)*.

§166.   Decision constructions divide in terms of surface grammar into those which contain a modal verb and those which do not. The latter subdivide into imperatives and subjunctives (including the periphrastic subjunctive).

§167.   The role configurations of decision constructions not containing a modal verb are as follows:

(a)   Jussive imperative: $[(Dr:S) \neq (Pr:A)]$ e.g. *Come here*

(b)   Joint imperative: $[(Dr = Pr):(S + A)]$ e.g. *Let's go*

(c)   Fiat imperative: $[(Dr:S) \neq (Pr:3)]$ e.g. *Let the prisoner stand forward*

(d)   Optative imperative:[1] $[(Dr:A) \neq (Pr:S/3)]$ e.g. *(Please) let John come too*

(e)   Optative subjunctive: $[(Dr:3) =/\neq (Pr:S/A/3)]$ e.g. *God save the Queen*

(f)   Hortatory subjunctive: $[(Dr : 3) \neq (Pr : 3/S +/- A)]$ e.g. *Let each man speak the truth/Let us pray* (cf. Quirk *et al.*, 1972: 404)

All these constructions have: (Teller : Speaker).

§168.   The suggested category (c) of 'fiat imperatives' is, perhaps, rather doubtful. It depends on the notion that in some *let* constructions it is the (Teller : Speaker) who decides.

The distinction between fiat imperatives and hortatory subjunctives is tenuous, depending principally on the status of the speaker, as voicing his own decision in the first case, or acting as 'mouthpiece' teller for some greater or wider authority whose decision he relays, in the second. In the latter case, the speaker is seen as a party to the decision, and may be included among the occupants of the performer role. The difference between *Let us* forms in this category and the 'joint' imperative is that the former do not take the *shall we* tag whereas the latter do: *Let's go shall we*, but not **Let us pray shall we*. This reflects the exclusion of the addressee from occupancy of the decider role in the hortatory subjunctive.

The form *Let me see* presents a problem for this analysis. It can be an optative imperative, //1 Let me see// with (Decider: Addressee), but, where the speaker decides for himself, (//1 Let me see//) it scarcely belongs under fiat imperatives and is perhaps best regarded as an unanalysable fossilised expression.

In constructions such as *Let him know tomorrow, let* perhaps retains something of a causative sense from an earlier stage of the language.

§169.   *Summary*

(i)   All imperatives have participant occupancy of the decider role. Subjunctives have third-party occupancy of this role.

Imperatives sub-divide as follows:

(a)   (Decider : Speaker): jussive and fiat imperatives
(b)   (Decider : Addressee): optative imperatives
(c)   (Decider : Speaker + Addressee): joint imperatives

(ii)   All imperatives (except the 'joint' type) have separate occupation of the decider and performer roles: [Decider $\neq$ Performer] is the typical imperative role pattern. Joint imperatives combine decider and performer by virtue of having multiple (participant) occupancy of both.

Subjunctives divide between the optatives, which are neutral to this distinction (*God save the Queen* with [Decider = Performer], and *Long live the King* [Decider $\neq$ Performer] are not syntactically distinct), and the hortatory type, which have [Decider $\neq$ Performer].

(iii)   Imperatives subdivide according to the inclusion of the addressee in the Performer role. The feature (Performer: Addressee +/− Speaker) groups jussive and joint imperatives together in contrast to fiat and optative imperatives which have (Performer: not-Addressee).

Subjunctives subdivide according to whether or not the addressee can optionally occupy (or share) the performer role. This distinguishes the periphrastic optatives (e.g. *May he/you succeed*) and the hortatory type (e.g. *Let us pray*) from the inflected optatives, such as *God save the Queen*, which have obligatory third-party occupancy.

§170.   With respect to directness (cf. §153) as assessed in terms of participant/non-participant role occupancy of secondary roles, the following 'scale' emerges (ordered from maximum to minimum degrees).

(i)   Jussive and joint imperatives: Both performer and decider occupied by participant primary role players (Speaker/participating addressee).

(ii)   Optative and fiat imperatives: Decider occupied by a participant primary role player; Performer role may (optative) or must (fiat) be occupied by a third party (non-participant primary role-player).

(iii)   Subjunctive: Decider role occupied by non-participant primary role player (third party); Performer role may be occupied (indifferently from the point of view of mood status) by participant/non-participant role player. (Occupancy realised only in person, not mood.)

§171.   Placement of operations:

(i)   Decision. All imperatives have the deciding operation placed within the confines of SU. The subjunctive has unplaced decision; it is certainly not confined to SU, although neither is it definitely excluded from it, or confined to SP, which is itself indeterminate.

(ii)   Performance: Imperatives on the whole indicate the placing of the performance operation with SU; but this may easily be overridden by adverbial specification to the contrary, e.g. *Come tomorrow/Let the prisoner be remanded until a week from today/ Let John come with us next week/Let's go this evening.*

Subjunctives all indicate a performance which, while not excluded from beginning in SU, is certainly presented as extending (indeterminately) beyond it.

(iii)   Telling (presentation): All imperatives are told by the speaker within SU. All, except the optatives, have direct telling of the teller's decision (Teller:Speaker). Optative imperatives have telling of teller's wish and, in this respect only, resemble the subjunctive.

Optative subjunctives have semi-indirect telling (of the speaker's wish) in that they are not directed at a participating addressee. Here they contrast with optative imperatives, which are so directed (and where that addressee is the decider).

Hortatory subjunctives are directed at a 'collective' addressee: they are not addressed to a particular individual but to a group, either severally (*Let each man/anyone . . .*) or as a whole (*Let us pray*). Fiat imperatives share this feature, even in informal use, e.g. *Let John play Kojak.*

Optative subjunctives divide into those in a main clause where the description sign is not opposed to occurrence value (cf. §138), and those in a dependent clause following a lexical verb of decision/wishing (cf. §146) where this opposition obtains.

This distinction is partly a matter of telling. The former have full telling, the latter, derived.

§172.   In terms both of secondary role occupancy and the placement of operations, imperatives as a group are more direct than the subjunctives.

§173.   Modal verb decision constructions are distinguished as a group from imperatives and volitional subjunctives taken together by the fact that they realise attitudes (chiefly wishes) of the performer as well as the teller, and also of the addressee. In this way, they realise as elements of their LMM features which are supplied by context in the use of non-modal constructions. For example (cf. §46), an imperative used in circumstances where it is clear that the addressee wishes to perform the action in question functions as permission; but the modal verb construction, *You can do x* does so irrespective of circumstances, and has 'Addressee wishes to do *x*' as an element in LMM. *Come in*, when it is clear that the addressee does not want to, functions as a command; *You can come in* in the same circumstances would have a sarcastic effect, which the imperative would not, precisely because of this extra element in its LMM: it means 'I assume you want to', whereas the imperative is neutral to distinctions of performer's wish.[2]

Similarly, one distinction between obligation *should* constructions and the (periphrastic) subjunctive is that the former usually convey the performer's wish/intention not to, whereas the latter are neutral, and give no indication of this feature. Compare *Jane should brush her teeth after meals* with *May the best man win.* (Both constructions realise teller's wish for a positive Ov.)

§174.   Modal verb constructions divide between direct and indirect along very similar lines to those distinguishing imperative from subjunctive mood: according to the occupancy of secondary roles and the placement of operations. They all have basically unplaced performance, in the sense that the decided on event is not presented as tied to occurring in SU. In constructions in which the lexical verb is marked for pastness (*have* + V-ed) the occurrence of this event is excluded from SU.

§175.   Modal verb constructions of direct decision have participant occupancy of the decider role and placement of the decision operation in SU. (This excludes relayed speech decision, §186 below. Cf. hortatory subjunctives, §171 above.)

They subdivide as follows:

Declarative: (Decider : Speaker)
Interrogative: (Decider : Addressee)

(The contrast between speaker as sole 'static' occupant of the teller role in declaratives, and the transference of this role to the addressee in interrogatives, is the same for both decision and knowledge constructions and is discussed as a feature of telling in Chapter 5 below.)

§176.   Direct decision modals divide into two groups: those involving the question of performer's choice as an LMM feature, and those in which this is not at issue (except where performer and decider 'accidentally' combine). The first group I shall call 'countermanding' modals, the second, 'volitional'.

§177.   Countermanding modal constructions contain one of the following verbs: *must/can't/can (may)/needn't; couldn't/might(n't)*. They comprise constructions of compulsion, prohibition and permission. They involve two decision operations: one (the teller's) is presented as made in SU; the other (the performer's) is presented as still open in SU, and placed in SP (which may, but needn't coincide with, or overlap, SU). It is the teller's decision which the construction realises; but it also conveys whether or not the performer has choice, and, further, if he has, whether this is assumed to be in harmony or conflict with that decision.

§178.   I use the term 'countermanding' because all constructions of this type realise a teller's decision which reverses an assumption concerning the performer's freedom or lack of freedom to choose with respect to carrying out his performance. *Must/can't* constructions impose constraint and remove previous freedom of choice; *can/*

needn't constructions remove constraint and confer freedom. I shall group the first pair together as 'conflict' forms, and the second as 'consent' forms.[3]

§179.   Conflict forms realise: (i) the teller's decision to remove the performer's choice; (ii) the teller's decision concerning the Ov of the performance; (iii) opposition between this decision and the assumed wish (and intention) of the performer. The role configuration feature [Decider ≠ Performer] is an essential element in their LMM (as it is in that of imperatives). This dominates accidental combination of Teller–Decider and Performer in constructions with first person subject, so that *I must go* means 'someone else is making me' [Performer ≠ (Decider = Teller)], giving relayed speech (speaker as 'mouthpiece' teller of another's decision).

§180.   Consent forms realise: (i) the teller's decision to confer power to choose on the performer; (ii) the teller's expectation concerning the Ov of the performance; (iii) expectation of harmony between this Ov and performer's decision (and between both and his assumed wish).

§181.   Conflict forms realise the teller's decision concerning the Ov of the performance, but consent forms do not: they realise the conferring of the power to make this decision on the performer. I shall say that conflict forms realise implemented teller's decision, and consent forms unimplemented performer's decision, with respect to Ov, and refer to them as 'decided'/'undecided' respectively (positive/negative decision operation sign).

§182.   The underlying semantic features of these constructions can be given as follows for the declaratives:

A. Conflict Forms

$$\left\{ \begin{array}{l} [(\,(Dr^+ = Tr) : S) \neq (Pr : A/3)] \\ [D^+ ; P^-] \text{ Decision} \searrow Ov \end{array} \right\}$$

Description sign: positive.

(i)   Inertia value: negative (performer's wishes assumed to be negative).

e.g.   *You/John/ must be back before six o'clock*

(ii)   Inertia value: positive (performer's wishes assumed to be positive).

e.g. *You/John/ can't come with us.*

B. *Consent Forms*

Decision 1: Decision ↘ Performer's freedom to choose

$$\left\{ \begin{array}{l} [(Dr^+ = Tr) : S] \\ [D^+] \end{array} \right\}$$

Decision 2: Decision ↘ Ov

$$\left\{ \begin{array}{l} [(\,(Dr^+ = Pr) : A/3) \neq (Tr : S)] \\ [D^- ; P^-] \end{array} \right\}$$

Description sign: positive

(i) Inertia value: negative (performer's wishes assumed to be positive).

e.g. *You/John can have the day off/can borrow my car*

(ii) Inertia value: positive (performer's wishes assumed to be negative).

e.g. *You/John needn't come to the lecture*

§183. The interrogative forms differ from declaratives principally in terms of occupancy of the decider role (addressee rather than speaker). They all have unimplemented decision, and realise teller role transference from speaker to addressee. In the conflict forms, the contrast is between expected or assumed addressee's decision and speaker's wish.

A. *Conflict Request Forms*

$$\left\{ \begin{array}{l} [(Dr^+ : A) \neq (Pr : S/3)] \\ [D^- ; P^-] \text{. Decision} ↘ Ov \end{array} \right\}$$

Description sign: positive

(i) Expected decision: that no: Ov^- (Speaker's wish: that yes: Ov^+).

e.g   *Can't I/John come too?*

(ii)   Expected decision: that yes: Ov^+ (Speaker's wish: that no: Ov^-).

e.g.   *Must/need I go to that lecture?*

B. Requested Consent Forms

$$\left\{ \begin{array}{l} [(Dr^+ : A) \neq (Pr : S/3)] \\ [D^- ; P^-] \text{ Decision } \searrow \text{ Performer's freedom to choose} \end{array} \right\}$$

Description sign: positive

(i)   Expected decision: open (no particular expectation) (Speaker's wish that yes: Ov^+).

e.g.   *Can I/John come too?*

(ii)   Expected decision: that no: Ov^- (Speaker's wish: that no: Ov^-).

e.g.   *Needn't I go to that lecture?*

§184.   In the declarative constructions, surface polarity attached to the modal verb realises the opposite of inertia value, irrespective of decision operation sign (the conflict/consent distinction). In the interrogatives, surface polarity realises the Ov which is expected (or assumed) to be chosen by the decider, again irrespective of operation sign. This is standard for decision constructions.

§185.   Description sign is positive throughout these constructions. That is, polarity does not attach to the lexical verb in the cases given. For example, the form for asking 'Can I not-go?' is *Must I go?* Oppositeness of meaning in the description is realised lexically, by an autonym: *Can I go/can I stay.*

There is one exception to this, however: the form *must not/ mustn't*, e.g. *You mustn't be late/John mustn't throw stones.* Here surface polarity realises negative description sign. The topic selected for presentation is 'your not-being late'/'John's not-throw-ing stones'. 'Not-must' is realised by *needn't. Mustn't* is distinguished from *can't* along these lines. *You can't go* has 'your going' as topic and positive description sign. *You mustn't go* functions as a weaker command than *You can't go*. Telling an obligation not to perform an act conveys a weaker force of compulsion than telling a prohibition. This distinction is not paralleled in systems of deontic logic (e.g. Von Wright, 1951: 36-41, where $O \sim A \equiv \sim PA$).

Mustn't also realises negative description sign in the interrogative. *Mustn't I go to that lecture* means 'Am I commanded/obliged not-to-go' as distinct from *Can't I go* which does not mean 'Am I allowed not-to go' but 'Don't/won't you allow me to go'.

Declarative *mustn't* may be used in circumstances where one instance of performance to which it applies has already taken place, as in a reprimand to a child, e.g. *You mustn't throw stones*, when he has just done so. This is not true of *can't*.

§186.   Relayed decision. All countermanding modal decision constructions share the feature [Decider ≠ Performer]. This over-rides all other role combinations. Therefore, when a declarative has first-person performer, as in *I must go*, the [Decider ≠ Performer] constraint takes precedence over the feature [(Decider = Teller) : Speaker]. Such constructions realise an external compulsion, attributable to an unspecified third party, a decision taken outside SU by a non-participant. Their role configuration is [(Decider: third party) ≠ (Performer : Speaker)].

The speaker voices a constraint placed upon him by another agency, rather than his own decision, and in this way acts as a 'mouthpiece teller', relaying another's decision. With first person plural the 'relaying' is optional. Here there is partially different occupation of the decider and performer roles even where the speaker occupies the decider role because his fellow occupant(s) of the performer role do not generally share it with him, which permits a non-relayed interpretation: (Dr : S) ≠ (Pr : S + (A/3)). *We must go* is ambiguous between (Dr : S)/(Dr : 3) as well as between (Pr : (S + A +/− 3)/(Pr : (S + 3)). Possibly the relayed sense occurs more often with addressee-exclusion in adult speech, and with addressee-inclusion in that of children.

Declarative first person *can't* constructions are ambiguous between relayed decision and a capability sense; *I can't come* may mean 'I am not being allowed to come' or 'I am not able to come'. It normally has the latter sense in adult speech, but in the speech of children it sometimes has the former. This applies also to *can*, e.g. (My father says) *I can come*. First person declarative *needn't* generally realises relayed decision.

Interrogatives realise relayed decision when they have a second-person performer. Hence, *Must you go?* asks not 'Do/will you decide to go', but 'Are you obliged to do so'. That is, it has the form of querying some apparent third-party constraint on the addressee's choice of action as performer. The use of this construction in circumstances where it is clear that the addressee—performer is also the decider (and there is no third-party constraint) has a sarcastic effect, as in *Must you make that noise?*

Interrogative second person *can/can't* usually have a capability sense, but may realise relayed decision; interrogative *needn't* in the second person is rare, e.g. *Needn't you go (after all)*, and is generally relayed.

§187.   Items: (ignoring relayed decision).

(a)   *Can* in all its decision occurrences (positive/negative; declarative/interrogative) has the sense of 'allow'. We may gloss as follows:

Declarative positive :	'I allow Ov^+'
Declarative negative :	'I don't allow Ov^+'
Interrogative positive :	'Do/will you allow Ov^+?'
Interrogative negative :	'Don't/won't you allow Ov^+?'

The pleading tone which may be associated with *can't* interrogatives is linked with their 'won't you allow' paraphrase and relates to the properties of the negative interrogative in general (cf. Chapter 6). *Won't you allow* does not paraphrase as 'Will you not-allow'. This suggests that the surface polarity in *can't*, at least in interrogatives, does not realise sign relating to an operation of 'allowing'.

(b)   *Must* in all its decision occurrences has the sense of 'command'/'order'. We may gloss as follows:

Declarative positive :	'I command Ov^+'
Declarative negative :	'I command Ov^-'
Interrogative positive :	'Do you command Ov^+?'
Interrogative negative :	'Do you command Ov^-?'

(c)   *Need* in all its decision occurrences has the sense of 're-quire'/'demand'.

> Declarative positive   :   Rare (*You need know nothing* is
> equivalent to *You needn't know
> anything*)
>
> Declarative negative :   'I do not require Ov^+'
>
> Interrogative positive   :   'Do you require Ov^+?'/
> 'Does someone/something
> require Ov^+?'
>
> Interrogative negative: :   'Don't you require Ov^+?'/
> 'Is there no requirement
> for Ov^+?'

Need in the negative interrogative is unlike both *can* and *must* in the same construction. 'Don't you require' paraphrases as 'Do you not-require'.[4]

§188.   Let us summarise some of the elements of meaning in the modals which we have taken into account so far, as follows: ('+' and '−' in Table 4.1 refer to positive and negative Ov respectively).

Table 4.1

Inertia value	Performer's wish	Decided that		
+	+	−	*Can't*	Conflict
−	−	+	*Must*	forms
+	−	ϕ	*Needn't*	Consent
−	+	ϕ	*Can*	forms

Conflict forms have the same Ov for inertia and performer's wish; it is the opposite of the Ov decided on by the teller. Consent forms have opposing Ovs for inertia and performer's wish; the teller's decision consists in permitting that Ov for which the performer is assumed to wish. Conflict forms countermand the Ov of the performer's wish and the inertia value. Consent forms allow the performer's wish to countermand the inertia value. Conflict forms remove the performer's choice. Consent forms confer performer choice.

§189.   The analysis of English countermanding modals suggested here differs in certain interesting respects from the outline of the basis of a first order deontic logic given in Von Wright (1951, 1957, 1968, 1971).

(i)   Von Wright (1971: 161) gives 'two different typical meanings' of saying that 'something may be, or may be done'. The first he states as 'a *denial* of the statement that the contradictory of this thing ought to be (done)', and the second as 'an affirmation to the effect that the being or doing of the thing in question is a sufficient condition (guarantee) of something else'. The first, which he calls the *weak* meaning of 'may', he asserts 'can be rendered as a "need-not" statement'; the second, which he calls the *strong* meaning of 'may', he claims is 'frequently couched as a "can"-statement'.

This view contrasts with the analysis of (declarative) *needn't* given above as meaning 'I do not require A' ('A' = 'Act'), which corresponds in Von Wright's terms not with a denial of the statement that the contradictory of this thing ought to be (done), which might be expressed as 'I deny that not-A ought to be (done), but, rather, with the denial of the statement that this thing ought to be (done); 'I deny that A ought to be (done)'. (These glosses work roughly if 'deny' is taken to mean 'don't say' as opposed to 'say that not'.) The conversion into terms of denial of statements is awkward, partly because *needn't* does not realise a statement about the status of an act, 'It is permitted that A'/'it is not obligatory that A', but simply realises the act, 'α' of removing a requirement that A must occur.

The main point at issue, however, is that in English, declarative *needn't* constructions involve 'A' (positive description sign in my terms) as opposed to '∼ A'.

(ii)   The 'strong' meaning of *may* as distinguished by Von Wright involves conditionality, but this does not seem to apply in the form in which he gives it to either *can* or *needn't* constructions in ordinary usage, although it does apply to those with *should/ought to* (cf. §197 below). However, both *can* and *needn't* constructions are conditional in another sense, that in which each is dependent on the assumed performer's wish. *Can* declaratives convey an implicit 'if the performer wants to'; *needn't* declaratives convey an implicit 'if the performer does not want to'. That is, it is an assumption concerning the performer's wish which makes it relevant to remove a sufficient obstacle to the performance of 'A' (*can*) or a sufficient cause of the performance of 'A' (the requirement that it must be carried out) with *needn't*.

Because of the feature of performer's wish which both *can* and *needn't* constructions realise, with opposite values, a construction of one type does not imply one of the other directly, but they do when their conditionals are made explicit: 'You can come if you want to' implies 'You needn't come if you don't want to', and conversely. The nature of the relationship between dependent and main clause in conditional sentences is a topic to which I return in Chapter 8.

(iii)   In Von Wright's system of deontic logic (where the deontic operators are 'P' ('Permitted') and 'O' ('Obligatory')), OA → PA (1957: 61; 'what is obligatory is also permitted'). The case is not quite the same in English where *You must go* does not imply *You can go* in the sense that a construction which realises removal of performer's choice cannot imply one which realises conferment of performer's choice. Further, *must* realises the performer's assumed wish for Ov^-, *can* for Ov^+. For parallel reasons, *You can't go* does not imply *You needn't go*.

(iv)   The interdefinition schema: 'P' = df '$\sim$ O $\sim$' in a deontic logic gives the following equivalences:

$$P(A) \quad \equiv \ \sim O(\sim A)$$
$$P(\sim A) \equiv \ \sim O(A)$$
$$\sim P(A) \equiv O(\sim A)$$
$$\sim P(\sim A) \equiv O(A)$$

I have claimed that the countermanding modals (with the exception of *mustn't*) have positive description sign. This amounts to claiming that only some of the expressions above are paralleled in English grammar, as follows:

$$P(A) \qquad : \quad can$$
$$\sim O(A) \ : \quad needn't$$
$$O(A) \qquad : \quad must$$
$$\sim P(A) \ : \quad can't$$
$$O (\sim A) \ : \quad mustn't$$

(v)   Compatibilities:

(a)   *Can* and *must* appear to be compatible and can be jointly applied to the same description when given in that sequence: *You can, and (indeed) must, come* (but not **You must and can* *come*). This may involve relayed decision in *can*: 'Someone else allows you to come and I command you to come'. The case is parallel for *needn't* and *can't* (*can't* and *needn't*): 'No one allows you to come, and I do not require you to come.'

(b)   *Can* and *needn't* are generally compatible in relation to the same performance, but, since they realise opposite values for both performer's wish and inertia, are generally linked by contrastive *but* rather than *and*: *You can, but needn't, take two papers in advance of the final examination.*

(c)   *Can't* and *must* are incompatible in relation to the one performance; so also are *must* and *needn't*, *can't* and *can.*

(d)   Let us take *You needn't come* as the deontic equivalent of a contradictory of *You must come*, and *You can't come* as the deontic contradictory of *You can come*. We can then, on the basis of the foregoing analysis, draw a deontic parallel to the predicate logic square of opposition for the four countermanding decision modals with positive description sign, as follows:

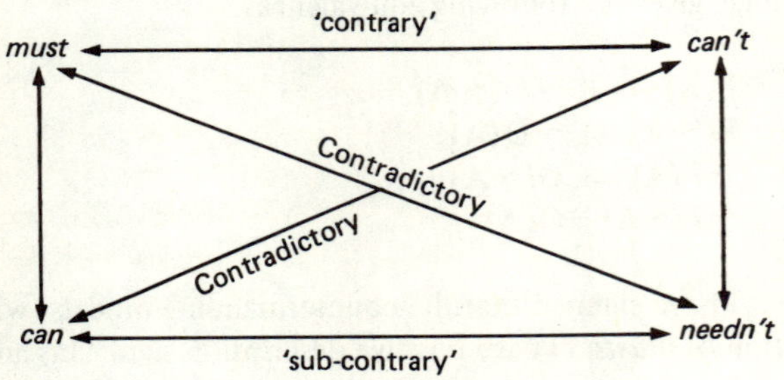

§190.   *Must* as a determinate countermanding modal now occurs in many cases where the form in earlier stages of modern English would have been *shall.* This applies also in the case of *can't* and *shall not.* Compare the use of *Thou shalt/thou shalt not* in the King James version of Exodus XX, 2-17 (the ten commandments). *Must* in contemporary English is not as forceful as *shall* in those examples, but *shall* in that usage has now died out.

§191.   *Shall* in contemporary English varies considerably both in the semantic features it realises and in its frequency of occurrence, between different dialects. What I have to say about it applies only to southern standard British English (and perhaps in some details only to my own dialect). I take it as a 'volitional' modal, cf. § 176.

In that dialect, *shall* realises two different role configurations in the declarative, depending on the occupancy of the performer role:

(i) $(Pr : S)$; $[Tr = Dr = Pr]$
(ii) $(Pr : A/3)$; $[((Tr = Dr) : S) \neq Pr]$.

For both (i) and (ii):

$[Decision^{+} ; Performance^{-} ; Telling^{+}]$.

In both cases declarative *shall* may have the significance either of a promise or a threat, according to the (contextually supplied) wishes of another: the addressee (or third party) in (i), the performer in (ii). For example, *I shall love, honour and obey you* would generally count as a promise, *I shall report him to the magistrate*, as a threat. *You shall have those piano lessons* might be either.

Shall not/shan't is relatively little used, but where it still occurs, as in *I shall not disappoint him/I shan't be ready until this evening*, it is more likely to do so with a first-person performer. Examples such as (?) *You shall not be disturbed*/(??) *You shan't have an ice-cream if you don't behave properly*, are now rare.

Three points can be noted:

(a)   *Shall* constructions do not realise another's wish as an element of their LMM. Hence their potential significance either as promise or threat. (In this way they differ from the countermanding modals and resemble imperatives.)

(b)   They realise description sign. *Shall not* gives a negative description (as does *must not*).

(c)   They realise a performance beginning after the end of SU. (In this they differ from the countermanding modals which realise a performance which may take place within SU.)

(c) is the most frequently remarked on. The use of *shall* with a first-person subject to realise non-decision constructions of prediction, as in, *I shall be seventy next birthday*, derives from this feature. In this use, *shall* is synonymous with *will* and the reduced form *'ll* does not distinguish between them.

Shall in interrogative constructions is only possible in the dialect under discussion, with a first-person subject (although in other dialects *shall you . . ./shall he . . .* are fully acceptable).

Shall I do x realises:

$$[(Dr : A) \neq (Pr : S)]$$

and may be paraphrased as 'Would you like me to do *x*?'. The performer in transitivity terms is agent and not goal. In this dialect *Shall I get a copy?* means 'Would you like me to fetch one?' rather than 'Am I going to receive one?', as it may do in others. (*Shall John help?* is perhaps possible as an offer made on behalf of another for whom one has the authority to speak. If so, it is relayed speech. It does not mean, in this dialect, 'Is he going to?'.)

§192.   *Will* to some extent parallels *shall*, and complements it. In SSBE, declarative *will* is synonymous with *shall* in constructions with a first-person subject (realising either teller-decision or prediction). In those with a second/third-person subject it is also basically synonymous and is very much the dominant form in non-decision prediction, as in, *You will find a pub on the corner/John will be here in a few minutes.* In decision constructions it can realise the same role configuration as *shall* in such constructions:

$$[((Tr = Dr) : S) \neq (Pr : A/3)] \, .$$

The distinction between *Jones shall* and *Jones will (play centre-half on Saturday)* seems to be that the former suggests that Jones wants to do so (or the addressee wants him to), and the latter does not. But we have seen that *shall* may be used where the performer/addressee can be assumed not to want to, and so can *will*, e.g. *You will eat that porridge (however much you don't like it).* Both verbs are neutral to the wishes of non-deciders.

However, declarative *will* also realises performer-decision in second/third person, which *shall* does not. This is its major decision sense in all three persons.

$$[(Dr = Pr) = /\neq Tr]$$
$$[\text{Decision}^{+} \, ; \, \text{Performance}^{-} \, ; \, \text{Telling}^{+}] \, .$$

This is the area of 'volitional' *will*, which includes that of performer's determination (in the face of contrary advice, etc.), where the modal verb carries the tonic, e.g. //1 John <u>will</u> park on double yellow lines//.

Wherever *shall not/shan't* may be used, *will not/won't* are the more common forms. They realise a negative description. They are used in the second and third person interrogative, which *shall not/ shan't* cannot be.

Interrogative *will* with second person subject realises the combination of [Decider = Performer] with [Decider = Teller] with addressee occupancy throughout. It is a standard form for polite request precisely because it realises a role configuration in which the authority in all respects is assigned to the addressee.

Interrogative *will/won't* in SSBE does not occur with a first-person subject where the verb is active and the subject actor (although in other dialects this is the standard form, equivalent to *Shall I* in SSBE). *Will I be admitted?* is acceptable, *Will I go?* is not. This reflects a distinction between a decision which is made by the performer (i.e. the referent of the mood subject) and one made by another (the unspecified agent in the passive construction). The former does not occur in the interrogative form, since this, as it realises (Decider : Addressee) would contravene the underlying feature [Decider = Performer] where (Performer : Speaker). The latter can occur in the interrogative, which then realises a query on third-party decision with respect to a future event. *Shall* is the form for addressee decision where [(Decider = Teller) ≠ Performer] (cf. §191).

In this area *will* and *shall* are fully distinct in contemporary SSBE, retaining the separation in their senses between [Decider ≠ Performer], (often with [Decider = Teller]), (*shall*), and [Decider = Performer], (*will*), which existed to a greater degree at an earlier stage in the language (cf. Mustanoja, 1960: 490-4 for a discussion of *shall* 'used to indicate that an event is ordained to take place in accordance with divine will or fate', and *will* 'used to express a future action dependent on the will of the person in question' in Middle English).

Otherwise, they are nearly synonymous. The features (a)–(c) listed in §191 for *shall* also apply to *will*, and serve to distinguish both from the countermanding set of modal verbs.

§193.   *Would* is the equivalent of *will* in all uses (but cf. §307) except that it realises non-immediate telling, a distancing of this operation from SU to an uncertain elsewhere. It is less direct for this reason, and therefore used as a polite form, particularly in second person interrogatives where it also mutes the demand for an immediate and definite reply (cf. Chapter 5). It also realises past time in declaratives of performer-decision, e.g. //1 John <u>would</u> park in the wrong place//, 'was determined to'. Other senses of *would* belong under prediction and do not realise decision factors (cf. Chapter 7 below).

§194.   Indirect decision modals: *should(n't)/ought(n't) to*.

Whereas the relation between *will/would* is basically one of type of telling, that between *shall/should* is more complex. They are in fact best seen as separate modal verbs.

Should is used in the periphrastic subjunctive (cf. §§143-4 above), which relates to performance and telling. It also realises probability of occurrence (cf. Chapter 7 below). I discuss it here in its obligation sense, in which it is closely related to *ought to*, as in *Children should/ought to brush their teeth regularly after meals*.

Should(n't) and *ought(n't) to* are indirect countermanding forms and resemble each other in the following respects:

(i)   Their polarity realises description sign (i.e. negation applies to the lexical verb).

(ii)   Description sign is the opposite of inertia value Ov.

(iii)   Inertia value Ov corresponds with the Ov assumed to be wished for or intended by the performer.

(iv)   The Ov told as wished for by the speaker 'mouthpiece teller' is that of description sign.

(v)   They present as opposition between the Ov for which the speaker voices the wish that it should occur/obtain, and that which he assumes the performer to choose.

(vi)   They present the final authoritative decision as belonging to the performer.

(vii) This decision is placed in SP, and so may be altogether outside SU where the two situations do not overlap.

This is the basic pattern and applies in both declarative and inter-rogative constructions.

Feature (vii) provides the motivation for distinguishing these forms from the other countermanding modals, as realising indirect decision. Alone among the countermanding modals they may take a lexical verb marked for past tense (*have* and V-ed), and realise a comment on a performance already ended before SU begins.[5] In this case the construction realises knowledge in addition to decision factors. For example, *He should have seen to the car this morning* conveys the common knowledge that 'he' did not do so. But this is not what is told. Polarity realises the wished for Ov, not that which is known to have happened.

With respect to feature (i) they resemble *must(n't)* (as opposed to the other countermanding modals).

In feature (ii) they resemble *must(n't)* and *can* (as opposed to *can't* and *needn't*).

In feature (iii) they resemble *must* and *can't* (as opposed to *can* and *needn't*).

In (iv) they are distinct from all the declarative direct decision modals because these realise either the teller-speaker's decision about Ov, or his decision to let the performer choose to do what he is assumed to want to; (and the latter constructions are neutral to speaker's wish). Countermanding modal interrogative constructions realise speaker's wish, which is for the Ov of the description sign in *can't/can*, but the opposite of it in *must/needn't*.

In (v) they differ not only from the declarative direct modals (which are neutral to speaker's wish) but also from the countermanding interrogatives, which realise (Decider : Addressee).

With respect to (vi), *should(n't)/ought(n't) to* resemble declarative *can* and *needn't*, in contrast to *must* and *can't*.

§195.　　　The network of contrasts just sketched is not symmetrical, but *should/ought to* fit into Table 4.1 for the countermanding modals (§188) in the same line as *must*, if we substitute 'performer's assumed choice' for 'Performer's wish', and 'Speaker's wish' for 'Decided on Ov'. The relationship between the negative forms is parallel.

In one sense they represent a 'half-way house' between conflict and consent countermanding modals, for performer's decision concerning Ov implies performer's choice, but they also realise another's decision on the Ov although this is unimplemented and is often relayed.

§*196.*　*Summary*

Should(n't)/ought(n't) to are essentially forms for realising third-party decision, even where they have (Performer : Speaker). They present a constraint originating in an outside, third-party agency, which the speaker accepts as legitimately governing the freedom of choice of the performer with respect to his own action, but they simultaneously realise acceptance that the latter may/does/has ignore(d) this. They are used typically with the significance of advice or of reproach, the distinction depending on contextual factors. One of the clearest examples of the opposition which they realise between constraint and performer's decision, comes from an earlier stage of Modern English in *The Book of Common Prayer*

(General confession): 'We have left undone those things which we ought to have done; And we have done those things which we ought not to have done; And there is no health in us.'

Should/ought to imply *is/does not.*
Shouldn't/oughtn't to imply *is/does.*[6]

§197.   These forms involve conditionality (cf. §189). They convey that the performance to which they relate is a necessary condition for an Ov of another (or others) for which the performer and/or addressee is assumed to wish. For example; *Children ought to brush their teeth regularly* (if you/they want them to have good teeth)/*Latecomers should wait in the lobby until the first interval* (if they want not to be turned back at the doors or interrupt the performance)/*Athletes shouldn't smoke* (if they want to succeed)/*Lecturers oughtn't to assume any previous knowledge of the subject* (if they want to be understood).

Must(n't) is also conditional in this way.

§198.   *Should(n't)* and *ought(n't)* are not always exactly synonymous. For example, declarative *should* is often stronger than *ought to*. Compare: *Latecomers should wait until the first interval* with *Latecomers ought to wait* . . . The latter conveys less sense of unpleasant consequences if ignored, and also a greater acceptance that latecomers are unlikely to wait.

§199.   There are exceptions to the basic interpretation outlined above for these obligation forms. They do not always imply the actuality of the opposite Ov. For example, *That's just what you should do*, can be used in response to a statement that *that* is being/has been done: //1 You <u>should</u> eat raw vegetables// (where it is known that you do so). Some examples of this kind are potentially confusing where it is not clear from the context that the speaker accepts that the event/state of affairs is already the case.

§200.   Interrogative *should(n't)/ought(n't) to* transfer to the addressee the role of mouthpiece teller. In this way they have the effect of requesting him to say whether or not a constraint applies, or whether or not the performance is desirable. In querying the desirability of the Ov realised in surface polarity, the speaker conveys his own opinion that it is not desirable. *Should John smoke?* conveys 'I think he should not'; *Oughtn't John to write to them?* conveys that 'I think that he ought to'. As *should(n't)* is sometimes more forceful in declaratives, so *ought(n't) to* is sometimes more forceful in interrogatives, conveying a greater degree of query, and so of challenge, to the desirability of the Ov realised in surface polarity.

§201.   We divided non-modal verb decision constructions into those realising participant decision (imperatives) and non-participant decision (subjunctives). Within modal verb constructions a parallel division obtains between the direct modals and the indirect forms.

Notes

1. The optative imperative resembles interrogative ('permission') *can* in many respects, and realises an element of speaker's wish rather than exhortation, hence my choice of the term. Compare, *Let John come too* with *Can John come too?* Both constructions readily take *please*.

2. I take imperatives + *do* to realise speaker's rather than addressee's wish, although they are often used in polite permission. Cf. Appendix I.

3. The notion of imposing/removing constraints is closely connected with the problem discussed in Von Wright (1968: 88-91) that to argue according to a principle that 'whatever is not prohibited is, *ipso facto*, permitted' (from '∼O' to 'P ∼') is somehow felt to be 'safer' than to argue according to the principle that 'whatever is not permitted is, *ipso facto*, prohibited' (from '∼P' to 'O ∼'). He concludes that the 'impression of an asymmetry' between the two (logically equivalent) inferences, derives from questions of relative decidability. Since there are fewer (legal) obligations than permissions, the former are more likely to be known, and it is the former which are encoded in laws.

In ordinary life assumptions concerning which acts are such that they require permission to be performed and which are not underlie conventions of polite and acceptable behaviour. There is a vast, unstated, body of 'laws' regulating ordinary social behaviour, which divides acts into four classes: (1) those which are forbidden unless expressly permitted, e.g. (?) borrowing someone else's bicycle, (2) those which are permitted unless expressly forbidden, e.g. cleaning one's shoes, (3) those which are permitted not to be done unless expressly required, e.g. a guest making his own bed in a hotel, (4) those which are required unless expressly permitted not to be done, e.g. writing letters of thanks for Christmas presents.

Use of a determinate countermanding modal in ordinary language may sometimes make explicit the assumption that the act to which it is applied belongs to set (3) with *must*, or to set (2) with *can't*. Use of an indeterminate countermanding modal may realise the assumption that the act belongs to set (1) with *can*, or to set (4) with *needn't*.

4. I have omitted consideration of the use of *needn't* in examples such as *You needn't think I'm going to ask you again. Needn't* here appears to realise 'need not-to'. If so, it would represent a stronger version of *mustn't*, as I have analysed the latter. I take this as a specialised, non-central use.

5. The modals *can't/must/may/needn't* in their epistemic sense can take *have* + V-ed. This possibility is a marker of a construction realising knowledge.

6. *Should* in the declarative, where future time is referred to, realises an assumption that the performer does not intend to; e.g. *He should give up smoking* ('but I don't think he will'). Similarly, *shouldn't* realises an assumption that the performer does intend to, e.g. *He shouldn't take the afternoon*

off ('but I think he's going to'). In the first person it can represent a device for indicating one's own intentions, in this way, especially if *should* is the tonic syllable, e.g. //1 I <u>should</u> write to Jim today// ('but I think I'll put it off').

However, *should* may be used in cases where an action has already been performed, e.g. ('John pays his taxes'). *So he should.*

5   TELLING

§202.   The telling plane is that area of the semantics in which features to do with relationships and reactions among participants in a conversation towards one another, as expressed in linguistic social moves, are distinguished and systematised. These features chiefly consist in occupancy of the teller role, placement of the telling operation, and the mode of this operation. They include not only the feature of implementation, but also a 'static'/'dynamic' distinction, deriving from continuity or transfer of occupancy, and associated distinctions of 'direction of transfer'. This chapter gives a broad outline of what I take to be the major distinctions in this area, and discusses their realisation. Appendix I contains an outline of the surface grammar of interrogatives and defines names of classes as used here.)

§203.   I introduced the notion that the telling operation has different aspects in Chapter 3 (§§115-19), where I distinguished 'proposition construction' from 'presentation', and mentioned different manners of teller-role assignment ('mode of telling') as a separate, but related, issue. I develop these last two topics here. Type of presentation is realised syntactically; mode of telling chiefly by the phonological system of tone (Halliday, 1967a).

§204.   In its presentation aspect, telling applies to a description + sign, or to a mediating operation (knowing/deciding) as it applies to that combination (cf. §154). Telling in relation to decision has been touched on in the last chapter, and it is considered in relation to knowledge in the next. Here I deal with features of telling as it applies to either (e.g. the declarative/interrogative distinction) although most of the examples involve knowledge. (In what follows I use the term 'telling' to refer to the presentation aspect of this operation, unless otherwise specified.)

§205.   Telling applied to an operation is an essential element in establishing discourse units of agreement/contradiction (cf. §52). (These terms may be extended to cover initiative and reply pairs of utterances in which the elements are imperative (or declarative modal verb construction) plus consent/refusal form, as well as those consisting of an indicative knowledge declarative and rejoinder. I illustrate, however, from the latter.)

Contradiction in English may be realised by a response utterance in which the construction has positive polarity, realising positive description sign, and agreement by negative polarity. For example; A: //1 John isn't coming this evening//. B: //5 Yes he <u>is</u>//, and, A: //1 He doesn't <u>drink</u>//1 <u>does</u> he//. B: //1 No, he doesn't//.

What is at issue is the relationship between the description sign value in the first and second construction in each case. Agreement is realised by sameness of sign value, contradiction by opposite values. Neither is realised by a given surface polarity as such. (This is the simple case; contradiction can also be achieved indirectly via implication relations, cf. examples in §52.)

§206.   Neither knowing nor deciding can be realised independently of the application of a telling operation (in addition to the construction of the description). I take there to be two elements in the traditional concept of 'assertoric force': knowing and telling. In making an assertion I tell what I present myself as knowing.

§207.   The operations of knowing and telling combine to give a full assertion realised by an indicative declarative sentence. But there are many distinctions of grammatical meaning which are explicable chiefly in terms of the separate status of the knowledge and telling planes. For example, different types of 'comment adjuncts' (Davies, 1967) can be established along these lines ('presentation comment': telling, e.g. *frankly*; 'interpretation comment': knowledge, e.g. *certainly*). I hope to show below (Chapter 8) that different types of constructions of condition and reason can also be so distinguished.

The problem of assumed knowledge which may be conveyed without being presented, as in declarative *should have* + V-ed constructions (cf. §194), also indicates the potential separation of these two operations.

§208.   The telling plane covers the semantics of what is done *with* a description in a verbal interaction, including the degree of speaker's commitment with which it is put forward, and the relative status accorded it in comparison with other descriptions within the same sentence. Realisation of telling features involves syntactic dependency as well as (related) distinctions of indicative/subjunctive mood, finiteness and sequence of tenses restrictions, together with the phonological systems of tonality which relates to the scope of the telling operation, and tonicity, which relates to its focus (cf. Halliday, 1967a).

§209.   The telling operation is typically located in SU, but it may be distanced from it. I distinguish between immediate and distanced telling according to this feature of placement, and shall take immediate telling first, beginning with features of teller-role assignment.

§210.   I suggested earlier (§82) that the speaker assigns the occupancy of both primary and secondary roles in relation to his utterance. There are different 'manners of assignment' of the teller role, realised principally in the phonological system of tone. The major distinction is between what I shall call 'static' and 'dynamic assignment'. The former applies to the utterance to which it attaches, in isolation; the latter relates its own utterance to one immediately preceding or following it.

I suggest the following rough analysis of tones as the realisations of such features, using the description of standard British English given in Halliday (1967a).

§211.   Static assignment is realised by falling tone (tone 1). Dynamic assignment is realised by the other tones (2–5) all of which have an element of rising pitch change.

Static assignment is the unmarked case. Tone 1 typically realises: 'Speaker occupies the teller role with respect to this description without competition.'

There is, however, one major exception to this. Where tone 1 occurs with first-order non-polar interrogatives such as //1 Where are you going//, teller role transference is involved and the construction points 'forwards' to an expected reply. Transference is made, however, only with reference to the element(s) specified by the *wh*-interrogative items, and not with respect to the description as a whole, nor to its sign. This limited transference is not realised intonationally, except in second-order (echo) interrogatives which typically have a rising tone (2/4) on the queried element(s), as in //2 Who did what//.

Tone 1 may be used at any point in the structure of a conversation: initially, medially or finally. It gives no indication of the relationship between teller role assignment in a preceding or subsequent utterance and that in its own. (For this reason tone 1 can be used in a 'flat' contradiction, since as it realises no link with a preceding utterance, it conveys no acknowledgement that the previous speaker has said anything worth taking into account.) It may be used equally where a preceding utterance has rising tone and is made by a different speaker, or where it has falling tone and is made by the same speaker as teller; equally it may be followed by either.

§212.   'Dynamic assignment' involves the transfer of the teller role between two different individuals occupying the roles of speaker and addressee respectively. The speaker of the utterance to which the rising tone concerned attaches makes this transference.

There are different types of transference, according to 'origin' and 'destination' and different 'directions' of utterance relationship, according to relative sequence.

§213.   The notion of 'origin' refers to the primary role-player who is shown as 'holding' the teller role with respect to the initiation of the transference involved; that of 'destination' to its subsequent occupant.

§214.   The clearest case of transference, typically associated with polar interrogative constructions, is from speaker to addressee. Here the rising tone 2 marks a relationship between its own utterance and one which is expected to follow it ('cataphoric direction'). I shall call this manner of transference 'imposition'. Tone 2 may be used initially or medially in a conversation, but not, normally, finally.

§215.   A second type of transference, typically associated with declaratives (chiefly in contradiction 'units'), is from addressee to speaker. Here tone 5, in its initial rising element, marks the speaker's active taking of the teller role from another to himself. The final falling element indicates his retention of it. Here the direction of linkage between utterances is 'backwards', to a previous ('anaphoric direction'). Tone 5 may be used medially or finally in a conversation, but not initially.

§216.   Tone 1 may also realise a transference feature, but of a different type from those of the other tones: namely the acceptance of a teller role assignment made by the previous speaker. This may be either by that speaker to himself, as in,

A: //1 It's snowing hard//
B: //1 Is it// (//1 I see//)

or to the speaker of the second construction, as in question and answer exchanges, e.g.

A: //2 Is it snowing//
B: //1 Hard//.

In the first example B's non-committal response indicates the reaction that A, who has assigned the role of teller to himself in his first utterance, should be allowed to keep it, but without the encouragement to continue/challenge to justify his remark which a rising tone on the isolated tag would give him by positively assigning it to him.

§217.   Tone 4 realises two transfers. It is typically associated with a sequence of three declaratives. For example,

> A: //1 3 Peter will come round at <u>three</u> I <u>think</u>//
> B: //4 I might be <u>out</u>//
> A: //1 That's <u>awkward</u>//.

The initial falling element in tone 4 realises acceptance of a previous assignment of the teller role to the current speaker by the previous speaker (current addressee). The following rising element realises its return: the current speaker 'reimposes' it on its previous occupant, from whom he temporarily accepted it. Linkage to other utterances is in both directions, and tone 4 generally occurs only in medial position in a conversation.

§218.   Tone 3 differs from all the others in that it realises an uncertain, potential transference. It indicates uncertainty, on the part of a speaker who is currently teller, about how, or if, to continue (and hold the teller role) or whether to transfer it to another. It occurs, for example, in hesitant replies, or in listing items, especially when the speaker is uncertain whether to end the list at a given point or not, or in cases where the speaker wishes to transfer the teller role to an addressee whom he is not sure is willing to accept it. Tone 3 links 'forwards' to a succeeding utterance.

§219.   We can summarise these observations about teller-role transference (with respect to whole descriptions) in Table 5.1.

Table 5.1

	I Manner of transference	II Direction of transference Origin	Destination	III Tone	IV Direction of utterance linkage
A C T U A L	Imposition	Speaker	→ Addressee	2 (rise)	cataphoric
	Claim + Retention	Addressee	→ Speaker	5 (rise-fall)	anaphoric
	Acceptance + Reimposition	Addressee	→ Speaker → Addressee	4 (fall-rise)	both
	Potential yielding	Speaker	→ Speaker/ Addressee	3 (low rise)	cataphoric

§220.   Seen in this light, the tone system has more to do with the
structure of discourse than with the traditional categories of speech
function. It is only because 'question' is included in the latter
that a connection exists. I would see the traditional category of
question as combining factors to do with teller-role transference
and occupancy, on the one hand, with features of mediating role
occupancy, on the other. In the former respect it realises the discourse feature of cataphoric utterance linkage, and predicts a
reply; it is this aspect of a 'question' which is realised in tone. The
fact that declaratives with rising intonation may be perceived as
questions perhaps lends support to this view, for the declarative
typically realises [Knower : Speaker] . That is, such forms are
'questions' only in the discourse sense, which may help to explain
why they are generally strongly 'loaded' towards expecting an
answer corresponding with their own polarity. (If I say //2 You're
going//, I can convey my assumption/expectation that you are.)

§221.   Distinctions of tone realise one aspect of making a verbal social
move towards another, as summarised in column I of Table 5.1 in
§219 (to which we may add the ''acceptance' move discussed in
§216). They are closely bound up with the establishment of discourse units ('exchanges') within the developing structure of a
conversation. If we take column IV of that table we can summarise
their discourse features as shown in Table 5.2.

Table 5.2

Tone	Position(s)	Linkage direction(s)	Discourse function(s)	Discourse type
1 (fall)	Initial/ medial/final	Neutral	Static	Unmarked
2 (rise)	Initial/medial	Cataphoric	Predicts response	Initiator
3 (low rise)	Initial/medial	Cataphoric	Predicts further utterance	Initiator
4 (fall-rise)	Medial	Anaphoric and cataphoric	Assumes initiator, predicts response	Reply— Initiator
5 (rise-fall)	Medial/final	Anaphoric	Assumes initiator	Reply

Rules governing patterns of tone combinations in exchanges and
the construction of more complex discourse units on this basis

would belong under the semantics of discourse and constitute one aspect of phonological meaning. It seems that they might relate to categories of first, and higher, orders of significance in interesting ways. This is beyond my scope to consider, but it is worth noting that tone on its own is insufficient to realise a category such as contradiction, and that discourse units are established by the combination of features from all four planes and derive from the interplay of elements of both interactional and interpretational semantics. All types of linguistic meaning are combined in the formation of texts.

§222.   The notion that the tone system plays a part in the realisation of discourse structure and the establishment of discourse units complements the ideas put forward in Halliday (1967a) that the placement of the tonic syllable, as defined in terms of surface elements of clause structure (tonicity), and the placing of tone group boundaries (tonality) realise features of 'information structure'.

I suggest that tonality realises the scope of a telling operation (of whatever kind, full/derived, immediate/displaced). It indicates the part of a description (usually the whole) to which a given telling operation applies. Tone group boundaries delimit the extent of what is presented by that operation.

Tonicity represents a phonological device for highlighting one element in a description as that which is the main focus of the telling operation. Unmarked tonicity (tonic syllable on last lexical item in the tone group) realises the presentation of that item (and the element of clause structure in which it occurs) as the major element of new information presented in the telling operation. Marked tonicity realises contrastive emphasis on the item on which it falls: *that* item, and not any other, is what the speaker presents. Marked tonicity often occurs in selective (implicit) contradiction (oppositeness of one item), as in: //1 Bromley <u>South</u> is the station in the high street// (//1 Bromley North is near the <u>Town Hall</u>//). In this use it may be associated with tone 5. Where marked tonicity attaches to the finite verb, or to the sentence-negating item, in a clause it realises the contrastive telling of the description sign, rather than of any particular element. Compare: //1 John <u>does</u> play tennis//, //John does <u>not</u> play tennis// with //1 John doesn't <u>play</u> tennis// (but he watches it a lot), in this connection. (Marked tonicity may also realise non-contrastive emphasis, as in //1 Bromley North is <u>miles</u> away from the shops//.)

In terms of the semantics of telling, a near-equivalent to marked tonicity, as a means of realising the foregrounding of one element as the particular focus of the telling operation, is the cleft sentence construction (referred to in Halliday, 1967c, 1967d, 1968 as 'Theme predication'). This would give, for example: *It's Bromley South which is in the High Street.* (This may of course combine with marked tonicity to realise stronger emphasis: //1 It's Bromley South which is in the High Street//.)

Theme predication is less available for contrastive telling of description sign, but compare: *It's (just) that John plays tennis/ It isn't that John plays tennis* with **It's/It isn't playing that John does to tennis.* The related form for telling focused on the predicate is the pseudo-cleft sentence, *What John does (do) is play tennis/ What John's doing is laughing*, but there is no syntactic device for realising telling focus on the lexical verb separately from the rest of the predicate: **What John does to tennis is play/*What John did to the cat was feed.*

§223.   We have discussed manners of teller-role transference relating them to the dynamics of the verbal interaction, but the teller role is usually combined with either that of knower or decider. Where this is so, the mechanisms transferring the teller role operate to transfer simultaneously the other secondary role(s) with which it is combined. It is probably more satisfactory to see polar interrogatives as realising transference of the knower role from speaker to addressee (by virtue of its combination with the teller role) than to view them as realising a simple 'static' assignment of that role to the addressee. In such constructions, the speaker occupies the teller role with respect to that aspect of the telling operation which involves constructing the description. I suggest that, in taking on that role, the speaker simultaneously assigns to himself the role of one who knows that the description is relevant to the discourse (cf. Grice's relevancy maxim, 1975: 46) and that it is well-formed (in terms of interpretational meaning). What he presents himself as not knowing is the Ov of the event/state of affairs to which the description relates. The knower role as transferred to the addressee in polar interrogatives relates specifically to knowledge of Ov, and the telling operation demanded is focused on description sign. (A comparable interpretation applies to transference of the decider role in decision polar interrogatives.)

Such an interpretation links polar interrogatives more closely to their non-polar counterparts, which realise transference of the knower role with respect to (a) specified element(s) in the description, but not with respect to Ov, knowledge of which is presented as common to both speaker and addressee (cf. §254 below).

§224.   Immediate telling is located in SU. Distanced telling, to which I turn now, is detached from SU in one respect or another. Distinctions in this area are realised mainly in syntax, and I shall restrict the discussion to that area.

§225.   I earlier suggested (§127) two independent dimensions in terms of which telling may be assessed, to give four major types:

(i)   Full and immediate
(ii)   Full and distanced
(iii)   Derived and immediate
(iv)   Derived and distanced

Both the distinctions full/derived, immediate/distanced are realised syntactically, and not by intonation. So far in this chapter we have referred only to constructions involving type (i), as realised in non-subjunctive main clauses.

§226.   There is at least one full telling operation associated with every sentence. A full telling operation applies to any main clause, and sentences with more than one main clause realise more than one full telling operation. Clauses dependent upon, or embedded within, a main clause have derived telling. They are presented for discussion not in their own right, but as appendages/qualifications/constituents of the main clause.

§227.   The description in a dependent clause is not asserted and the element of assertion which is lacking to it is that of full telling, not knowing. For example, *John having eaten his breakfast, Jane left* cannot follow a preceding sentence indicating that John was not having breakfast. The description is presented as known, and constitutes a part of what is told by the sentence as a whole (as shown by the restrictions on combination with preceding co-text). It represents in one sense 'given' information, a topic touched on, or at least shown to be relevant, before. It is not what is chiefly presented for consideration by the sentence as a whole, and does not constitute the 'jumping-off point' from which further discourse will develop. In terms of discourse structuring in relation to content (the interpretational meaning of descriptions), its links are 'backwards' (into preceding discourse).

The notion of full/derived telling relates to the dynamics of verbal interactions. Dependent clauses usually have tone 1, and embedded clauses carry no tone, unless they happen to realise the final element in the structure of a main clause (or in cases of marked tonicity). This seems to indicate that they are not directly involved in teller-role transference within the ongoing SU; but they are syntactically marked as subordinate to another clause which can be so involved, and so it is not necessary for them to enter into such exchanges directly.

However, teller-role transference outside the SU is realised in dependent clauses. I take this feature to underlie dependent clauses introduced by *if* both in indirect speech and in conditional sentences. The former claim is conventional and needs little further support. In a sentence such as, *John asked (Peter) if Jane was/were coming*, the performance given in the main clause description is one of teller-role transference and the dependent clause is marked (by *if*) to show that, in the distanced SU in which it was told, it was presented in a form which realised teller-role transference from the then speaker to the then addressee. This addressee may, but need not, be indicated in an indirect object in the reporting clause.

I would link the dependent clause in some conditional sentences with this pattern of interpretation. Where this is an 'open' condition, as in, *If it snows the train will be late*, the speaker presents knowledge in this respect as located if at all, outside SU, and belonging to some unspecified third party at a future time. In as far as the (non-modal) indicative typically realises the combination [Teller = Knower], whether 'statically' or in transference moves, assignment of the knower role to an unspecified outsider in a distanced situation can be seen as combining with a similar assignment of the teller role. Perhaps it is not too far-fetched to suggest that what is realised by such dependent clauses is the transference of the teller role to an unspecified destination outside SU. I shall call this 'undirected asking'.

§228.   Some dependent clauses serve to link the main clause to which they are subordinated to previous discourse in terms of pre-suppositional factors. This applies particularly to one type of dependent clause introduced by *if*, which I treat below (§286) as 'telling conditions'. In examples such as, *If John's a great walker, there's some lovely country round here*, the description in the dependent clause is presented as known on the basis of preceding discourse. Such constructions convey that the speaker accepts that the description holds good, on the grounds that someone has just claimed to know that it does, or has said something else which strongly suggests so. This 'accepted knowledge' is presented as the grounds for making the statement in the main clause. It is put forward as a sufficient condition for the relevancy of telling the main clause. The dependent clause in such cases has a clearly cohesive function in discourse structure. In such cases the only role transference which *if* could be thought to realise is that of the speaker taking up the teller role from another.

§229.   Syntactic dependency, often in combination with non-finiteness, also relates to the structuring of information within the sentence in terms of the relative prominence of presentation of different descriptions. (In this it can be compared with tonicity and theme as devices for realising the ordering of different elements within one description in this respect.) For example, taking *Looking at the damage, John blamed himself* and, *John looked at the damage and blamed himself*, the distinction appears to be at least partly a matter of the relative prominence with which 'John's looking at the damage' is presented in comparison with 'John's blaming himself' (lesser in the first example, and equal or slightly greater in the second). This is in addition to possible distinctions of relative sequence in time of the two events: (?) simultaneous/consecutive.

I do not suggest that syntactic dependency realises only telling features. Clearly it is intimately connected with features in the performance plane, particularly those to do with relations between events, such as cause and effect.

What I do suggest is that no subordinate clause realises full telling, and that this is one reason why they do not carry independent assertoric force.

§230.   I have used the term 'distanced telling' to describe the notion that the telling operation may be shown to take place outside the ongoing SU. One way of accounting for the tentative quality conveyed in constructions such as, *I wanted an application form (please)* (where the activity denoted in the 'past' verb clearly occurs in SU) is to say that they realise the separation from SU, not of performing, but of telling. In such examples, the speaker conveys that, under other circumstances, in some unspecified elsewhere, this is the description which he would tell, but he cannot quite bring himself to present it directly in the here and now. The addition of *please*, however, undoes this polite fiction. The form is 'polite' not only because it presents a wish which does not explicitly involve the addressee in any action, but because it presents that wish marked for 'non-immediate presentation'.

Modal, as well as lexical verbs, may be marked in a way which corresponds with 'unreal past'.[1] The distinction between *Will you/ would you come in now* is perhaps along these lines. Distanced telling in some cases of this kind introduces more scope for a delayed or not explicitly relevant reply, as in *Would it be convenient for you to come tomorrow*, to which it is slightly easier to reply, 'I'll check my diary', than it would be to the *will* equivalent.

Constructions of this kind realise a distanced (non-SU) placement of the telling operation, but they are directed at a participant in the ongoing SU. When interrogative they realise teller-role transference to an 'immediate' destination: the addressee in SU.

§231.   Distanced telling constructions discussed so far have had full telling. Dependent clauses, with derived telling, may also have immediate or distanced telling. Subjunctive mood in conditional clauses (where the verb is marked for 'unreal pastness') as in '*If it were to rain/if it rained*, the match would be cancelled', realises distanced telling. The distinction between these forms and the present indicative in such constructions is often said to be one of degree of reservation or doubt on the speaker's part. I suggest that this effect derives from the non-actual manner of presentation of their presentation.

While it may not be necessary to invoke a notion of distanced telling in the interpretation of the sequence of tenses rule as it applies to the dependent clause in constructions of reported speech, it is nevertheless in harmony with the facts there: the reported clause is told outside the SU in which the reporting clause is told. One may note also that one type of conditional which is marked for unreal past is also the standard form for reported speech: *(He said that) if it rained the match would be cancelled.*

§232.   Marking for unreal pastness (subjunctive mood) realises a displaced origin of the telling operation. I have suggested that conditional clauses realise a distanced destination of teller-role transference (an unspecified third party outside SU). Those with the present tense indicative realise an immediate origin of that transference (derived telling beginning in SU), those with subjunctive mood realise distancing of origin as well as of destination. The feature of derivative telling realised in the subordinate clause accounts for the awkwardness/(?) unacceptability of *If it were to rain the match will be cancelled*. It is inappropriate to mark the subordinate clause for a distanced origin of the telling operation, when the main clause to which that operation principally applies is marked for immediate telling.

§233.   The telling operation may be recursively applied. Constructions which realise the application of one telling operation to another I shall call 'constructions of re-telling'.

§234.   Re-telling involves more than one SU. I shall call that in which the sentence as a whole is uttered the 'current' SU (CSU), and that in which the other telling operation takes place the 'original' SU (OSU). Different construction types are distinguished according to the relation between SUs, and according to which of them is the dominant focus. I shall use 'TL_2' to refer to the telling operation in CSU, and 'TL_1' for that in OSU; 'TC' refers to the teller in CSU, 'TO' to the teller in OSU. I reserve the term 'speaker' for the individual in CSU. The notion of the speaker as a 'mouthpiece' teller (cf. §74) is relevant in places.

I distinguish four types of re-telling: repeated, relayed, reported and represented speech.

§235. Repeated Speech

Repeated speech consists in a reporting clause followed by direct quotation. There are two independent SUs, neither of which is dominant with respect to the other. There are two main clauses, each with full telling, and no marker of grammatical relation between them. For these reasons, repeated speech may sometimes be misunderstood in spoken language; the tone group boundary between the clauses is insufficient to distinguish it from reported speech, which does not always conform to the sequence of tenses rule in informal usage. *John said I'm being transferred* might be ambiguous in this way (*John =/≠ I*).

Person in the repeated sentence realises occupancy of the performer (and other, transitivity, roles) in terms of primary role status in OSU. Tense in this sentence realises the relation between SP and OSU. The repeating verb may be in the 'historic present' in colloquial speech.

In written language, the repeated sentence is enclosed in quotation marks. The use of quotation marks by logicians to distinguish the mention of a term or sentence as opposed to its use (e.g. Quine, 1951: 23-6) reflects the use of quotation marks in natural language to distinguish an item which is spoken, but not told in CSU. In *'Socrates' has eight letters*, the quotation marks set off the item *Socrates* as not told in CSU. The proposition has as its subject not an item referring to an entity in extra-linguistic reality, but the telling of such an item. The sentence is a report of a verbal event of naming.

The speaker does not tell the description + mediating operations realised in the repeated sentence: he tells *that* another did tell them, but merely speaks what that other told. Since he does not tell any knowing or deciding operation which is realised in the construction which he repeats, he does not commit himself to the force, any more than to the description, of what the other said.

This feature of repeated speech as indicated by quotation marks underlies the use of 'scare' quotes as illustrated in the following letter to the *Daily Telegraph* (22 Sept. 1969):

> SIR: Please may we have the term 'students' set in inverted commas when used in publicising the squalid and wasteful activities of some of them?

Repeated speech provides motivation for establishing the distinction which I have maintained between the roles of speaker and teller.

§236.   Relayed Speech

I have already made use of this category in introducing relayed decision (§186). It differs from repeated and reported speech in not requiring an explicit re-telling clause, although it may have one. Compare: *She says I've got to go*, with *We can go now*. Where there is no re-telling clause, constructions are often ambiguous between full immediate telling and relayed telling. The two differ according to whether or not the teller role combines with an authoritative mediating role, and often this question is decidable only from context. 'Relaying' is found most commonly in the speech of children, especially when conveying the authoritative pronouncements of adults to other children, often without explicitly labelling them as such: *(Miss Jones says) we can go now*.

For our purposes there are four features of interest.

(i)   The speaker generally commits himself to what he retells, both to the force and description. But he cannot be held to it. If challenged on either, he can evade responsibility by saying 'He said so'. The rules of hearsay evidence recognise this feature of relayed speech.

(ii)   TC is non-authoritative; he acts as a 'mouthpiece teller' voicing the decision (or sometimes the knowledge) of TO. The construction which TC speaks realises [TO = Decider/Knower].

The standard challenge to a relayed speech is 'Who says so?'

(iii) Person in the relayed construction realises performer-occupancy in CSU. In this respect CSU receives dominant focus. In cases where there is a re-telling clause the sequence of tenses rule does not apply.

(iv) Relayed speech need not make explicit *that* another has carried out a telling operation.

§237. Reported Speech

Here CSU receives the dominant focus and OSU is related to it. This is realised by person and tense in the reported clause, which are both derived from CSU. As with repeated speech, TO is the occupant of the performer role in the re-telling clause. (TC may, or may not, be the same individual.)

The speaker of the whole construction does not commit himself to telling the force and description of the reported element. He may often explicitly dissociate himself from the whole, or a particular part, of what he reports another as telling, as in this example from BBC Radio Four's programme 'Today in Parliament' (27 July 1965): 'For the opposition, Mr Anthony Barber said this was a very grave statement indeed . . . He blamed *what he called the* Government's inept and incompetent handling of our economic affairs.' Here the distinction between TO and TC is emphasised so that there is no possibility of attributing partisan criticisms of the government to the broadcasting corporation.

As in repeated speech, TC tells *that* TO tells (something else). The difference is chiefly that, in reported speech what TO tells is not given verbatim, but adapted to relate to CSU.

Reported speech allows wide variation in the lexis of the reporting verb, so that this may not only contribute to realising the LMM of the reported construction in OSU (e.g. *say/ask*) but also convey its first-order interactional significance there (e.g. *state/query*), or a higher level significance (e.g. *warn/threaten*) or its discourse status (e.g. *answer/reply/counter/repeat*) or a combination of some of these factors (as in *claim/argue/challenge*). It may also describe manner of speaking, as in *whisper/shout/mutter*. Both discourse status and one of the other features can be realised in an extended variant of the construction with S V-finite (O) (A) *by* V-ing . . . as in, 'Mr Jones *concluded* (his speech) (angrily) by *warning* that the future of Wales was at stake.' (The perlocutionary effect of TO's utterance may also be reported, in the extended construction: *Mr Jones roused the crowd by claiming . . .*). Reported speech allows maximum opportunities for describing how something was told in addition to conveying that it was told (and who by) and giving an adapted version of what was told.

The sequence of tenses rule in reported speech does not always apply. Jespersen (1924: 294), commenting on the example *It was he who taught me that twice two is four*, gives an interpretation which I quote in full and adopt.

The use of the unshifted present tense here implies that the actual speaker is himself convinced of the truth of the assertion, whereas the shifting of the tense also shifts the responsibility for the saying onto the original speaker; hence the difference in 'He told us that it *was* sometimes lawful to kill' (but he may have been wrong) and 'I did not know then that it *is* sometimes lawful to kill' (but it is).

Usage may vary on this point, and the distinction may be weakening. Even so, I would feel *John said that Jane is coming* conveys greater belief that she is coming than *John said that Jane was coming* would do. This suggests that the feature 'past tense' in a reported clause realises not principally (or at least not only) the relationship in time between SP and CSU, but, rather, the feature of distanced telling: 'knowing operation on reported description not told within CSU by TC'.

§238.   Represented Speech

I adopt Jespersen's term (1924: 219, 290-5) for a type of reported speech which is only partly adapted to CSU (that of narrative).

The equivalent of the reporting verb, where there is one, is usually *think*, but this typically occurs in a separate sentence. Represented speech need not have a re-telling verb and presents little opportunity for comment by TC. In this it resembles relayed speech. Person and tense are related to CSU, as in reported speech. I reproduce part of Jespersen's quotation from Thackeray as illustration:

I don't envy Pen's feelings as he thought of what he had done. *He had slept, and the tortoise had won the race. He had marred at its outset what might have been a brilliant career.* [My italics.]

Third person in the sentences in represented speech realises the speech role status of the performer-occupant in terms of CSU, the situation of narration. The pluperfect in each sentence realises two degrees of real pastness in relation to CSU, but also, I would claim, distanced telling in terms of CSU, shown too, in *might have been.*

Represented speech differs from reported speech chiefly with respect to the form of the interrogatives and imperatives. They have the word order of direct speech, but shift tense and person. Further, change between declarative and interrogative sentences does not require the introduction of a verb of asking, which is required in reported speech (although in the latter one reporting verb may govern several consecutive sentences if all are declarative).

Jespersen quotes from the same novel to illustrate these features:

All that the Rector could say could not bring Helen to feel any indignation or particular unhappiness, except that the boy should be unhappy. *What was this degree that they made such an outcry about, and what good would it do Pen? Why did Doctor Portman and his uncle insist upon sending the boy to a place where there was so much temptation to be risked, and so little good to be won? Why didn't they leave him at home with his mother? As for his debts, of course they must be paid – his debts! – wasn't his father's money all his, and hadn't he a right to spend it?* [My italics.]

Interrogatives in represented speech are not adapted to the CSU of narration by marking for teller-role transference in OSU (*if*). This might suggest that this is a fashion of reporting which recognises that no such transference takes place in OSU, which would reflect the reflexive nature of the 'asking' involved. If there is anything to this notion, represented speech would come nearest in English to a syntactic device for realising 'monologue'.

§239. We can now distinguish a notion of non-authoritative telling in addition to the types of distanced and derived telling suggested earlier. This rests on the occupancy of the teller role by someone other than the speaker. It does not always combine with distanced telling (repeated speech), but often does so (reported and represented speech). Relayed speech represents a grey area in this respect, for the speaker has some share, if not the major one, in occupation of the teller role.

§240.   If we accept that some kinds of syntactic dependency realise
semantic distinctions falling within the telling plane, this area of the
grammar relates to the 'interface' between telling and performance.

Notes

1. It is possible to think of some instances of *would* as showing marking
for 'unreal past' because others realise a real past, e.g. *He would go to the same
place every evening* ('used to'). This applies also to *could*, (i) as past capability, and (ii) as permission operative in the past, e.g. *I could play my radio
until 10 p.m. in those lodgings* ('used to be allowed to'). This contrasts with
Could I borrow your car? The case is harder to argue for *might*.

I suggest that marking for 'unreal past' is one way in which subjunctive
mood is indicated, but do not suggest that the subjunctive is always shown by
unreal past. Further, although I claim that the subjunctive can realise
distanced telling, I do not claim that it always realises this semantic feature.
There is a strong case in some instances for seeing the subjunctive as realising
distancing of performance from SU. Main clause decision subjunctives, such as
God save the Queen are the chief examples, but embedded clauses following
a decision verb in the matrix sentence may also realise this feature, as in
I demand that he (should) go. This is connected with the relatively frequent
occurrence of the subjunctive in dependent clauses. I would take examples
such as '*Whether it be the case . . .*', as realising lack of speaker commitment,
and so distanced telling. This construction also realises lack of knowledge.

6 KNOWLEDGE

§241. The knowledge plane covers semantic distinctions to do with who (in terms of primary roles) knows what, how they know it (from another/by deduction/with independent authority), whether they know or believe, and whether what they know is what they say. The chief factors concerned are occupancy of the knower role, and the placement and implementation of the knowing operation (together with features of its operand). Connections with telling features are relevant throughout.

§242. The grammatical constructions which I treat in this connection include those containing an epistemic modal verb, different types of declaratives with tag, and polar/non-polar interrogatives.

§243. I use the term 'direct knowledge' for cases where the knowledge operation is placed in SU and the knower role is occupied by a participant there. 'Indirect knowledge' covers cases where the operation is distanced from SU, which is generally associated with third-party occupancy of the knower role. Direct knowledge constructions have positive operation sign, indirect, negative operation sign (knowing +/−).

§244. Operation sign governs the relation between description sign (DS) and occurrence value (Ov) as follows:

$$\text{Knowing}^+ \; : \; DS = Ov \text{ (parity relation)}$$
$$\text{Knowing}^- \; : \; DS \neq Ov \text{ (opposition)}$$

I examine this claim below.

§245. Knowing$^+$ is relevant to the discourse category of contradiction. Where it applies to a single proposition (cf. §52) both utterances realise constructions with knowing$^+$, but they have opposed description sign (and, hence, opposed Ov). The contradiction relation between constructions whose operations apply to the same description is that of opposition between DS values. The agreement relation is that of parity between DS values. In both cases, both constructions have full immediate telling and direct knowing.

$$[(\text{Teller} = \text{Knower}) : \text{Speaker}]$$
$$[\text{Telling}^+, \text{Knowing}^+]$$

The opposition/parity relation is between what is told as known (asserted) : the DS values.

§246.   In declarative indicatives, the operand of the knowing operation is a DS value. For the moment, I shall distinguish terminologically between positive knowing applied to DS^+, which I call 'affirmation', and positive knowing applied to DS^-, 'denial'.

Negative knowing applied to DS^+ I term 'believing', and applied to DS^-, 'doubting'.

§247.   Constructions of positive knowing (direct knowledge) have speaker and/or addressee occupancy of the knower role, those of negative knowing (indirect knowledge) have neither. For example, we may gloss standard cases of each (all with DS^+) as:

$Knowing^+$

Declarative indicative
It's raining: 'I know that it is but I think that you do not know until I tell you so.'

Polar interrogative indicative
Is it raining?: 'I do not know whether or not it is, but I am confident that you do know which it is. (Please tell me.)'

$Knowing^-$

Declarative modal verb
It may be raining: 'Neither you nor I know (but someone else perhaps does).'

The interrogative modal verb construction is awkward (unacceptable for me) with *may*: **May it be raining?* A positive interrogative construction realises (Knower : Addressee). With a construction which realises 'Addressee not an occupant of the knower role', as here, the interrogative is semantically ill-formed. Variations in occupancy of the knower role underlie several surface grammar distinctions in constructions of positive knowing.

§248.   I suggest 'Query' as a knowing operation.

We have :   affirmation as: $K^+\!\searrow DS^+$
            denial as: $K^+\!\searrow DS^-$ for (Knower : Speaker)
Let us take query as: $K^+ \searrow (DS^+ ? DS^-)$ for (Knower : Addressee)

'?' has the truth table A (Table 6.1).

Table **6.1**

p	~p	?
T	T	F
T	F	T
F	T	T
F	F	F

I make use of '?' for convenience only as a means of emphasising
the relevancy assumption realised in polar interrogatives. They
assume not only that 'not (both p and not-p)' but also 'not (neither
p nor not-p)'.

§249.   Scope

The operand in positive knowing is a DS value. I introduce the
notion of 'scope of operation' to refer to the description over which
that DS value ranges. I shall say that tags realise 'shared scope'. They
present a knowing operation applied to a DS value, but not the
description over which it ranges, except in terms of subject–predicate symbols: pro-forms (although marked for person, gender and
number at S, and tense, number at V). The description which is the
scope of their operation is realised in a different clause, or in another sentence. Isolated tags (occurring as separate sentences), as in
agreement/contradiction, I shall call 'truncated' forms.

§250.   Where a tag occurs within the same sentence as the clause realising the description which the tag operation shares as scope, I shall
say that the sentence as a whole realises a double knowing operation.
Where main clause and tag realise the same type of operation
(affirmation/denial) I shall say that the construction realises a
'repeated' operation: where the operations differ, that it realises
'alternating' operations.

§251.   I distinguish the notion of double (including repeated) operations
from that of recursive operations. The difference is that, in the
former, each operation applies to a DS value, but, in the latter, one
operation has the other as its operand.

§252.   Some types of direct knowledge constructions in British English
can now be summarised within this framework. (I postpone for the
moment problems raised by negative interrogatives, cf. §259 below.)
Since I discuss only constructions realising a complete description

(cf. §112 above) I use the term 'proposition' in what follows.

Table 6.2
Single Knowing Operation: (positive polarity only)

Knower role occupancy	Operation scope		
Single: speaker	unshared	(a)	Full declarative: *John plays chess.*
	shared	(b)	Truncated declarative: *He does.*
Single: addressee	unshared	(c)	Full polar interrogative: *Does John play chess?*
	shared	(d)	Truncated polar interrogative: *Does he?*

Table 6.3
Double Knowing Operation

Knower role occupancy	Operations	Scope
Single: speaker	Repeated 1.1 Aff + Aff 1.2 Den + Den	Shared
	Repeated 2.1 Aff + Aff 2.2 Den + Den	Split Op. 1. Full predicate Op. 2. Full subject
Joint (sharing of knower role): speaker + addressee	Alternating 3.1 Aff + (pos) query 3.2 Den + (neg) query 4.1 Aff + (neg) query 4.2 Den + (pos) query	Shared

(e) Declarative + tag
1.1 *This is a good game, it (really) is.*
1.2 *Mary can't bake a cake, she (just) can't.*
2.1.1 *He's a good player is (our) John;*
2.1.2 (?) *He's a good player (our) John is.*
2.2.1 *He can't kick straight can't John;*
2.2.2 (?) *He can't kick straight John can't.*
3.1 *John enjoyed it did he.*
3.2 (?)*John didn't come didn't he.*
4.1 *John plays chess doesn't he.*
4.2 *John doesn't play chess does he.*

§253.   In constructions with a repeated operation the same individual
as speaker occupies the knower role in both applications of that
operation.

Those with alternating operations realise, in the tag, the assignment of the knower role to the addressee. Whether or not the role
of teller is simultaneously transferred to the addressee depends on
tone: rising tone (2/3) gives transference, falling tone (1) does not.

Where there is no such transference, the assumption realised
is that the addressee knows that which the speaker knows in terms
of DS value. Such constructions invite no reply, but make explicit
an assumption of joint knowing. This holds good whether the
surface polarity of the tag is the same as, or the opposite of, that of
the main clause. The distinction between parallel and contrastive
polarity, between main clause and tag, relates to discourse factors
and not to same/opposite with respect to the DS values of the
operations (i.e. not to whether or not the tag realises an assumption that the addressee affirms where the speaker affirms, and denies
where he denies). Constructions with parallel polarity explicitly
realise the discourse feature 'reply'; those with contrastive polarity
do not. The difference between, for example, //1 John plays chess
does he// and //1 John plays chess doesn't he// is chiefly that the
former is marked (by the feature of parallel polarity) to indicate
that it represents a deduction from, or summary of, what another
has previously said, or perhaps from context; whereas the latter is
not so marked, and represents only an appeal to common knowledge.
Constructions with contrastive polarity lack a telling (relevancy,
discourse) feature which is present in parallel polarity forms.

We may also distinguish parallel polarity forms as realising
(current) addressee (= previous [(Knower = Teller) : Speaker]) as
the dominant occupant of the knower role, and contrastive polarity
constructions as realising (current) speaker as dominant there.

Where there is transference of the teller role, with rising tone on
the tag in these constructions, the addressee is invited to reply, and
more allowance is made for a knowing operation which he tells to
be the opposite of the speaker's in terms of DS value known: the
assumption of joint knowing is weaker. The distinction between
constructions of parallel and contrastive polarity when they have
rising tone is similar to that with falling. The former with rising tone
represents a more tentative summary than with falling (the speaker
may be less sure that he has heard the other's remarks aright, or that
this is an appropriate summary/deduction to make). This gives

increased dominance to the addressee as (primary) knower.

§254.   So far we have considered constructions in which the operation scope is a fully specified proposition. Non-polar interrogatives realise a proposition which contains at least one indefinite quantifier. This proposition is known by the speaker. That is, for example, underlying *Where did John go?* I take there to be an incompletely specified proposition: 'John went somewhere', which is the scope of an affirmation. Query attaches only to the indefinite quantifier: 'which where?'

It is clear that the description of query given in §248, and realised in polar interrogatives, does not apply here. Lack of speaker's knowledge in these constructions does not relate to 'which DS value', but to the selection of 'which lexical item(s)', from an indefinitely long list of possibilities, to substitute for the indefinite quantifier. It does not concern sign.

We may specify this 'selective query' more easily as an 'unknown element' in terms of speaker's knowledge, and reserve the term 'query' for the operation applying to DS value. We have then a case where occupancy of the knower role is 'split' between speaker and addressee in such a way that one (or more) element(s) in the proposition is presented as known to the addressee but not to the speaker. The construction itself realises (a) one knowing operation with an incompletely specified proposition as scope, (b) split occupancy of the knower role, and (c) assignment of the knower role to the addressee with respect to those elements which are not lexically specified in the proposition. The addressee is presented as knowing everything which the speaker does, together with elements in the description which the speaker cannot specify lexically. 'Split occupancy' refers to both these aspects of speaker–addressee knowledge, and seems preferable to the 'split operation' notion in § 94.

The non-polar interrogative could be viewed as a construction marked for sharing part of its operation (affirmation) scope with a following construction, and compared with single knowing declaratives containing one or more pro-forms, which realise an operation scope partially shared with a preceding construction. (For a full description of the latter type, cf. Halliday and Hasan, 1976.)

§255.   There are several types of non-polar interrogatives, including (syntactic) 'echoes', and 'recollection forms'. The latter realise previous joint knowledge by speaker and addressee, as in *Who was it (did you say) who/that mended their clock?* They all realise split occupancy of the knower role; variation occurs according to:

(i) the number of elements given as lexically unspecified: (ii) the grammatical status of unspecified elements in terms of clause structure; (iii) reference to surrounding discourse.

What the speaker knows in such constructions (the incompletely specified proposition), is generally 'accepted' knowledge: he knows it on the basis of something which has earlier been said, or on that of some factor in context. He does not present it as new. For example, although, *Where have you been?* could be used to begin a conversation, knowledge 'that you have been somewhere' would be derivable from context in such an instance.

Echo non-polars, e.g. //2 Is <u>who</u> driving back//, //4 John sent him the <u>what</u>//, //4 Let's go <u>where</u>//, are marked for anaphoric reference to an immediately preceding construction. This is realised by repetition of the syntactic form of that construction, with the substitution of a *wh-* interrogative for the lexically specified item(s) at one or more places in its structure. Echoes relate to a previous telling operation as well as to one of knowing. Bearing in mind the possibility of an echo of a non-polar interrogative, as in //4 Where did John put <u>what</u>//, it is clear that the relations involved are highly complex; but I do not pursue them here.

Recollection forms relate to previous knowledge, which may be at some distance, and outside SU. Where they have interpolated *did you say/you said*, they explicitly realise a link to a previous telling operation; otherwise only knowing need be involved.

If we accept the suggestion in § 254 that non-polar interrogatives as a whole realise a connection with succeeding discourse, by virtue of their partially shared operation scope, we can now see them as linking constructions realising both anaphoric and cataphoric 'cohesive bonds'.

§256.   We can add non-polar interrogatives, as a group, to Table 6.2 in §252 (constructions with single knowing operation), as in Table 6.4.

Table 6.4

Knower role occupancy	Operation scope
Split	Partially shared

§257.   So far we have discussed only positive interrogatives of either kind. Negative interrogatives are of two types, both in polar and non-polar constructions, according to whether they have positive or negative force. Compare, //1 Haven't we met somewhere before//: //1 Didn't John enjoy it (then)// and //1 Where hasn't he been//: //1 What haven't I done now//. The distinction is not accountable for in terms of tone, although in the non-polars marked tonicity plays the major part in realising it.

§258.   There are different ways of presenting what is at issue in the non-polar interrogatives. I take what I hope is the briefest.

Positive non-polars realise an incompletely specified proposition which is affirmed. Let us take, //1 Where did he go to today//. This realises an affirmation that 'He went to somewhere today'. This, in turn, implies 'He did not go to no where'. Finite verb tonicity in a positive non-polar can have the effect of reversing the sign of this implied description, to give: 'not (he did not go to no where)'/'He went nowhere' as the description which is affirmed. Compare: //1 What has he done// (Nothing). Tone 5, however, in such constructions emphasises the speaker's lack of knowledge of 'which': //5 Where has he been// (I have no idea/can't imagine 'which where').

Negative non-polar interrogatives similarly realise an incompletely specified proposition which is denied (i.e. has negative DS). For example, //1 What hasn't he seen// realises the speaker's knowledge that 'He hasn't seen something' (There is something which he hasn't seen). This in turn implies: 'He has not seen everything'. Marked tonicity on the finite verb in negative non-polars reverses this polarity to give: 'not (He has not seen everything)'/'He has seen everything', as the meaning of the construction. Compare: //1 Where hasn't he been// (He has been everywhere), //1 Who doesn't he know// (He knows everyone).

The underlying *some-* in positive non-polars can be taken as 'not-none'; that in negative non-polars as 'not-all'. Both constructions convey 'You have asked me the wrong question: it is easier to answer that with the opposite polarity, for there I can give a universal quantifier in reply.' This is achieved by the marked tonicity.

§259.   Negative polar interrogatives divide into two types according to whether they have a positive or negative force. Compare: //1 Isn't that nice// with //1 Didn't he enjoy it (then)//. The types can be distinguished by matching with declarative + tag constructions. For example:

(a)   //1 Isn't that <u>nice</u>//: (a′)   //1 That's <u>nice</u>//1 <u>isn't</u> it//
(b)   //1 Haven't we met <u>before</u>//: (b′)   //1 We've met <u>before</u>//
//1 <u>haven't</u> we// (or: //2 <u>haven't</u> we//)

as contrasted with

(c)   //1 Didn't he <u>enjoy</u> it (then)//: (c′)   //1 He didn't <u>enjoy</u>
it (then)//1 <u>did</u> he//.

The division reflects the degree and type of the speaker's knowledge. In (a) and (b), the speaker knows a positive Ov, and the interrogative element realises a move to include the addressee as an occupant of the knower role sharing in carrying out the same knowing operation. (They sometimes may, but generally do not, have tone 2, realising transference of the teller role also. In such cases the positive force is weakened, but not altogether lost.) Negative polarity here could be thought of as realising 'no query', as opposed to denial.

Constructions such as (c) are closely related to summary tags/ declaratives + tags. They realise the addressee as dominant knower, and the speaker as accepting what the current addressee (as previous [(Teller = Knower) : Speaker]) has told him. Negative polarity realises the Ov^- which the addressee knows. This type can be seen as realising the 'query' (in the sense of assignment of knower role to addressee) of a denial.

Declarative + tag constructions with alternating operations and contrasting polarity, might be seen as realising a move by the speaker to include himself among the occupants of the knower role, which already include the addressee. Those with parallel polarity realise the speaker's acceptance of the addressee as dominant knower, and of what he has previously told that he knows.

Declarative + tag constructions, on the whole, convey positive/ negative description sign value more clearly than their corresponding negative interrogatives, because it is explicitly realised in the polarity of the main clause. This applies rather more in the case of a positive main clause.

§260.   Indirect knowledge is the area of belief and deduction. Constructions of this type realise non-authoritative knowledge, and third-party occupancy of the knower role. Declaratives may be glossed as

as 'neither you nor I have independent knowledge of whether or
not p is the case, but I (have reason to) think so/think not'. Interrogatives may be glossed as 'Neither of us knows, but do you think
so/not?' There are fewer interrogatives for the reasons outlined
in §247; where they occur they are either marked for distanced
telling, 'in other circumstances (i.e. if you knew), what would you
say?' or occur in negative interrogatives with positive DS, e.g.
'*Might it be raining* (do you think)?' or *May it not be raining?*
(Don't you think it is?)

§261.   I distinguish two types of indirect knowledge, belief and doubt.
In belief constructions the Ov which is 'believed in' corresponds with
the DS value (that which is selected for discussion) realised in
surface polarity. In doubt constructions, the Ov believed in is the
opposite of DS value in surface polarity. This corresponds with the
relation:

I believe that x ≡ I doubt that not-x ≡ I don't believe that not-x.

I take *doubt* to be synonymous with *do not believe*. Deduction
represents a belief arrived at on the basis of some evidence: it is
explicitly motivated belief.

§262.   There are both explicit and implicit constructions of belief and
doubt. The explicit type may be compared with reported speech.
Contrast, however, (a) *John said Jane was at home*/ (b) *John knew
Jane was at home*/ (c) *John believed Jane was at home.* In (a),
although the teller's knowledge in CSU of 'Jane's being at home'
is indirect, a knowing operation applying to this description is told
as known in CSU definitely to have taken place in OSU, and the
occupant of the knower role in OSU is identified. This is distanced,
but placed, indirect knowing, an analysis which applies also to (b).

In (c), however, knowledge of 'Jane's being at home' is unplaced,
and it is not specified that there is any occupant of the knower role.
We have unimplemented, unplaced knowledge. Further, compare:

(d)   *John didn't say that Jane was at home : John said that
Jane wasn't at home.*
(d')   *John didn't know she was there : John knew she wasn't
there.*

with

(e)   *John didn't think that Jane was at home* : *John thought Jane wasn't at home.*

Scope of negation in (d), (d$'$) is restricted to the clause (matrix/complement) in which the negative particle occurs. In (e) scope of negation applies to the complement clause irrespective of whether it is that verb or the one in the matrix sentence which is negatived.

Where we have unimplemented unplaced indirect knowledge, lack of such knowledge of a positive DS value is equivalent to the presence of such knowledge of a negative description sign. This returns us to the equivalence:

Don't believe x $\equiv$ *believe that not-x*
    (and *Doubt x* $\equiv$ *believe that not-x*)
also: *Don't doubt x* $\equiv$ *Believe x*

§263.   We can outline constructions of explicit belief as follows:

Belief affirmation : believe/think
                    don't doubt   } that x
Belief denial   : don't believe/don't think
                    doubt   } that x

Belief query :

(i)   Loaded   Doubt if x (almost synonymous with belief denial)
(ii)   Open   (a) Wonder if not-x (possibility of not-x as topic)
                 (b) Wonder if x (possibility of x as topic)

(I have taken only the basic lexical verbs of believing; there are many other possibilities, e.g. *bet* (in its non-performative sense). There are also variant constructions, especially in (possibly non-standard) British English, e.g. *I wouldn't wonder if he was(n't) there*, 'I think he probably is there'.)

Constructions with *wonder if* resemble the other constructions listed in realising unplaced, unimplemented knowing, with an unspecified knower. For this reason, they can be used as polite questions: they do not explicitly demand a reply since they do not realise assignment of the knower role to the addressee. For example,

I wonder if John's coming gives an addressee freedom not to reply.

§264.   Constructions of explicit belief present the scope of the believing operation with derived telling in a complement clause. They 'downgrade' *what* is believed and realise full immediate telling and direct knowledge *that* it is believed. The believing operation is the operand of the knowing and telling operations. They represent one type of recursive application of knowing. Constructions of implicit belief realise a single operation, and its operand is fully told in a main clause.

§265.   Implicit belief is realised by modal verbs which realise a distinction between determinate/indeterminate, usually carried in adverbs (e.g. certainly/perhaps) and not realised in the matrix verbs of explicit constructions. We may summarise as follows:

> Belief affirmation : determinate *must* (be) x
> indeterminate *may* (be) x/*could* (be) x
> Belief denial: : determinate *can't* (be) x/*couldn't* (be) x
> indeterminate *needn't* (be) x/*may not* (be) x
> Belief query   :
> Loaded (to positive) *may-not (be)* x
> *might-not (be)* x   (possibility of x
> Open   *might (be)* x   as topic)

The status of *might(n't)* in declaratives raises difficult problems. I shall take it, for the moment, as equivalent to *may (not)* in terms of belief operations, but say that it realises distanced telling (and hence greater tentativeness). But the distinction, if any, is slight. *May (not)* and *might(n't)* are both capable of combining with lexical verbs in either the 'present' (V base) or past (*have* + V-ed) tenses, e.g. *John may/might have come yesterday/He may/might come tomorrow.* This suggests that *might* is distinguished according to manner of telling rather than in terms of what is known (relative sequence and overlap of SU–SP). *May/might* is not a distinction of tense. The same point applies in principle to *can't/couldn't*.

§266.   The main clause in sentences which I term 'knowledge conditionals' (cf. §§310-19 below) often contains a belief modal verb. For example, 'If John's away from work *he must/may be ill*'; 'If his car isn't outside *he can't/may not, be here*'; 'Even if there is someone in the house, *it (still) needn't be John*'.

Belief modals also operate freely in constructions where deduction is not explicitly at issue. For example, *John may be out now/That must be John*. I take this as a modality applying to the proposition as a whole (cf. §§278-9 below), and analyse as follows:

Let x = 'now'
  p = the proposition 'John is out'
  S = the indefinite set of $S\theta$s to which p is relevant
  A = the set of $S\theta$s of which p is true
  A' = the complement of set A (the set of $S\theta$s of which p is not true)
  $A \subset S$
  $A' \subset S$
  $A \cup A' = S$
  $x \in S$

Let us take 'knowing' as a modal operator, and use our notion of operation sign:

  K = K^+
  $\sim K$ = K^-

Then I would analyse as follows:

(1) $K\,(x \in A)$ 'John *can't be* out now'
(2) $K\,(x \in A')$ 'John *must be* out now'
(3) $\sim K\,(x \in A)$ 'John *may not be* out now'
(4) $\sim K\,(x \in A)$ 'John *could be* out now'
(5) $\sim K\,(x \in A')$ 'John *may be* out now'
(6) $\sim K\,(x \in A')$ 'John *needn't be* out now'

  [(3) is equivalent to (6); (4) is equivalent to (5)]

Indeterminate belief modals have an underlying indefinite quantifier: 'sometimes p is true, sometimes p is not true.' *John may be out now*: 'sometimes John is out and sometimes John is not out'; and, 'we do not know that this $S\theta$ ("now") doesn't belong to the set of $S\theta$s of which p is true'.

The determinate pair can operate in cases where deduction is not explicitly arrived at, for example, where the grounds for belief are supplied by context, as in *That must be John* (following a knock on the door). Cf. also the cliché phrases, *You must be joking/You can't mean it* with implicit 'if you say that'.

§267.   The same set of items realises both countermanding decision and belief. One difference is that in the decision constructions *may not*, where still used, is synonymous with *can't* and contrasts with *needn't*; but, in belief, *may not* is synonymous with *needn't*, and contrasts with *can't*.

> Decision: *may not* x 'not-may x' e.g. '*You may not enter the competition* if you are employed by the firm.'
> Belief: *may not* x 'may not-x' e.g. *That may not be John.*

§268.   I have suggested earlier that determinate belief contrasts with direct knowledge, not along the dimension of certainty, but in terms of the placement and implementation of the knowing operation and the unspecified occupancy of the knower role; and that the contrast between *John's out now* and *John must be out now* is one of the relative authority of the knower to vouch for what he says, and not principally one of conviction. But if we accepted the analysis

> (7)   K (x ∈ A) as underlying *John is out now*; and
> (8)   K (x ∈ A′) for *John isn't out now*,

as an extension of the list in §266, the determinate modals would contrast with indicative constructions on the basis of what is known, and this would underlie the distinction in 'manner of knowing' which they realise. (7) and (8) express direct knowledge. (7) gives 'x is a member of set A', which contrasts with (2) on exactly this dimension: (2) gives: 'x is not a member of set A′' and *therefore*, 'x is a member of set A'.

In traditional logic, *John is out now* and *John isn't out now* are contradictories; they cannot both be true, and they cannot both be false.

But if we accept the introduction of the epistemic modal operator 'K' as present in the underlying semantics of such constructions, then they are 'epistemic contraries'; for although it cannot be that I both know that *John is out now* and know that *John is not out now*, it can be that I neither know that *John is out now* nor know that *John is not out now* (a semantic feature realised by the indeterminate knowledge modals, and related in our previous analysis to non-participant occupancy of the knower role).

Such an approach enables us to to account for the point made by Dummett (1973: 335) that 'By saying *It may be so* I undo just what I previously did by saying *It is not so*'. That is, in our terms, this is the opposition between $\sim K (x \in A')$, $K (x \in A')$: between not-knowing and knowing the same thing. The two are 'epistemic contradictories'. This applies equally to *may not* and *is*, where the opposition is between: $\sim K (x \in A)$, $K (x \in A)$.

§269.   Constructions of implicit belief relate to events/states of affairs which are presented has having a knowable or known Ov. What they realise as lacking is not occurrence itself, but knowledge of occurrence value, cf. *John may have come yesterday*.

§270.   In suggesting a set of belief modals, I wish to distinguish them from 'prediction modals' (cf. Chapter 7 below). This can be done largely in terms of items for the determinate pairs: *must/can't* (belief); *will/won't* (prediction). Usage varies, however, and for many speakers, *will* can be used deductively, e.g. *That will be the milkman*, and may be preferred to *must*. (*Won't* is, perhaps, less common as an alternative to *can't*.) The indeterminate modals present more problems of identification, which I reserve for the next chapter, but *needn't* x (= *may not*-x) does not realise prediction.

Roughly speaking, belief constructions can be grouped with knowledge indicatives in terms of presenting an event whose Ov is somewhere known or knowable, and with prediction constructions in terms of realising the modal distinction of certain/uncertain (determinate/indeterminate) as opposed to unarguable direct knowledge.

§271.   If we accept the analysis suggested in §266 and §268, a case can perhaps be made for saying that English distinguishes between 'verifiable' and 'deduced' knowledge (i.e. between 'manner of knowing') in this area of the grammar, as follows (using the examples there):

Verifiable knowledge
    $K (x \in A)$ John is out now
    $K (x \in A')$ John is not out now
    $\sim K (x \in A)$ John may not be out now
    $\sim K (x \in A')$ John may be out now

Deduced knowledge
    $K (x \in A)$ John can't be out now
    $K (x \in A')$ John must be out now
    $\sim K (x \in A)$ John could be out now

~ K (x ≡ A′) John needn't be out now

In deduced knowledge *can't* and *must* are 'epistemic contraries'; *can't* and *could* are 'epistemic contradictories', as are *must* and *needn't*. (*Could* and *needn't* in such a scheme would be in a 'sub-contrary' relation.)

We might re-phrase this interpretation of deduced knowledge forms as follows:

(i)   *can't* realises 'No possibilities that (x ∈ A)'
(ii)   *must* realises 'All possibilities that (x ∈ A)'
(iii) *could* realises 'Not-none possibilities that (x ∈ A)'
(iv)   *needn't* realises 'Not-all possibilities that (x ∈ A)'

and draw a 'square of opposition' as below.

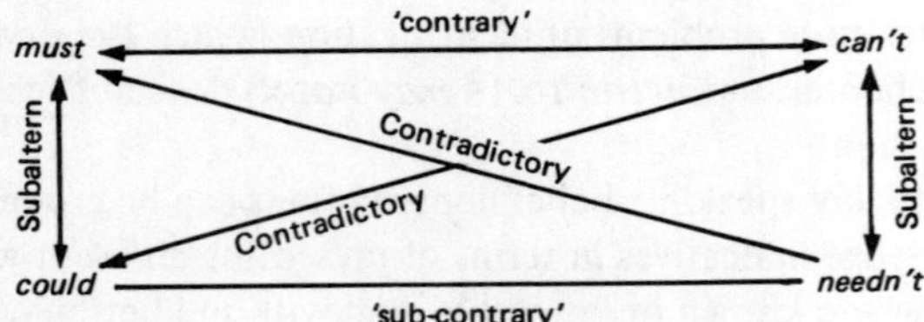

7 PERFORMANCE

§272. The performance plane is largely outside the scope of this study.
It is that area of grammatical semantics which underlies distinctions
of case and transitivity relations (cf. Fillmore, 1968; Anderson,
1971; Halliday, 1967b, 1968). Distinctions within this plane relate
to the analysis of events and states of affairs as such, and not to
how they are told, or known or decided on. The notions coming
within this area which I have made use of are principally: (i) the
performer role; (ii) the performance operation; (iii) occurrence
values; and (iv) the situation of performance. All four are necessary in linking the performance plane with those of telling, decision
and/or knowledge. It is principally in these areas that performance
distinctions relate to mood. I suggest, however, that probability
features of the performance operation and the '+/− authority'
feature of the performer role ('+/− capable') relate to mood more
directly, and are realised by modal verbs. This proposal is the main
topic of the chapter.

§273. I suggest a set of prediction modals, as distinct from those of
belief, with the following core members[1]:

Determinate
$$\begin{cases} will \text{ x} = \text{'not (may not-x)'} \\ won't \text{ x} = \text{'not (may x)'} \end{cases}$$

Indeterminate
$$\begin{cases} may \text{ x} = \text{'not (will not-x)'} \\ may\ not \text{ x} = \text{'not (will x)'} \end{cases}$$

This may be presented, on analogy with the square of opposition
in traditional formal logic as[2]:

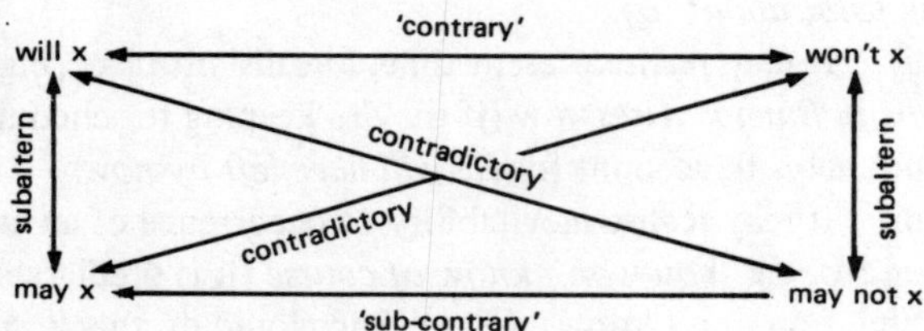

§274. *Will* is generally taken to realise, 'future time of the occurrence of
an event, in relation to SU'. The present indicative may also realise

this, with or without explicit marking for the feature (*be going to/ be about to*). For example, *John leaves/is leaving/is going to leave tomorrow/John is about to leave (now)*. The belief modal *must* can also occur when reference to future time is realised, as in *John must be leaving tomorrow*, but it does not realise 'future' itself: 'It must be the case that John is going to leave tomorrow.' The role of the time adverbial, *tomorrow*, is crucial in specifying a future sense in most of these examples. Without it, *John leaves* is incomplete (except in certain specialised contexts such as stage directions), and *John is/must be, leaving* indicate 'now'. (Cf. Crystal, 1966, for a detailed treatment of the role of the adverbial in realising distinctions of time in English.) With *John will leave*, reference to future time, the presentation of the event as occurring in an SP which extends in time after SU has ended, and may not begin until that point, is unambiguous. This is the case for regarding *will* as the realisation of a (periphrastic) future tense in English. *Will have* + V-ed presents some problems for this view, but these can be approached by saying that *will* realises the relation of SP to SU, and *have* + V-ed realises the relation of one SP to another. For example, *He will have left by then* : SP_1, *then*, SP_2 that SP in which he leaves; SP_2 begins before (and ends as/ before) SP_1 begins. SP_1 begins after SU ends. The relation between SP_2 and SU is unspecified: they may or may not overlap in time; they are linked only through SP_1. Consider, however, *He will have left by now*, where SP_1 = SU, and SP_2 is past with respect to both of them.

§275.   Objections to treating *will* (in its non-decision sense) as the realisation of future tense, are principally as follows:

(i)   It is not the only marker of 'future time' in the verb which is unambiguous without the need for adverbial specification (*be going to/be about to*).

(ii)   It may realise present time, but distant place, e.g. '*They will be in Buenos Aires now* (if they're keeping to schedule)'. This feature helps to account for *He will have left by now*.

(iii)   It may realise inevitability of occurrence of an event within SU, e.g. *You won't know of course* (it is predictable/I predict that you don't know). Cf. //1 She <u>would</u> do that//, 'past action fully predictable/inevitable'.

(iv)   It may realise inevitability of occurrence in an unspecified number of SPs, a 'general predictability', e.g. *Babies will cry* : this is an activity generally associated with anything which is a baby; this predicate applies to all members of the set at subject; *All babies cry* (on more than one occasion).

§276.   I suggest that the distinction between *will* and the present indicative, irrespective of time reference (since each can refer to either present or future), is one of knowledge. The indicative realises direct, independently authoritative knowledge of the occurrence of an event; *will* realises the inevitability of occurrence of the event (usually in one SP rather than several) and is neutral to knowledge. I take inevitability as the limiting case of probability. It is not a knowing operation which is presented in *will* prediction declaratives, but a feature of the event itself: its probability of occurrence in an SP. Present indicatives present an event as actually occurring, but not as inevitably occurring (things might easily have been otherwise).

§277.   If this is accepted, then the distinction between prediction and belief modals is also one of 'neutral/non-neutral to knowledge'. Compare, *You won't have heard of course*, with *You can't have heard. Won't* realises 'I predict that you haven't heard'; *can't* realises, 'I deduce (and so know non-independently from supporting evidence) the conclusion that you have not heard'. This is related to an underlying distinction in scope of modality which corresponds with the notion that performance involves the relation between a performer and his 'activity' (or attributes), and knowledge applies to the combination (performer–performance) taken as a whole. Knowledge modality applies to the proposition as a unity, with established subject–predicate bond; performance modality applies to restrictions on the establishment of the subject–predicate bond itself. (Because of potential confusion between 'subject–predicate' and SP ('situation of performance'), I use 'Sθ' ('situation of thesis') for the latter below.)

§278.   Let us take prediction modality first.

The distinction between determinate/indeterminate prediction appears to be as follows:

(i)   Where there is generic reference at S, the *will/may* distinction realises: 'this predicate applies to all/some members of the set at S'. e.g. (a) *Babies will cry*: 'this predicate applies to all members of the set at S on some occasions'. (b) *Babies may cry*: 'this predicate applies to some ('not-all and not-none') members of the set at S on some occasion(s)'.

(ii)   Where there is specific (including unique) reference at S

the *will/may* distinction can be looked at in two ways. Either
(1) 'This individual is definitely included within/is not definitely
excluded from a set at subject to which this predicate applies with
respect to one Sθ' or, (2) 'This predicate is definitely included
within/not definitely excluded from the set of predicates which
apply to that individual at S with respect to one Sθ.' e.g. (c)
Nijinsky will win the Derby: (1) 'The individual Nijinsky is
definitely included within a set at S to which the predicate *wins
the Derby* applies with respect to a given Sθ (e.g. this year).'
Or, (2) *Wins the Derby* is definitely included among the set of
predicates which apply to the individual *Nijinsky* at S, with
respect to one Sθ (Epsom on a particular day).

The example is atypical in that only one horse wins a given
race. I would prefer the second interpretation as more appropriate
in this case. It might be glossed more freely as, 'Winning the Derby
is definitely among the things which Nijinsky is going to do.'
(d) *Nijinsky may win the Derby*: (as with *will* less likely to be (1)).
(2) *Wins the Derby* is not definitely excluded from the set of
predicates which apply to the individual *Nijinsky* at S, with respect
to one Sθ.' More freely, 'Winning the Derby is not definitely
excluded from the set of things which Nijinsky is going to do.'

In these last two examples the modality applies to a future
event. Compare *They will/may be there now*.

§ 279.   The distinction between determinate/indeterminate in belief
modality is of a different order: 'always/sometimes'.

(i)   Where there is generic reference at subject, the *must/may*
distinction realises: 'this proposition applies with reference to all/
some (= not-none and not-all) Sθs.' It assumes: 'this predicate
applies to all members of the set at S.' e.g. (a) *Whales must be
mammals*: 'The proposition "all whales are mammals" applies to
all Sθs' (is true in every SU of all Sθs). (b) *Bulls may be dangerous*
(in the sense that all bulls have their off days): 'the proposition
"all bulls are dangerous", applies to not-none and not-all Sθs.'
(ii)   Where there is specific (including unique) reference at
subject, the *must/may* distinction realises either: (1) The given
Sθ is definitely included among/not definitely excluded from
the set of those to which this proposition applies (of which it is
true). Or, (2) This proposition is definitely included among/not
definitely excluded from, the set of propositions which apply in

this $S\theta$. Both assume: 'this predicate is included within the set of predicates which apply to the individual at S.' e.g. (c) *John must be busy these days*: (1) 'The range of occasions specified by *these days* is definitely included within the set of $S\theta$s to which the proposition "John is busy" applies.' Or, (2) 'this proposition is definitely included within the set of propositions which apply to the $S\theta$ specified as *these days*.' (d) *The land may be flooded*: (1) 'This occasion is not definitely excluded from the set of $S\theta$s to which the proposition "the land is flooded" applies.' Or, (2) 'This proposition is not definitely excluded from the set of propositions which apply in this $S\theta$' (the 'now' in this case: $S\theta$ = SU).

I would prefer the first interpretation for (c) and the second interpretation for (d).

§280. The distinction between determinate belief and determinate prediction can be illustrated by *Babies will cry*. This means: 'All babies cry sometimes', and not, 'All babies cry all the time'. *Cry* is a predicate which applies to all members of the set at S ('babies') but not on all (and not on no) occasions. Determinate prediction generally relates to one occasion ($S\theta$) rather than to several.

§281. Indeterminate belief and indeterminate prediction often merge in practice, especially with *may*, which can realise either. For example, *John may have 'flu* is ambiguous along these lines: (i) 'The proposition "John has 'flu" is not definitely excluded from applying to the $S\theta$ of "now" (belief)'. (ii) (a) ' 'flu may be the illness (or among the illnesses) which John has', (b) 'John may be among those who have 'flu' (both prediction).

The ambiguity of an example such as *Lions can be dangerous*, as between 'All lions are sometimes dangerous' (belief) and 'Some lions are dangerous, some are not' (prediction) could itself be dangerous if the first interpretation is true and second were the one understood.

On the whole, there is some tendency for *could/can (needn't)* to realise belief, and for *may/(may not)* to realise prediction; but this is not sufficiently clear-cut to be a reliable guide.

§282. The analysis of belief and prediction modals in terms of quantifiers suggested above, accounts for the fact that one can draw a square of opposition, comparable to that obtaining in predicate logic, for each of these sets of verbs (cf. §§ 271, 273).

§283. *Can/can't*, in one of their uses, realise the performer's ability to carry out the performance in question. *John can('t) swim*:

'is able/unable to'. In this usage they can be marked for 'real' past tense: *could(n't)*, 'used (not) to be able to'. They relate to prediction modality in the sense that an activity cannot be predicted of a performer who is shown as incapable of carrying it out. So that one contradicts oneself if one says both: 'John can't swim' ('is unable to') and 'John may swim this morning' ('it may be one of the things that he does'). But capability modals do not realise properties of the subject—predicate bond: they are part of the predicate. As such, they are part of what can be known and told. It is in this way that 'real' past tense applies to them, as to any lexical verb.

§284.   I take *would(n't)/might(n't)*, for the moment, to realise distanced telling as opposed to immediate telling in *will/may*. *Would* in combination with *have* + V-ed can occur in the consequent clause of a counter-factual conditional, where it conveys 'but didn't', as in *If the Germans had invaded England in 1940, they would have won the war.* (Similarly for *wouldn't* in such uses, which conveys 'but did'.) But we have already seen that not all such constructions are counter-factual (cf. §149). Even where they are, I suggest that *would(n't)* realises a *present* (SU) assessment of probabilities of that predicate applying to that subject, but in a past Sθ (which is specified only as succeeding that in which the event in the antecedent clause did not take place). That is, I suggest that the past marking in *would(n't)/might(n't)* does not realise 'past probabilities', nor, necessarily 'unreality'; so that, perhaps, one may account for it more simply in terms of the speaker's reservations and lack of immediate commitment realised in distanced telling. This is a highly complex area, and I return to it below under 'performance conditionals' (Chapter 8, §§306-7). *Might(n't)*, like *may (not)* is ambiguous between belief and prediction modality.

Notes

1. I ignore, for present purposes, *should(n't)/ought(n't) to* as prediction modals, but they can certainly be used in this way; e.g. *John should be ready soon*, 'It is probable that he is going to be'/*John oughtn't to be more than ten minutes*, 'It is probable that he is not going to be'. Like *will*, they are not restricted to future reference; e.g. *This should be the place*, 'It is probable that this is the place'/*He shouldn't have heard yet*, 'It is probable that he hasn't'. It is possible to relate *should* (*ought to*) to *mightn't*, and *shouldn't* (*oughtn't to*) to *might*, as follows: To say '*should* x' implies the admission, '*mightn't* x' (might not-x); to say '*shouldn't* x' implies the admission '*might* x'. That is to affirm the probability of x implies not excluding the possibility of not-x;

and to affirm the probability of not-x implies not excluding the possibility of x. *Should (n't)/ought (n't) to* and *might (n't)* can be seen as a set of indeterminate prediction modals.

2. I take *will* x and *may not* x to be in a 'contradictory' relation. It cannot be both inevitable and non-inevitable that x happens; nor can it be neither inevitable nor non-inevitable that x happens. (The same applies with respect to x not-happening in relation to *won't* x and *may* x.)

On the other hand, although it cannot be that, both it is inevitable that x happens and inevitable that x does not happen (*will* x and *won't* x), it can be that it is both not inevitable that x happens and not inevitable that x does not happen (*may not* x and (/'but') *may* x).

§285.   I have suggested four areas, or planes within the grammatical
semantics, and associated different types of surface grammar distinctions with each, and with the fashions in which features in one
plane interlock with those in others.

I now propose to consider constructions of condition and
reasoning in English from the viewpoint of these planes; and suggest
that they can be usefully divided into four types, according to the
semantic status (in terms of planes) of the relation between their
subordinate and main clauses. I claim that, according to this status,
different kinds of logical relation are involved.

I shall refer to 'telling'-, 'decision'-, 'knowledge'-, and 'performance'-conditionals. (For a related discussion of some features of the
surface grammar of conditional sentences, cf. Davies, 1976: 391-
421).

§286.   Telling Conditionals

These constructions have been mentioned in §228. Other examples
include: (a) *There are biscuits on the sideboard if you want them*
(cf. Austin, 1961: 210); (b) *If you like watching tennis, Wimbledon's being televised this afternoon.*

The distinguishing semantic feature of such constructions is that
knowledge of what is presented with derived telling in the *if* clause
is given as the reason for the full telling (saying) of the main clause.
There is no connection between the Ov of the antecedent event,
and the Ov of the consequent event. The biscuits are there whether
or not you're hungry, and Wimbledon is being televised irrespective
of whether or not you like tennis.

The two examples differ with respect to *if*. In (a), *if* is 'open'.
The subordinate clause realises lack of speaker's knowledge, and
represents a use of undirected asking (cf. §227), addressed in
practice to a participant in SU, which is 'polite' because it
excludes the need to reply. What is presented here as the reason for
telling the main clause is that the question of whether or not 'you
might want them' has occurred to the speaker, who produces this as
a reason for telling you where they are. (The permission to help
yourself conveyed by this remark derives from the query on *you*

want in the subordinate clause, but the connection is more a matter of high-level significance, as governed partly by conventions of polite behaviour rather than a question of LMM.)

In (b), *if* is closed. The subordinate clause realises the speaker's acceptance of knowledge concerning its proposition, based on something another (probably the addressee) has said, or on something which has arisen in context. 'Your liking to watch tennis' is treated as information relatively newly introduced, or as something the speaker has recently been reminded of. He uses such knowledge as the pretext for giving full telling to his direct knowledge concerning Wimbledon. His (recently acquired) knowledge of p is given as the justification for telling his knowledge of q; but it is not otherwise related to his knowledge of q. He knows 'that q' irrespective of accepting knowledge of p (and his acceptance of knowledge of p is not conditioned by his knowledge of q). Similarly, the speaker of (a) knows where the biscuits are irrespective of whether or not he knows if you want them (and he is unsure of whether you want them irrespective of knowing where they are).

Although both constructions realise knowledge features in each clause, the *relation* between clauses is neutral to both knowledge and performance in both cases (and also to decision); the relation involves telling only.

The subordinate clause is introduced in order to show that the main clause is a relevant thing to say in relation to preceding remarks, and belongs in the conversation. This applies similarly when the main clause is interrogative, as in (c) *If you're keen on boxing, are you staying up to watch the fight tonight?*; 'the information that you're interested makes it relevant for me to ask if you're doing something which someone who was interested might do' (I wouldn't ask my grandmother).

The antecedent clause in a telling condition presents a stage in a chain of thought which the speaker feels that another might not follow if it were not made explicit. They can be introduced before any main clause, but are mostly left out as unnecessary. (Frequency of use varies considerably between different speakers.) The function of such clauses is principally cohesive (discourse).

§287. Decision Conditionals

All constructions in this group realise a decision feature in their main clause. They divide into those which also realise a decision feature in the dependent clause (constructions of 'double decision') and those which do not. Both, one, or neither clause may contain a modal verb. Where neither clause does so, the main clause is generally imperative. In some instances, the dependent clause contains a capability modal verb.

Constructions of this type also divide according to the value of *if* which they realise. There are three main possibilities:

(i)   *if* related to *when(ever)*, as in,
(a)   *If John comes, phone Mary*
(ii)   *if* related to query, as in,
(b)   *If you'll just take this bag, I'll pay the taxi*
(iii)   *if* related to *as* (similar to that in telling conditionals), as in,
(c)   *If John plays tennis, let's ask him to make up a doubles*

This last type of example is very close to a telling conditional. Accepted knowledge that 'John plays tennis' is my reason for saying 'let's ask him'; but, also, I wouldn't make the decision realised in *let's* without such knowledge, so that it is not the case that only a telling relation obtains between the clauses. An example such as, (d) *Tell me if you're coming* is ambiguous between (i) and *if* = *whether* in a reported speech complement clause.

§288.   The relation between dependent and main clause realised in (a) is such that the command in the latter only becomes operative if the condition given in the former is fulfilled. If John doesn't come, there is no command either to phone Mary or not to phone her. The matter is left undecided on: the teller makes no decision. Similarly for other constructions of this type, such as (a') *If it rains, you must take your umbrella.*

In the case of constructions with a determinate decision modal in the main clause, we may summarise this feature as: 'If x then O y' implies 'If not-x then ~ O y' where 'x' = the event in the dependent clause (with the Ov given in surface polarity), 'y' the event in the main clause (with the Ov realised in surface polarity), and 'O' the determinate modality realised in the main clause modal verb.

If we recall the 'square of opposition' suggested for countermanding decision modals in §189, we can make the following statements:

'If x, *must* y' implies 'If not x, *needn't* y.'
'If x, *can't* y' implies 'If not x, *can* y.'

But, since *can* and *needn't* are 'sub-contraries' on that model, where '*needn't* y' is implied, '*can* y' is not excluded, and vice versa. Hence, if given your command in (a′) it turns out not to be raining but I still take my umbrella, I have not disobeyed you, but simply done something which you didn't expect me to (because *must* realises your assumption that I don't want to take my umbrella).

What is negated by non-fulfilment of the condition in such constructions is the decision modality attaching to the Ov of the event in the main clause (as opposed to negation of the Ov and retention of the modality).

§289.   *Will* (cf. §192) may realise performer decision. Some conditional constructions with *will/won't* in the main clause belong under decision rather than performance. For example, (a) *If it's fine on Saturday, I'll do some gardening.* Some have *will* in both clauses, as in (b) *If Jane won't baby-sit for us, I won't go.* Some have a capability performance modal in the dependent clause, in combination with *will* in the main, as in (c) *If you can find a baby-sitter, I will gladly come*, or with a countermanding modal, as in (d) *If Paul can't start his car, you must go by bus.* They may also have a countermanding modal in the dependent clause, as in (e) *If you must do that I won't have it in the house.* An example such as, (f) *If we can't find a baby-sitter I can't go with you*, is ambiguous between realising relayed speech decision and capability in the main clause. Decision conditionals may freely have an interrogative main clause, e.g. *If it's fine on Saturday, can I go swimming?*

§290.   The foregoing examples illustrate two features of the surface grammar of decision conditionals which distinguishes them from conditionals of performance and knowledge, but link them with telling conditionals:

(i)   They may have a modal verb in the dependent clause;
(ii)   They may have a non-declarative main clause. (Where this is imperative it distinguishes them from telling interrogatives also.)

§291.   Decision constructions in which the dependent clause contains a decision modal I shall call 'double decision'. They are often used in making polite requests. For example:

(a)   *If you'll just wait a moment, I'll fetch the cases.*
(b)   *If John would look after Sam for five minutes, I must go and change.*

In such constructions, the decision told in the main clause is made irrespective of the fulfilment of the condition in the dependent clause. Lack of fulfilment does not imply undecidedness. Rather, the main clause decision is given as the reason for making the request in the *if* clause. In (a) it is because I decide to fetch the cases that I ask you to wait, and in (b) it is because I must go and change that I ask John (indirectly, through the addressee) to look after Sam.

The relationship between the clauses is 'double-layered'. In terms of performance, the Ov (realised in surface polarity) of the event in the dependent clause is presented as a sufficient cause for the Ov realised in main clause polarity. 'Your waiting' is a sufficient condition of 'my fetching the cases'. 'John's looking after Sam' is a sufficient condition of 'my going and changing'. But in terms of decision, the relation works in the opposite 'direction', and involves telling. That is, the decision in the main clause is presented as a sufficient condition for telling the decision in the dependent clause, i.e. for presenting that proposition as an indirect request. In this sense such constructions could be thought of as telling conditionals 'in reverse'.

If in such cases is related to the *if* in reported speech interrogatives. The politeness element in such constructions lies chiefly in the fact that *if* realises transference (in this case of the decider role) to a third-party 'destination', although the request is intended in practice for a participant in SU.

Not all constructions of double decision contain a dependent clause with 'reported query *if*'. Those which do not, such as *If John won't go you must take the car*, can be analysed in the same terms as other decision conditionals.

§292.   One type of decision conditional with a non-modal dependent clause and a modal in the main clause is of particular interest, as the equivalent of a construction of purpose. Compare: (a) *If I'm going to do that job I must have the right tools*; with (a′) *I must have the right tools (in order) to do that job*. Here the Ov of the main clause event is told as a necessary condition of that in the dependent clause. But *must* does not seem a countermanding modal. It appears to realise a feature of the relationship between the two clauses, and occurs in the one realising the event presented as a necessary cause of that in the other. One the other hand, in (b) *If he's going to get that job he must pass the exams*; (b′) *He must pass the exams to get that job*, it is easier to see *must* as countermanding, at least if a third-party decider is allowed. Both constructions could be thought to realise relayed decision. Taking into account that *is going to* in both examples could be substituted for by *want(s) to*, and the correspondence with the purpose construction in each case, it is tempting to analyse the former as realising performer-decision (intention) and to analyse such forms as one type of double decision. If so, they are similar to those in §291 in having decision and performance relations which run counter to each other.

The two types of construction may be compared as in Table 8.1.

Table 8.1 Double Decision

		Given Ov of dependent clause	Given Ov of main clause
A		Sufficient cause —————————————⟶	
B		⟵—————————————	Necessary cause
		Decision in dependent clause	Decision in main clause
A		⟵—————————————	Sufficient cause of telling
B		Sufficient cause —————————————⟶	

In Table 8.1 the A lines describe request double decision, the B lines describe purpose double decision. In the latter wanting/intending to perform the action in the dependent clause ('doing the job'/ 'getting the job') is a sufficient cause for the decision realised in the main clause, a requirement to 'possess tools'/'pass exams'.

Must in these examples may be substituted for by *need(s)*. This might be taken as a marker of relayed decision, or, at least of an unspecified third-party (non-performer) decider. Compare the distinction between, *You must be back at six* and, *You need to be back at six*, in this respect.

§293.   All decision conditionals, except for purpose double decision, share the following semantic characteristics:

(i)   They are not forms of argument, and do not realise a conclusion in their main clause.

(ii)   It is not the case that either Ov in the main clause is presented as influencing the Ov of the event in the dependent clause.

Let   p = description + DS value in the dependent clause
          q = description + DS value in the main clause

Then, it is not the case that decision constructions follow the rule of propositional truth functional logic that:
'$(p \supset q) \equiv (\sim q \supset \sim p)$'.
The case with purpose constructions of double decision is less clear cut. I reserve discussion for the treatment of purpose below (§§326-7).

§294.   The main use of decision conditionals is in contingency planning. They are a standard form for one type of 'practical reasoning' (cf. Kenny, 1966; Hare, 1971).

§295.   Performance Conditionals

There are three main types of conditional sentences in which the relation between the dependent and main clauses realises a feature in the performance plane, and in which a prediction modality is told in the main clause. I term them, 'open prediction', 'induction', and 'counterfactual' constructions.

§296.   Open prediction conditionals include examples such as,

(a)   *If the weather's wet, the roads will be treacherous.*
(b)   *If they don't come soon we'll be late.*

Such constructions realise lack of speaker's knowledge of the Ov presented with derived telling in the dependent clause (i.e. the DS value, the Ov chosen for discussion and realised in surface polarity). They present a 'cause' and 'effect' relation between the Ov of the dependent clause event, and the prediction modality attaching to the Ov realised by surface polarity in the main clause.

I use the terms 'cause' and 'effect' as they are used in ordinary language, rather than as philosophically defined concepts, and take them also to cover cases where set inclusion relations are at issue, as in

(c)   *If the painting is signed it will be genuine.* ('All paintings which are signed are paintings which are genuine.')

Let A be the set of paintings which are signed.

$$A : [a_1, a_2, \ldots, a_n]$$

Let B be the set of paintings which are genuine.

$$B : [b_1, b_2, \ldots, b_n]$$

Then (c) realises:

'$A \subset B$'.

§297.   Taking into account this rather wide notion of 'cause' and 'effect', we can extend the approach as follows:

Let   'α' and 'β' be the names of events;
Let   '+' be a positive occurrence value for an event;
Let   '−' be a negative occurrence value for an event;
Let   'x' be the name for an event which is a cause;
Let   'y' be the name for an event which is an effect;

Then 'x' may be specified as either 'α^+' or 'α^-'; and 'y' may be specified as either 'β^+' or 'β^-'.

Further,

Let   'W' be the determinate prediction modality realised by *will*;
Let   'M' be the indeterminate prediction modality realised by *may*.

Using these definitions, we can draw up the following table of some types of open prediction conditional sentences in English (distinguishing between a necessary and a sufficient cause).

$$\text{Let us take } x = \alpha^+ \quad y = \beta^+$$

	Type of cause relation	Modality on effect	Realisation Dependent clause Conjunction	Polarity	Main clause
(i)	Sufficient	W	*if*	pos	*will*
(ii)	Necessary	W	*if*	neg	*won't*
			unless	pos	
(iii)	Not sufficient	M	*even if*	pos	*(still) may not*
(iv)	Not necessary	M	*even if*	neg	*may (still)*

Examples:

(i)   *If the weather's wet, the roads will be busy.*
(ii) $\begin{cases} \textit{If the weather isn't wet, the roads won't be busy.} \\ \textit{The roads won't be busy unless the weather's wet.} \end{cases}$
(iii)   *Even if the weather's wet, the roads may not be busy.*
(iv)   *Even if the weather isn't wet, the roads may be busy.*

Related tables can be worked out for other specifications of x and y ($x = \alpha^-$, $y = \beta^+$; $x = \alpha^+$, $y = \beta^-$; $x = \alpha^-$, $y = \beta^-$).

Negation of the cause relation is realised by *even* modifying *if* in the dependent clause, and *may* (= 'not *will*') in the main clause.

§298.   Several points of interest in terms of a 'natural language logic' underlying English grammatical rules are relevant to this table:

(a)   The negation of *will* x is 'not-will x', rather than *won't* x. This parallels the case in decision conditions (cf. §288 above).

(b)   Surface polarity realises DS value = Ov of the events, throughout, but it realises the Ovs of cause and effect only in example (i), constructions of sufficient cause, where both cause and effect are positively occurring events.

(c)   Taking (i), it is not the case that we can argue on the basis 'if x, then will y', that 'if not-will y, then not-x' or that 'if not-will y, then not-will x'. E.g. We cannot argue on the basis of 'If the weather's wet, the roads will be busy' that 'If the roads will not be busy, the weather isn't wet', and still less that 'If the roads will not be busy, the weather won't be wet'.

Neither can we argue that 'if not-y, then not-will x', that is, not: 'If the roads aren't busy, the weather won't be wet.' That is, in saying 'If the weather's wet, the roads will be busy', we do not allow that either a prediction concerning the state of the weather, or knowledge concerning the state of the weather may be based on a prediction concerning the state of the roads; nor that a prediction concerning the state of the weather may be based on knowledge concerning the state of the roads.

We do not allow that the state of the roads has any influence on what the weather does.

§299.   The statement in (a) that the negation of *will* x is 'not-will x' involves one in arguing as follows with respect to the meaning in use of open prediction conditionals:

'If I say, for example, *If it's fine on Saturday, they'll go to the beach*, and it turns out to be wet but they still go, I have been "weakly", but not fully, proved wrong by events. For in saying what I did, I implied only that *If it isn't fine on Saturday, they may not go to the beach*, and not that they *will not*.' I believe that this does correspond to most ordinary usage.

§300.   If we accept this interpretation, then 'If x, then *will* y' constructions do not realise a relationship of material implication. But they fail to do so in any interesting way. That is, whereas the truth table for the sign of material implication is given in Table 8.2.

Table 8.2

p	q	⊃
T	T	T
T	F	F
F	T	T
F	F	T

(Where 'T' = 'True', 'F' = 'False').

An 'occurrence validity' table for 'If . . . then *will*' in prediction conditionals would read as Table 8.3.

Table 8.3

x	y	'If . . . then will'
+	+	V
+	−	SI
−	+	WI
−	−	V

(where	'+'	'event occurs'
	'−'	'event doesn't occur'
	'V'	'valid'
	'SI'	'strongly invalid'
	'WI'	'weakly invalid'.)

If I say, 'If the weather is wet, the roads will be busy',

(i)   I am proved right if the weather is wet and the roads are busy.

(ii)   I am proved completely wrong if the weather is wet and the roads aren't busy.

(iii)   I am proved partially wrong if the weather isn't wet but the roads are busy, because, in saying what I did, I explicitly did not predict that combination of events/state of affairs.

(iv)   I am not proved wrong if the weather isn't wet and the roads aren't busy.

I suggest that prediction conditionals in English realise a modal logic of occurrence, and not a truth functional logic of propositions.

§301.   If we accept the analysis of prediction modals suggested in Chapter 7 (§278) we can phrase this last limitation as a restriction that: 'one cannot argue from a modality on a subject—predicate bond either to a modality on another subject—predicate bond, or to a belief in (or knowledge of) another proposition.'

§302.   I suggest that prediction conditionals in English are, like decision conditionals, not constructions of argument. They do not realise telling of a conclusion in their main clause, but telling of a probability concerning the occurrence value of an event in an $S\theta$ which is partially specified in the dependent clause. They are used to make limited predictions: 'something inevitably happens in certain circumstances' (or, for the indeterminate case 'something is not prevented from happening in certain circumstances'). They relate to interrogatives with *happens*: *If it rains the match will be cancelled: what (will) happen(s) if it rains?*

Some prediction conditionals can be looked on as 'split' propositions, the *if* clause constituting an extrapolated adverbial element in a matrix sentence, given finite clause status. Our example, 'If the weather is wet the roads will be busy' may be rephrased as, 'The roads will be busy in wet weather'.

This suggestion matches the notion that a knowledge/belief construction realises the applicability of a proposition to $S\theta$, whereas a prediction construction realises the applicability of predicate to subject. The indicative *if* clause realises the feature that a proposition may apply in one/a number of $S\theta$s, and the prediction main clause realises a probability of applicability of the predicate to the subject of its proposition with reference to the $S\theta$(s) in which the *if* clause proposition does apply.

§303.   **Induction Conditionals**

These constructions are distinguished from open prediction conditionals mainly by the status of *if*, and the knowledge feature realised in the dependent clause. That is, where the former realise 'lack of speaker and addressee knowledge' and have 'open *if*', induction conditionals realise accepted knowledge, and have 'closed *if*', related to *as*. Examples include: (a) *If this plane has flown a thousand times without an accident, it won't crash now* (which is notoriously false as a piece of reasoning but nevertheless a well-formed inductive conditional in terms of grammatical meaning).

They represent a form for carrying inductive arguments leading to statements of probabilities (i.e. 'predictions' in my terms) and realise the implication relations of a modal logic of probabilities. In this, I would claim, they are closely related to prediction conditionals, as analysed above. They represent the special case of the latter in which the *if* clause proposition is known to apply to some/all $S\theta$(s). Here, also, one cannot argue from a lack of the occurrence value predicted as probable in the main clause to the lack of the occurrence value told in the dependent clause (or to the falseness of the proposition there, which in this case is the same thing since the proposition is told as 'known'). That is (a$'$) *If this plane may crash now it can't have flown a thousand times without an accident*, is not derivable from (a).

§304. Counterfactual Conditionals

Constructions of the form '*If* S *had* V-ed . . . (then) S *would/might have* V-ed . . .' are generally referred to as 'counterfactual conditionals'. For example, (a) *If the Germans had invaded England in 1940, they would have won the war.*

I suggest, however, that a 'contrary to fact' sense ('DS value $\neq$ known Ov' in my terms) is not automatically an element of LMM in these constructions. One might argue that it is not conveyed by the grammatical construction as such, but derives from features of common knowledge concerning the content of the propositions presented. It is true that such constructions may equally well be used when neither speaker nor addressee knows whether or not the event in the *if* clause occurred, as when both know that it didn't (or, in the case of those constructions with a negative *if* clause, that it did). Cases of such usage occur frequently in learned argument and in detective fiction. For example, consider the following argument.

(b) 'If the Laputians had invaded Ruritania in 200 BC, they would have won the war. We know that this would have been so because we know that Ruritania, after the sudden death of King Egbert the Magnificent in the previous year, was in no state to defend itself. We should therefore look for evidence of a Laputian victory since they had the capacity to invade. But there appears to be none. On the contrary, there is evidence which suggests that the war continued for a further five years. We must therefore conclude that they did not invade, although we do not know why they failed to do so.'

Consider also: 'If John had been at the scene of the crime at the time when the murder was committed, Mary would have seen him leaving. So we must get hold of her to find out if she did see him.'

§305.   I suggest that two points of interest here are:

(i)   The grammatical form of the construction does not invariably realise a feature 'false' with respect to either clause.

(ii)   What is consistently realised is the assignment of a probability of occurrence in the present, to a past event. Taking (a) we have 'I assign a 100 per cent probability of occurrence (inevitability) to the event of "the Germans winning the war" given that the event of "their invading England in 1940" took place', i.e. 'If x, then *will* y', where both 'x' and 'y' are past events.

§306.   'Counterfactual' conditionals, whether used in a 'closed' way ('we both know the opposite Ov to that realised in surface polarity'), or in an 'open' way (neither of us knows), realise a prediction modality applying to the main clause event. However, because that event is past, it may be known whether or not it took place. And where it is known that it did not happen, we may argue from that *knowledge* to *knowledge* that the event in the dependent clause did not take place either. But we cannot argue from the modality itself, the inevitability in (a), either to a modality applying to the event in the *if* clause, or to the falseness of the proposition which it presents, any more than we can do so in open prediction conditionals.

In both cases, open and 'counterfactual', prediction conditionals may be used as premisses in an argument leading to a deductive conclusion, but they do not themselves realise a conclusion concerning the truth of a proposition, or the validity of a fact, in their main clause. They both realise a limited statement of probability, defined as applying where the event in the dependent clause takes place with the Ov realised in surface polarity.

The argument concerning the Laputians in Ruritania which we looked at in §304 accepts the available evidence that they did not win the war (it continued for five years afterwards), and on the basis of this accepted *knowledge* proceeds to the deductive conclusion that it could not have been the case that they invaded. But it does not proceed from negating the modality in the main clause, 'not-*would* = *might* not' to a conclusion of any sort regarding 'their invading'.

Similarly, although using (a) above as a premiss: 'If the Germans had invaded England in 1940, they would have won the war' we can derive from the knowledge that they didn't win, the knowledge that 'they can't have invaded', we do not present any conclusion in using the construction itself. All we present is a statement of a probability concerning one performer—performance bond obtaining in the circumstance of another event occurring. In this case, common knowledge supplies the information both that the other event did not occur, and the performer—performance bond did not obtain. But this 'knowledge to the contrary' does not affect the relation told in the construction as holding between the event and the 'bond'. This relation is exactly the same as if we said 'If the Germans invade England in 1980 they will win the war'.

§307.   Nevertheless, although counterfactuals may realise present predictions about past events in cases where the Ovs of these events are presented as unknown, this construction type remains the only one available for use when those Ovs are known (by both speaker and addressee) to be the opposite of surface polarity in each clause. Further, when used in isolation, even in circumstances where common knowledge cannot be assumed, they usually have a contrary to fact meaning. If I say, as a conversation opener, 'If it hadn't rained the match would have been played', you would understand me to mean that it had rained, and that the match hadn't been played. It is generally the 'open' sense which requires a disambiguating context to make it clear.

I suggest that the construction is ambiguous in terms of LMM, between an indicative construction realising two degrees of 'real pastness' in the dependent clause, and a subjunctive construction which also conveys distanced telling (of the 'non-presentation' type). The reason for the sameness of grammatical form is the restriction (remarked on in §149) that English cannot indicate three degrees of 'pastness'. There is no grammatical device available for marking a 'real' pluperfect for distanced telling.

If we accept this view, the lack of speaker-commitment to what is said (the DS value) carried in distanced telling accounts for the opposition between surface polarity and the Ov which is assumed to be independently known by the speaker (and generally also by the addressee). The same argument applies to *would have* + V-ed in the main clause: there is no device available for further marking for past. Here, too, the feature of distanced telling underlies the opposition between the DS value realised in surface polarity and the Ov value assumed as known.

The existence of counterfactual constructions relating to present time and marked for 'unreal past' realising distanced telling, such as *I wouldn't do that if I were you*, or *If he were in town he would call* (Jespersen, 1940: 377) support this view. I treat these also as subjunctive. If we take this view, marking for distanced telling by subjunctive mood in these cases can be seen as realising a feature 'false', although not in any literal sense: merely 'presented as false'. The sentence *If the Germans hadn't invaded England in 1940, they wouldn't have won the war* is grammatically well formed.

§308.   Let 'x', 'y' be the names of events:

'x'   'it's raining'
'y'   'the match's being cancelled'
'W'   'inevitable'

We can describe the prediction conditional (1) *If it rains the match will be cancelled* as realising: Immediate telling of, 'If x, W y'. 'x' here is presented as a sufficient cause of 'y'. The related counterfactual conditional, (2) *If it had rained the match would have been cancelled* realises:

(i)   Immediate telling of, 'If x, W y'; 'x' is a sufficient cause of 'y'.

(ii)   Distanced telling of 'x', 'y' (indicating DSv ≠ Ov: Told Ov ≠ Known Ov) conveys assumed knowledge of 'not-x', 'not-y'.

But the relations with corresponding constructions of deduction, are exactly the same for both (1) and (2). Using either (1) or (2) as premiss and given (independently) 'that not-y', we can arrive at the deduction expressed in (3) *If the match wasn't cancelled it can't have rained*, and, given (independently) 'that x', at the deduction in (4) *If it rained the match must have been cancelled*.

This feature indicates that counterfactual constructions realise the same underlying performance relation; between the occurrence of one event as cause and a probability of occurrence of another event as effect, as do the prediction conditionals. They are not 'about' knowledge of propositions.

Subjunctive mood, and the dissociation of the speaker from what he tells (as the opposite of what he, and others, know) conveys that the events presented did not take place; but this does not affect the relation predicted between these events. It is only the events which are unreal. The counterfactual construction is useful in practice as a form in which to express relations between past events so that a statement of that relation can then be used as a step in an argument, or as a stage in explaining why things happened as they did, or in what ways they might have happened otherwise. A counterfactual relating to present time is useful as a premiss in working out a conclusion about what is currently the case if this is not available to direct, independent knowledge. For example: 'If they really wanted us to come they would make it a more pressing invitation than that.' That 'it' wasn't 'more pressing' as an invitation, is conveyed as commonly accepted knowledge.

'x' 'their wanting us to come'
'y' 'their making it a more pressing invitation'

Premisses: (i) 'if x, W y'; (ii) 'not-y'. Conclusion: Therefore, not-x (/*'can't x'*): 'They can't really want us to come.' The conclusion is arrived at by argument from knowledge of the non-occurrence of an inevitable effect to knowledge of the non-occurrence of a sufficient cause, and is often treated as obvious and left unstated in such examples of informal conversation. The succeeding remark is likely to be one suggesting a plan of action based on accepted knowledge that the conclusion holds. (In this example something such as 'So I think we can safely make our excuses'.)

Counterfactual constructions do not, in themselves, constitute forms of argument. This being so, they do not pose problems concerning argument from a 'false proposition'. Their status in terms of argument can only be that of a premiss.

§309. Truth functional logic is properly called 'propositional logic'. None of the three types of performance conditionals in English realises relations between propositions: none of them is a form in which a deductive argument can be couched. They tell a modality on a subject—predicate relation, as opposed to knowledge of a proposition, in their main clause. They all realise relations of a modal logic of probabilities.

§310. Knowledge Conditionals

I come, finally, to the one type of English conditional which does realise truth functional relations between propositions, and a deductive conclusion in its main clause.

Such constructions may freely have either two non-modal indicative clauses (constructions of full, independent knowledge), as in (a) *If whales are warmblooded then whales are mammals*, or a belief modal verb in the main clause, as in (b) *If he's a local man, he must know about the old mine workings* (constructions of non-independent knowledge).

I shall illustrate from the latter type, which are explicitly marked as telling a deductive conclusion, knowledge arrived at only by reasoning. These constructions have closed *if* (*if* related to *as*), and realise accepted knowledge in the dependent clause.

§311.　In order to consider the relationship between such constructions and performance conditionals, let us turn back to the notion that the latter realise a 'cause' event in the dependent clause, and an 'effect' event in the main clause.

There are four types of valid argument in terms of cause and effect:

(i)　Argument from knowledge of the occurrence of a sufficient cause to knowledge of the occurrence of its effect.

(ii)　Argument from knowledge of the non-occurrence of a necessary cause to knowledge of the non-occurrence of the effect.

(iii)　Argument from knowledge of the occurrence of an effect to knowledge of the occurrence of any event which is a necessary cause of that effect.

(iv)　Argument from knowledge of the non-ocurrence of an effect to knowledge of the non-ocurrence of any event which is a sufficient cause of that effect.

§312.　If we take these valid forms of argument, then:

(a)　From the first we can derive that knowledge of the non-occurrence of a sufficient cause is a necessary condition of knowledge of the non-occurrence of the effect. For, if a cause is a sufficient cause, we cannot know that its effect does not occur unless we know that all causes which are sufficient to 'produce' it do not occur.

(b)　From the second valid form, it is clear that knowledge of the occurrence of an effect is a sufficient condition of knowledge of the occurrence of a necessary cause of that effect (which is the form of valid argument given in (iii)).

(c)   From (iii) we can see that knowledge of the non-occurrence of a necessary cause is a sufficient condition of knowledge as the non-occurrence of an effect of that cause.

(d)   From (iv) we can see that knowledge of the occurrence of a sufficient cause is a sufficient condition of knowledge of the occurrence of the effect (which is the form of valid argument given in (i)).

(a) above underlies the logical equivalence '$(p \supset q) \equiv (\sim q \supset \sim p)$'; for, if 'x' is a sufficient cause and 'y' its inevitable effect, then if 'p' is the name of the proposition 'that x occurs' and 'q' is the name of the proposition 'that y occurs', '$p \supset q$' is true. Further, the non-occurrence of 'x' is a necessary cause of the non-occurrence of 'y', and knowing that x does not occur is a necessary condition of knowing that y does not occur. Where it is necessary to know that 'not-x' in order to know that 'not-y', we can argue from knowledge of 'not-y' to knowledge of 'not-x': '$\sim q \supset \sim p$'.

§313.   In cases where the argument realised in a deductive conditional is from knowledge of the occurrence of a sufficient cause to that of its (inevitable) effect, the construction resembles the performance conditional, which it assumes as an underlying premiss, in realising the cause event in its dependent clause, and the effect event in its main clause. It is in these cases, where the performance relation assumed runs in the same 'direction', between dependent and main clause, as the knowledge relation which is told, that the modal verb used in the main clause may vary in usage between *must* (realising deduced knowledge) and *will*, realising a prediction modality. The distinction does not so much need to be accurately made here, for there is no conflict between the status, in terms of cause and effect, of the event realised in the main clause of the assumed prediction, and that realised in the main clause in which the deductive conclusion is told.

e.g. Prediction as underlying premiss:
    If it rains the roads will be busy:
      'If x, W y.'   'x' = 'it's raining'
                         'y' = 'the roads being busy'
                         'p' = 'x occurs'

'q' = 'y occurs'
Given: that p
Deductive construction realising argument from sufficient cause:
If it's raining the roads must (/will) be busy:
'p implies q'.

The same points apply to constructions realising argument from knowledge of the non-occurrence of a necessary cause to non-occurrence of the effect. Compare: (Premiss)

If he isn't a local man, he won't know about the old workings.
(Only local people do know about them): 'If ~ x, W ~ y'.

Deductive construction:

If (= as) he isn't a local man he can't (/won't) know about the old workings:

§314.   However, in cases in which a deductive conditional realises argument from knowledge of the (non)-occurrence of an effect, the knowledge relation which it tells runs counter to the performance relation which it assumes in terms of 'direction' between dependent and main clauses.
For example:

Let   'x' = 'Its being a public holiday'
      'y' = 'the roads being busy'

Prediction as premiss:

If it's a public holiday, the roads will be busy: 'If x, W y.'
'p' = 'x occurs'
'q' = 'y occurs'
Given: that 'not-q'
If the roads aren't busy, it can't be a public holiday:
'not-q implies not-p'.

Here the performance relation 'runs' from non-occurrence of a sufficient cause in the main clause, to the non-occurrence of the effect in the dependent clause, but the knowledge relation of argument runs from the proposition in the dependent clause ('not-q') to the proposition in the main clause ('not-p'). *Won't* in such cases is not generally an acceptable alternative to *can't*. The same points apply in argument from the occurrence of an effect to the occurrence of a necessary cause. Compare: (Premiss)

> *If he isn't a local man, he won't know about the old workings*: 'If ~ x, W ~ y.'

Deductive construction:

> *If (= as) he knows about the old workings he must be a local man* (see Appendix II).

§315.　Deductive constructions with *may (not)/could* tell indeterminate belief in their main clause, and present, in the dependent clause either the occurrence of a necessary cause, or the occurrence of an effect (where the event in the main clause is a sufficient cause of that effect) or the non-occurrence of an effect (where the event in the main clause is a necessary, but not sufficient, cause of that effect) or the non-occurrence of a sufficient cause (where this is not the only sufficient cause). An indeterminate modal in the main clause corresponds with the realisation of a non-valid form of 'argument'.

For example:

Prediction as premiss:

> *If it rains the roads will be busy*: 'If x, W y.'
> 'x' = 'it's raining'
> 'y' = 'the roads being busy'
> 'p' = 'x occurs'
> 'q' = 'y occurs'
> Given: that 'not-p'

Indeterminate deduction:

> *If it isn't raining, the roads may not be busy.*
> 'If not-p, *may* not-q'.

(Non-occurrence of sufficient cause — indeterminate belief in non-occurrence of effect.)

Such constructions assume only conditions of determinate prediction as premiss.

§316.   The form *'Even if . . . (still) needn't/couldn't'* represents a type
of indeterminate deduction construction which is specifically marked
to show 'conclusion does not follow'. (*Even* (+/− *still*) realises the
denial of the implication relationship. Taking *Even if it isn't raining the roads could (still) be busy*, in relation to the last example,
we may write it as: 'If not-p, not necessarily not-q'. *Could*
in such constructions realises: 'not necessarily not-q'. *Needn't*
realises: 'not necessarily q'.

§ 317.   Constructions realising modalities in their main clause may
contain a modal verb of belief in their dependent clause. For
example, *If it may be living there must be some indication of
chemical processes taking place.* ('If we accept that it may be the
case that it is living this implies that it must be the case that there
are . . .') I do not discuss such examples further, but it is worth
noting that they have counterparts in decision, e.g. *If they may be
here by six we must be ready before then*, and also (?perhaps) in
prediction, *If it may rain the match will be cancelled.*

§318.   Deductive conditionals can be compared with those of performance in terms of what they realise in the dependent and main
clauses. In performance conditionals, this is cause and effect,
respectively.

Deductive conditionals always realise in the dependent clause
knowledge of a proposition, which knowledge constitutes a sufficient condition for knowing the proposition presented as the
conclusion in the main clause. The proposition presented as known
in the dependent clause may describe either a cause or an effect.
Where it is an effect, the knowledge and performance relations
realised in the construction 'run counter' to one another.

§319.   I suggest that, although 'If . . . then' in English does not realise
material implication in the case of decision or performance
conditionals (for reasons outlined in §§288, 299-300 above), it
does do so in the case of both knowledge constructions of
determinate belief (those with an indicative dependent
clause, and *must/can't* in the main clause, as discussed above)
and also in constructions of full, direct knowledge, with
both clauses in the non-modal indicative. This similarity between
this one kind of modal construction and the indicative can
be accounted for in terms of the analysis suggested in §§ 266,
268 above.

§320. The existence of a somewhat peripheral group of indicative
knowledge constructions supports the claim that 'If . . . then . . .'
in the indicative has this meaning. These are contrary to fact
constructions which depend on content and common knowledge to
indicate a 'true' or a 'false' value for one proposition, thereby
deriving, by *modus ponens/modus tollens* a value for the other.
A proposition assumed to be commonly known to be 'true' is
realised in the dependent clause (*modus ponens*), one presented
as self-evidently false is realised in the main clause (*modus tollens*).
E.g.: *Modus ponens*

(a) *She's fifty if she's a day.*
(cf. *He's a fast driver, if I've ever met one*, supported by 'and
I've met quite a few'.)

Modus tollens

(b) *If that's really gold I'm a Dutchman.*
(c) *If that song isn't a hit, I'm Father Christmas.*
(cf. The fossilised expression, *I'm blowed if that's true*.)

These constructions operate by exploiting the meaning of the sign of
material implication, '⊃', as given in the truth table (Table 8.4).

Table 8.4

	p	q	⊃
1.	T	T	T
2.	T	F	F
3.	F	T	T
4.	F	F	T

(T = True, F = False, p = any proposition, q = any other proposition)

Given that '⊃' is true (which excludes line 2 of the table), we may
argue on the basis of a false value for q to a false value for p (line 4),
as in (b) and (c), or on the basis of a true value for p to a true value
for q (line 1), as in (a).

These constructions realise an assertion that 'p implies q' where
p is the event in the dependent clause, and exploit (rather than
describe) this relation to arrive at a conclusion, which may be carried

in either main or dependent clause.

They would not 'work' unless 'if . . . (then) . . .' had the meaning of '⊃' here.

§321.   I turn now to constructions which realise neither a prediction nor a deduction in the main clause, but in which it is the relationship between the operation(s) told in each clause which is itself told as known. These are 'constructions of fulfilled condition'.

I suggest that a four-way division may be made amongst them, according to the four planes to which the operations which they assert belong, and that each such group parallels one of the major types of ('unfulfilled') conditionals which we have been considering. They represent constructions of 'reason' and explanation.

§322.   In terms of surface grammar, such constructions may be divided into two groups, according to the conjunction used: *because/as*; *therefore/so*. In all these constructions, with the exception of some of telling, both clauses are non-modal and indicative, and the main clause is declarative.

The distinctions between *because* and *therefore* sentences are to do with telling. The latter constructions have two main clauses (cf. Jespersen, 1940: 387), and carry full telling of knowledge of each event independently; the former have one main clause which is fully told and a dependent clause with derived telling. In *because* sentences the fully told clause realises a resultant operation, and the 'reason' element is less prominent in this respect, although, since the dependent clause usually comes last, it has the telling prominence associated with 'not given' (cf. §227). In *therefore* sentences, the 'reason' element is fully told. In the latter, the order of clauses is fixed: that is, a reversal of sequence creates a reversal of meaning in terms of reason and result. Compare, for example, (1) *She ate a lot of chocolate, so/therefore she got fat*, with (1′) *She got fat, so therefore she ate a lot of chocolates*. In *because* sentences the relative sequence of clauses is not fixed in this way.

(2) *She got fat because she ate a lot of chocolates* is cognitively equivalent to (2′) *Because she ate a lot of chocolates she got fat*. Where the dependent reason clause precedes the main clause, it tends to take *as* instead of *because*.

For convenience in what follows, constructions with *because/as* will be referred to as 'explanation' forms, and those with *therefore/so* as 'conclusion' forms.

Cognitively equivalent explanation and conclusion forms are paired in (1) and (2) above, and in the following examples of 'reason—result' constructions relating to different planes:

> (3) *John slid on the ice because he felt cheerful.*
> (3′) *John felt cheerful so he slid on the ice.*
> (4) *It was a Monday morning, because I'd just started the washing.*
> (4′) *I'd just started the washing, so it was a Monday morning.*
> (5) *Buy me an evening paper, because you're going out anyway.*
> (5′) *You're going out anyway, so buy me an evening paper.*

§323.   Each of these pairs of examples is related to one of the four planes in terms of what they give a reason for, as follows:

> (1), (2) give a reason for occurrence (or 'happening');
> (3), (3′) a reason for deciding (and performing);
> (4), (4′) a reason for knowing;
> (5), (5′) a reason for telling (or saying).

In the case of reasons for knowing and telling, it is *the fact that* the dependent clause is known which is treated as the reason for telling or knowing the given occurrence value, or the decision concerning it, of the main clause. In the case of occurrence and decision, it is *what* is known, the occurrence value itself (or the decision value concerning it) which is taken as the reason for the given occurrence value (or the decision value concerning it) of the event in the main clause.

§324. **Reason for Telling**

Constructions of this type present, in the one clause, some justification for saying the other clause. They are alone among constructions of explanation and conclusion in being able to have a non-declarative main clause as in (5) and (5′) above, and in

> (6) *John got here half an hour ago, so where's Fred?*
> (6′) *Where's Fred, because John got here half an hour ago?*
> (7) *We've lost anyway, so who's worrying?*
> (7′) *Who's worrying, because we've lost anyway?*

It is as much the knowledge itself as the known occurrence value of the event which is offered as justification: as much the fact that the speaker knows it as the identity of what is known. In this way,

(5) *Buy me an evening paper, because you're going out anyway*, may be glossed as 'The fact that I know that you're going out anyway seems an adequate reason for me to ask you to buy me an evening paper.'

There may be some connection on the performance plane between the events in the two clauses as in (5), which suggests that evening papers are bought 'out', and so the fact that 'you are going out' will make it easy for you to buy one. But the connection here is tortuous: 'your going out *anyway*' is neither a necessary nor a sufficient cause of 'your buying me an evening paper', nor is it a result of the latter; and 'your buying me an evening paper' is not a sufficient or necessary cause of 'your going out anyway', although it is a possible result. (There would be more connection between the events here if the item *anyway* were omitted, but this is fortuitous and a feature of this particular example.) The construction in general operates without the need for any performance relation between its clauses, as illustrated in (6) and (6').

Knowledge of one proposition provides an 'adequate reason' for telling another in much the same way here as that suggested for telling conditionals (cf. §286). Telling does not follow from knowing, neither is the knowledge presented as a necessary condition of telling. The justification which it provides is largely that of contextualising the telling operation and explaining its relevance in the ongoing SU. The clause realising the knowing operation which is the reason for telling, has a cohesive function. Constructions of reason for telling occur principally in colloquial speech.

§325.   **Reason for Decision: Constructions of Motive and Purpose**

Constructions of this type present a given occurrence value in one clause, as a sufficient reason for making a decision concerning the performance of the event in the other. But since the occurrence of that event is presented as known, it is impossible to separate the decision from its implementation in performance, and these constructions are very similar, with respect to their 'output', to constructions of reason for occurrence. However, there is a volitional element in (3) *John slid on the ice because he felt cheerful* which is not present in (2) *She got fat because she ate a lot of chocolates*, which suggests that the main clause in (3) realises telling of (performer's-) decision, as well as knowledge of occurrence.

A *why?* test may be used to distinguish (2) and (3) along these lines. That is, *Why did it happen?* is appropriate to query the main clause in (2), but not in (3); *Why did he do it?* is applicable to (3), but not to (2).

§326.   There are two types of 'reason for decision' constructions, according to the type of reason given. I distinguish between constructions of 'motive' and those of 'purpose'.

The former include examples such as (3), and another type which has a modal verb of decision in the 'reason' clause, as the motivation for the decision in the result clause, e.g. (8) *John won't buy a new suit so Jane must buy one for him.*

Purpose constructions have the structure, main clause plus dependent non-finite clause, e.g. (9) *She went to Bermuda to look for sunken treasure*. The dependent clause presents a sufficient reason for the voluntary action reported in the main clause: 'that's why she decided to go'. This reason is a wish for a not-yet occurring performance (rather than a decision as in constructions of motive): 'her desire to look for buried treasure'.[1]

A decision feature is realised in each clause. The decision relation 'runs' from the wish in the dependent clause to the decision in the main. The performance relation runs counter to that of decision; the known occurrence value of the event in the main clause is presented as a necessary cause of the putative occurrence value given for the wished for event in the dependent clause. This may be summarised in Table 8.5.

Table 8.5 Constructions of Purpose

	Main clause	Dependent (non-finite) clause
Decision	resultant 'decision' voluntary performance ◄────	wish as sufficient reason for
Performance	necessary cause of ────►	putative result

Table 8.6 Constructions of Motive: (i) *Because* Forms

	Main clause	Dependent clause
Decision	resultant 'decision' (voluntary performance) ◄────────	sufficient reason for OR
Performance		occurrence as sufficient cause of

Table 8.7 Constructions of Motive: (ii) *Therefore* Forms

	First clause	Second (*so/therefore*) clause
Decision	sufficient reason for ⟶	resultant 'decision'
	OR	(voluntary performance)
Performance	sufficient cause of ⟶	

Contrast Tables 8.6 and 8.7 with Table 8.5.

Constructions of purpose represent an intermediate degree of 'fulfilment' or 'closedness' between open decision conditionals on the one hand, and constructions of motive on the other. On the performance plane, the necessary cause is told as known to have occurred (and so is fully closed), but the result event is neither known nor yet occurring (and so is fully open). On the other hand, the wish for that resultant occurrence is presented as implemented and, as such, constitutes a sufficient reason for the decision to carry out the performance whose occurrence is a necessary case of the occurrence which is wished for.

§327.   Purpose constructions are related to the type of decision conditional mentioned earlier (§292), constructions such as (10) *If he's going to get that job he must pass the exam*, where, on the performance plane, the main clause also presents a necessary cause for the given occurrence value of the event in the dependent clause; and where the unfulfilled performer—decision (intention) in the dependent clause is given as sufficient reason for the decision feature realised in the main clause.

The fully closed equivalents of constructions of purpose are forms in which the wish element is lexicalised and told as known, as in: (11) *John slid on the ice because he wanted to be one of the gang*, as compared with (12) *John slid on the ice to be one of the gang*.

Constructions of purpose are explanation forms, giving the reason for the volitional performance of the event in the main clause in a dependent (non-finite) clause, even though the reason given is an unfulfilled wish.

§328.   Reason for Occurrence: 'Cause of Happening'

Constructions of this type realise full independent knowledge of the event in the dependent clause, as compared with lack of knowledge as realised in the *if* clause of an open prediction condition, accepted knowledge in the *if* of inductive constructions, and assumed knowledge of the opposite Ov in the dependent clause of counterfactual conditionals. Examples include (2) above. *She got fat because she ate a lot of chocolates.* Like their unfulfilled condition counterparts they realise cause in the dependent clause and effect/result in the main (or *so/therefore*) clause. (I use 'result' to cover an effect event which is known to have occurred.)

Where such clauses contain *because* they are ambiguous with a negative main clause. (13) *They didn't win because Tom played at goal* may mean either 'It wasn't because Tom played at goal that they won' or 'It was because Tom played at goal that they didn't win'. Negation in the main clause realises either a denial of that proposition or of the implication relation realised in *because*. Constructions with *as* unambiguously realise denial of the main clause proposition.

I include under this heading constructions in which the cause of another's event occurrence is itself a decision operation, as in (14) *I left him behind because he wouldn't move.*

Those with a performance cause are not restricted to past tense in either clause. Compare (3″) *She's getting/going to get fat because she's eating a lot of chocolates.* With *going to get* in the result clause, the performance there is presented as not yet occurring and so the construction is to some degree open.

§329.   Since all constructions of explanation convey knowledge of both clauses, the distinction made under conditional constructions between those of performance with *will/won't* in the main clause, and that type of deductive conditional in which the knowledge relation runs parallel with, as opposed to counter to, the performance relation (with *must/can't* in the main clause) is no longer easily discernible here. All constructions of reason for occurrence involve knowledge both of cause and effect, and a distinction cannot be made between closed performance conditionals and the closed counterparts of those deductive conditionals in which the knowledge relation runs parallel to that of performance.

An example such as (15) *She's busy because she's got six children* is regularly ambiguous (or perhaps 'indeterminate') between meaning 'that's why she's busy' (reason for occurrence) and 'that's why/how I know she's busy' (reason for knowing). Near equivalence to, or difference from, a construction of reason for occurrence, can be used as a test for distinguishing the two types of deductive conditionals.

§330.   Reason for Knowing: 'Adduced Proof'

Constructions of this type represent the fully 'closed' counterparts of deductive conditionals. They realise full independent knowledge of one proposition (realised in the *because* clause) as a sufficient condition for knowing the proposition in the main clause. The only distinguishable cases of reason for knowing constructions are those (shown in Tables 8.8 and 8.9) in which the performance relation runs counter to that of knowing (for reasons given in the last paragraph), as in (16) *He's a local man, because he knows about the old workings* ('only local men know about them').

Table 8.8 Explanation (*Because*) Constructions of Reason for Knowing

	Main clause	Dependent clause
Knowledge	Resultant knowledge ◄── Sufficient condition of knowing	
Performance	Necessary cause ──► Result occurrence	

Table 8.9 Conclusion (*Therefore*) Constructions of Reason for Knowing

	First clause	Second (*so/therefore*) clause
Knowledge	Sufficient condition ──► Resultant knowledge of knowing	
Performance	Result occurrence ◄── Necessary cause	

The performance relation in these constructions is between a necessary cause and an effect. Argument is from knowledge of the occurrence of an effect to knowledge of the occurrence of a necessary cause of that effect. Knowledge of the former is presented as a fulfilled sufficient condition of knowledge of the latter.

§331.   This analysis applies equally to (4) above: *It was a Monday*

morning, because I'd just started the washing, as much as to (16) or to (17) *It's been raining, because there are puddles on the pavement.*

Examples such as (4) are sometimes said to be 'illogical' probably for the following reasons:

(i)   The performance relation between necessary cause and effect, on which the construction is based, is not self-evident unless one knows that 'I' only do the washing on a Monday morning.

(ii)   The grammatical form of the construction is identical with that of a construction of reason for occurrence. This point applies to many constructions of reason for knowing, and there is some tendency to associate them particularly with colloquial or uneducated speech. Dislike of the use of these forms has some reasonable basis, for although an example such as (4) is not ambiguous in practice, one such as (18) *He went because I saw him* may either mean 'that's why he went (because he'd noticed that I'd spotted him)' or, 'that's how I know that he went (because I saw him go)', and this distinction matters.

§332.   Since a cause event cannot be shown to take place later than its result, and since 'reason for knowing' constructions may realise the cause in their main clause, and those of occurrence realise it in the *because/so* clause, tense relations between the clauses can be used to distinguish these construction types. Thus, (17) is unambiguously 'reason for knowing', and so is, (17') *There are puddles on the pavement, so it's been raining.*

§333.   Reason for knowing may also be distinguished from reason for occurrence by a *because* test. Applied to (2) this gives:

(2″) *It was because she ate a lot of chocolates that she got fat* which means the same as the original, but selects the cause relation for telling focus.

Applied to (17) it gives:

(17″)*It is because there are puddles on the pavement that it's been raining*, which demands *I know* before the main clause.

Reasons for deciding behave similarly to occurrence reason on this test; reason for telling constructions are more similar to those of knowing.

Note

1. The form of the purpose construction is potentially ambiguous, as in *He worked hard to be promoted* which may either mean 'His wish for promotion made him work hard (at his job)' or 'Being promoted is what he worked hard at' or 'I can see that he must have worked hard because I've just heard that he's been promoted'. The construction in its second interpretation is related to the question 'What did he work hard at?' and, in its third interpretation to the question 'How do you know?'. Only the first interpretation is related to the question 'Why did he do it?'.

9 CONCLUSION

§334.   The framework of the analysis which I have proposed for the semantic interpretation of syntactic form within the area of mood does not require the intermediate level of 'deep grammar'.

§335.   I suggest that the following points have arisen in the course of this study concerning the relationship between mood (force-indicating devices) and a natural logic in English.

(i)   The semantic factors underlying distinctions of mood are situational: principally, roles and operations.

(ii)   These factors govern the division of the semantic organisation of English into four different 'planes'.

(iii)   There are different types of constructions of reasoning each of which can be matched with one of the four planes.

(iv)   The types of reasoning construction so distinguished underlie different kinds of formal logic (both the truth functional propositional logic and different types of modal logic).

(v)   English has a rich system of natural logics, which are identifiable in terms of the surface grammar features of constructions realising them.

(vi)   This system is not co-extensive with that of formal logics. For example, the latter has no equivalent to a logic of telling.

(vii)   There are identifiable construction types in English grammar for use in contingency planning, inductive reasoning, predictions of probabilities in past and future; in deductive reasoning, and for justifying saying what one does say.

§336.   Mood and condition are intimately connected in English, principally through the modal verbs. Semantically, modality and reasoning are closely connected through the notions of the different operation types and of operation sign (e.g. the known/unknown distinction explored in §§266, 268).

§337.   The different types of operations and operation sign are both derivable principally from the secondary roles, and features of their occupancy.

§338.   I suggest, then, that the different fashions of reasoning realised in English grammar are dependent on different types of modalities;

that the modalities derive from the different operations and operation sign, and that the latter derive from the four socio-linguistic 'secondary' roles.

§339.   If these connections are allowed, complex modes of reasoning may be directly related to simple primes. Some of these may feature in animal communication systems. E.g. one might posit a role of 'knower' as forming an element in the semantics of the language of bees. On this basis it should not be entirely unexpected that a higher primate might learn some fragmentary rudiments of a human language (cf. Linden, 1976).

§340.   It seems possible that, if a roles-based semantics underlies the part of English syntax to do with mood and condition, it might underlie comparable areas in the syntax of another language, in a fashion comparable to that proposed for universal phonetic features (Jakobson & Halle, 1956). That is, although I would not predict that another language would share the same selection of roles and operations (and associated attributes) which I have proposed for English, I would suggest that situational factors of this kind might be elements in the semantics of comparable areas of the grammar in other languages besides English, great variation in selection and combination being possible.

I propose the notions of 'secondary' (socio-linguistic) roles, and their associated operations, as putative universals of syntactic semantics.

APPENDIX I

I give below outline diagrams of the surface grammar of some imperative
constructions (Diagram I) and of types of declaratives and interrogatives
(Diagram II). These are drawn up as system networks following the conventions and notation developed by Halliday (1966a, 1967a, 1969, 1973,
etc.). I depart from Halliday's approach in using this apparatus for the
description of surface, as opposed to deep, grammar (an intermediate level
which I suggest is unnecessary in relation to the analysis of mood).

The surface grammar taxonomy specified in the systemic network provides
a means of stating bundles of surface grammar features each of which
realises a bundle of semantic features (in LMM). Such an approach removes
the need to postulate e.g. an imperative morpheme, in an intermediate level
of deep structure. It also avoids any necessity to postulate an implicit verb
of ordering or acting (cf. Ross, 1970; Sadock, 1974). My belief is that an
analysis of LMM can be approached more economically in terms of features
of surface form than by postulating 'ghosts in the machine'.

Distinguishing Surface Grammar Features of the Imperative

1. Base form of the verb.
2. Optional subject or none.
3. If subject present verb cannot be marked for concord.
4. Neutral to tense.
5. Mainly neutral to aspect (except for a few forms, e.g. *Get going*).
6. Cannot take modal auxiliaries.
7. Mainly active (very few passives, chiefly with *get*).

Distinguishing Surface Grammar Features of the Four Basic Types of Imperative

1. Fiat: + *let*; − subject; − tag; − vocative; can't take *please* (*let* is
   obligatorily initial).
2. Jussive: − *let*; − *let's*; +/− subject; +/− tag (with second person subject);
   +/− vocative; may take *please*.
3. Optative: + *let*; +/− subject; +/− tag (with second person subject); +/−
   vocative; may take *please*.
4. Joint: + *let's*; +/− subject; +/− tag (with first person plural subject);
   +/− vocative; may take *please*.

I take the feature '+ *do*' to constitute marking of the construction as realising 'speaker's wish' ('weak' (v) §§27–9); and '+ subject' to give marking for 'speaker's decision' ('strong' (v), §§27–30). They are mutually exclusive options: *You do take one.* An imperative with '+ subject' cannot take *please* (which is an alternative/extra marker of 'speaker's wish'). *Please you take one.*

Optatives are closely related semantically to interrogative countermanding constructions with *can.* Compare, *Let John come with us, Can John come with us?* They share the feature [Decider : Addressee] , and both may be additionally marked for 'speaker's wish'; the optative by + *do* and/or *please*, the interrogative only by *please.*

The feature '+ tag' in jussives I take to realise a move to include the addressee among the occupants of the decider role. In optatives it may realise a move by the speaker to include himself among those occupants, particularly if the construction is '+ subject' a feature involving some conflict , since the optative basically realises [Decider : Addressee] . This may account for the potentially aggressive tone of *You let John come, will you.* It realises both recognition of the addressee as decider, and a claim by the speaker to override his authority and take over as dominant occupant of that role.

The negative tag in jussives and optatives can be seen as another device for realising 'speaker's wish' (for the positive action). It does not combine with '+ subject', *You let John take one, won't you.* The tag realises, 'inclusion of addressee in decider role' and 'speaker's wish'; both features are incompatible with 'speaker's decision', realised by *you.* Negative tags often convey an extra degree of 'politeness' as compared with their positive equivalents. This arises from their meaning of 'speaker wishes x' when they are used in circumstances where the addressee can be conventionally expected to want to perform the action x.

Please, do and a negative tag may combine, giving triple marking of speaker's wish, as opposed to decision, although this is rather unlikely in practice: (?) *Please do come in won't you.*

I take a 'path' statement, such as one of those given in 1–30 below, to be the surface grammar specification (SGS) of a construction.

The combination of an SGS with an LMMS gives the linguistic element ('X') in an FOS rule of the type, 'X counts as Y in context C' (cf. §§43, 54).

Let us illustrate with the 'plain' jussive imperative, e.g. *Take one* [(3) above] :

$$SGS_{IM_3} \text{ [jussive : } (- \text{ subject } I_1 \text{ positive}) : (- do/- \text{ tag}) : - \text{ vocative]}$$

$$\text{LMMS}_{\text{IM}_3} \left\{ \begin{array}{l} [((\text{Teller} = \text{Decider}) : \text{Speaker}) \neq (\text{Performer} : \text{Addressee})] \\[6pt] \begin{bmatrix} \text{Decision}^+ \\ \text{Performance}^- \\ \text{Inertia}^- \end{bmatrix} \end{array} \right\}$$

Let $C_{a\,\ldots\,n}$ be contextual features
$\quad C_a \;=\;$ 'Addressee does not wish to perform action'
$\quad C_b \;=\;$ 'Addressee wishes to perform action'

Let $Y_{1\,\ldots\,n}$ be categories of first order significance
$\quad Y_1 \;=\;$ 'command'
$\quad Y_2 \;=\;$ 'permission'

$$(\text{SGS}_{\text{IM}_3} + \text{LMMS}_{\text{IM}_3}) = X_{\text{IM}_\alpha}$$

Then:

$\quad$'X_{IM_α} counts as Y_1 in context C_a'

I.e. '(jussive) imperative counts as command in context where addressee does not wish to perform the action',

and:

$\quad$'X_{IM_α} counts as Y_2 in context C_b'

I.e. '(jussive) imperative counts as permission in context where addressee wishes to perform the action'.

Diagram II specifies a wide variety of construction types, some of which are discussed in Chapter 6.

The surface grammar features referred to in the system labels are roughly as follows:

1. Declarative/interrogative: Absence/presence of 'enclosed subject' (vSV order, cf. Davies, 1968b) and/or *wh*-interrogative item (i.e. 'neither' gives declarative).

2. Polar/non-polar interrogative: Absence/presence of *wh*-interrogative item.

3. Polar: predicated/non-predicated; Presence/absence of *was/is + it* before specifically queried element, + relative pronoun (*that/wh-*) introducing

Diagram I Surface Grammar of Imperatives

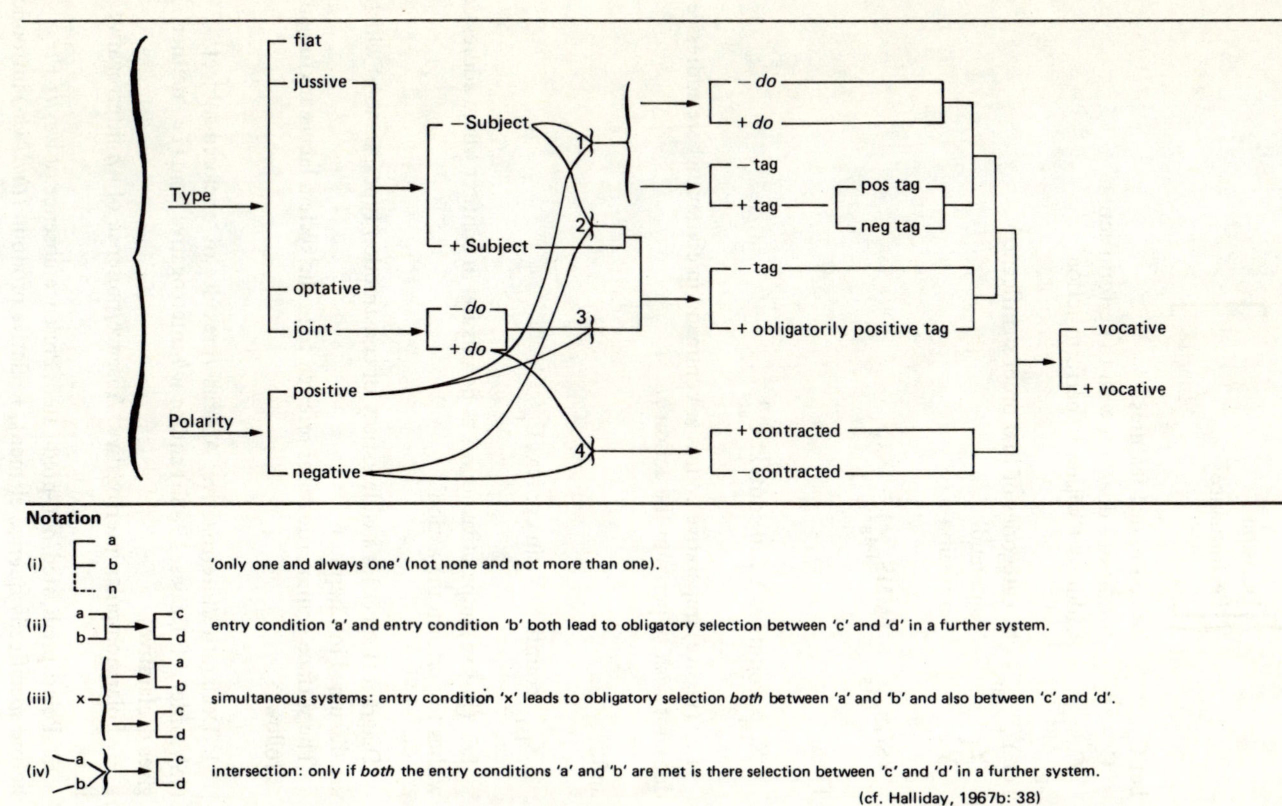

Notation

(i) a / b / n 'only one and always one' (not none and not more than one).

(ii) a b → c d entry condition 'a' and entry condition 'b' both lead to obligatory selection between 'c' and 'd' in a further system.

(iii) x → a b → c d simultaneous systems: entry condition 'x' leads to obligatory selection *both* between 'a' and 'b' and also between 'c' and 'd'.

(iv) a b → c d intersection: only if *both* the entry conditions 'a' and 'b' are met is there selection between 'c' and 'd' in a further system.

(cf. Halliday, 1967b: 38)

The system network in Diagram I generates the following types of imperative constructions: (/ simultaneity; : hierarchy; I intersection) (cf. Halliday, 1969: 82).

Examples	*Linear Statement of 'Path' through System*
1. Let the prisoner stand forward.	(fiat/pos.)
2. Let not your heart be troubled.	(fiat/neg.)
3. Take one.	[jussive : (− subject I_1 positive) : (− *do*/− tag) : − vocative]
4. Take one, will you.	[jussive : (− subject I_1 positive) : (− *do*/(+ tag : pos. tag)) : − vocative]
5. Take one, won't you.	[jussive : (− subject I_1 positive) : (− *do*/(+ tag : neg. tag)) : − vocative]
6. Do take one.	[jussive : (− subject I_1 positive) : (+ *do*/− tag) : − vocative]
7. Do take one, will you.	[jussive : (− subject I_1 positive) : (+ *do*/(+ tag : pos. tag)) : − vocative]
8. Do take one, won't you.	[jussive : (− subject I_1 positive) : (+ *do*/(+ tag : neg. tag)) : − vocative]
9. Don't take one.	[jussive : (− subject I_2 negative) : − tag : − vocative]
10. Don't take one, will you.	[jussive : (− subject I_2 negative) : + pos. tag : − vocative]
11. You take one.	[((jussive : + subject)/positive) : − tag : − vocative]
12. You take one, will you.	[((jussive : + subject)/positive) : + pos. tag : − vocative]
13. Don't you take one.	[((jussive : + subject)/negative) : − tag : − vocative]
14. Don't you take one, will you.	[((jussive : + subject)/negative) : + pos. tag : − vocative]
15. Let John take one.	[optative : (− subject I_1 positive) : (− *do*/− tag) : − vocative]
16. Let John take one, will you.	[optative: (− subject I_1 positive) : (− *do*/(+ tag : pos. tag)) : − vocative]
17. Let John take one, won't you.	[optative : (− subject I_1 positive) : (− *do*/(+ tag : neg. tag)) : − vocative]
18. Don't let John take one.	[optative : (− subject I_2 negative) : − tag : − vocative]
19. Don't let John take one, will you.	[optative : (− subject I_2 negative) : + pos. tag : − vocative]
20. You let John take one.	[((optative : + subject)/positive) : − tag : − vocative]
21. You let John take one, will you.	[((optative : + subject)/positive) : + pos. tag : − vocative]
22. Don't you let John take one.	[((optative : + subject)/negative) : − tag : − vocative]
23. Don't you let John take one, will you.	[((optative : + subject)/negative) : + pos. tag : − vocative]
24. Let's take one.	[((joint : − *do*) I_3 positive) : − tag : − vocative]
25. Let's take one shall we.	[((joint: − *do*) I_3 positive) : + pos. tag : − vocative]
26. Do let's take one.	[((joint : + *do*) I_3 positive) : − tag : − vocative]
27. Do let's take one shall we.	[((joint : + *do*) I_3 positive) : + pos. tag : − vocative]
28. Let's not take one.	[((joint : − *do*)/negative) : − vocative]
29. Don't let's take one.	[((joint : + *do*) I_4 negative) : + contracted : − vocative]
30. Do let's not take one.	[((joint : + *do*) I_4 negative) : − contracted : − vocative]

Diagram II Surface Grammar of Some Declaratives/Interrogatives
(notational conventions as for Diagram I)

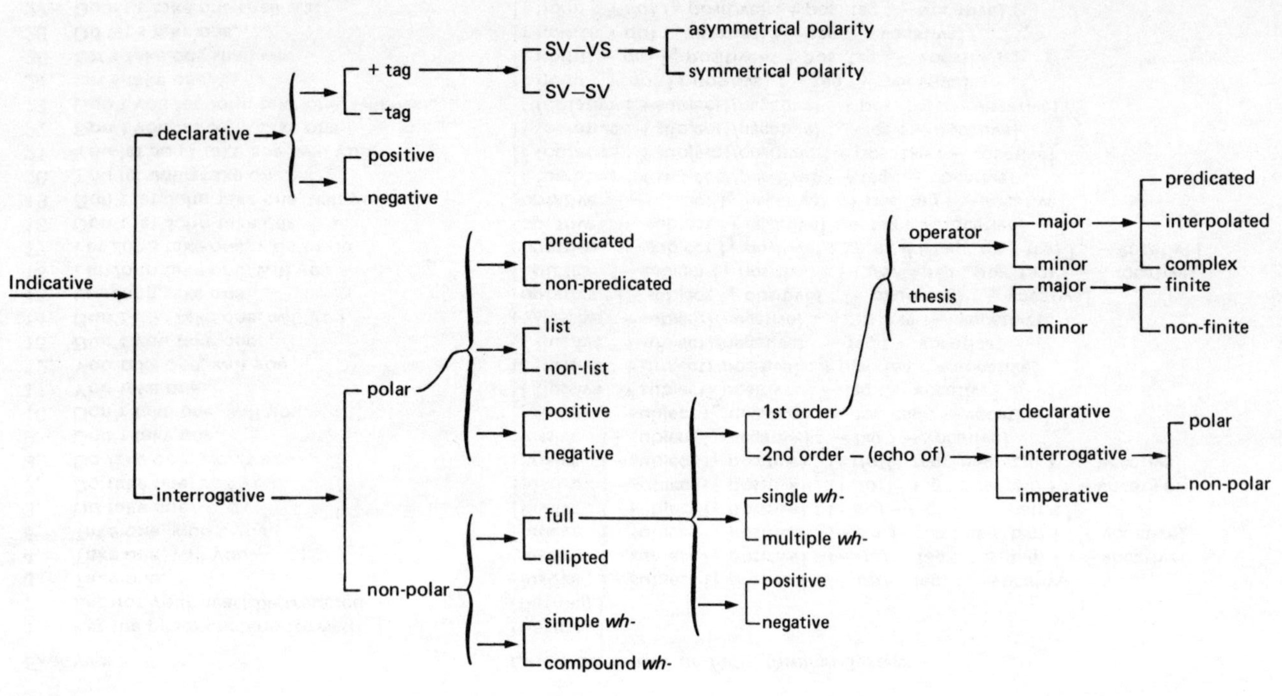

remainder of clause, i.e. 'predicated polar' gives an interrogative cleft
sentence, e.g. *Was it John who told you?*

4. Polar: list/non-list; Presence/absence of a list of co-ordinated items at
any element of clause structure, including the verb, e.g. *Was John coming or
going?* as well as *Would you like tea or coffee?*

5. Non-polar: full/ellipted; Presence/absence of other items in addition to
the *wh*-interrogative. e.g. *Which paper?/Where are you going?* as opposed
to *What?/Why?*

6. Non-polar: simple/compound *wh*-; Absence/presence of particle
'attached' to *what* as *wh*-item ('attachment' testable for by possibility of
particle preceding *what* in sentence initial position), e.g. *Where?/What in?*:
In what did you put it?

7. Non-polar: single *wh*-/multiple *wh*-; One/more than one *wh*- interrogative in first orders. One/more than one *wh*- substitution in second
orders (echoes). E.g. first orders: //1 Where are you going// (single) //1 Who
wants what// (multiple). Second orders: //2 When is who leaving// (single)
//2 When is who going where// (multiple). Cf. also, //2 Did who leave//
(single) //2 Did who go where// (multiple).

8. Non-polar: first/second order; discussed in Chapter 6. Second order
constructions involve the substitution *in situ* of a *wh*- interrogative for an
element (or part of an element) in a preceding sentence. For this reason they
may freely break rules for sequential position of *wh*- items in surface
structure.

9. Non-polar: first order: major/minor operator; Presence/absence of
was it/did you say (or both) following initial *wh*- item, and preceding
relative pronoun (*that/wh*-) + remainder of clause. Constructions with a
major operator are the 'recollection' forms (cf. Chapter 6), e.g. *Who was it
(did you say) who mended their clock?*

10. Non-polar: first order: major/minor thesis; Presence/absence of verb
in 'cognitively central component', i.e. in proposition, e.g. *What about John?/
How about some tea?* (minor thesis)/*How about hiring one?/Why worry?*
(major non-finite thesis)/*What are you doing?/Who's there?* etc. (major finite
thesis). Constructions with minor thesis take a negative only rarely.

Distinctions of meaning realised in the selections polar/non-polar, single/
multiple, first/second order, together with those realised by different types of
tags, are discussed in Chapter 6.

Non-polars with a major predicated operator realise recollection of
previous knowledge by the speaker, potentially aided by the addressee.
'Interpolation' in the operator explicitly realises 'Addressee the previous
teller (and also previous and current knower) of the whole proposition,

including the element queried' (cf. §255, above).

The two distinctions within polar interrogatives are not covered in the text:

(a)   Polar: predicated/non-predicated. A predicated polar interrogative is a cleft sentence device for applying a yes/no query to a specific element. That is, the affirmation/denial disjunction concerns whether or not a specific element belongs to the proposition which is affirmed or denied. Such constructions resemble first order *wh-* interrogatives in realising the speaker— teller's knowledge of the remainder of the proposition, e.g. *Was it Jane who fell downstairs?* realises knowledge of an incompletely specified proposition, containing an indefinite quantifier: 'Someone fell downstairs'. Cf. *Who fell downstairs?* The difference lies in the distinction between 'putting up' a particular member of a list of items which could substitute for the (lexically) unknown element (in this case subject) and requesting affirmation/denial of its correctness, and requesting a selection from a list presented as indefinite (except for certain grammatically specified restrictions, in this case '+ animate + human'). The extent of speaker's knowledge conveyed in the predicated polar interrogative is greater than in the corresponding non-polar, for the former conveys knowledge of the identity of one member of such a list. In this way predicated polar interrogatives represent a more restricted query than either non-predicated polars or *wh-* interrogatives: '+/− this particular *which/who/where*', etc. The cleft sentence as a device for realising forms of the telling operation is discussed in Chapter 5.

(b)   Polar: list: non-list. 'Alternative questions' (cf. Quirk *et al.*, 1972: 399—400). List polar interrogatives can be thought of, in one sense, as multiple predicated polars, but without grammatical marking for telling focus. (The two features may combine, in which case telling focus is shown, e.g. *Is it John or Mary who's coming?*) Their distinguishing characteristic is that they present the whole list from which selection is to be made. In this they differ from first order non-polars (where the list is indefinite, and no member of it is presented as known), and from predicated polars, where the list is also indefinite although one member of it is given. They partially resemble these construction types in realising knowledge of an incompletely specified proposition with an underlying indefinite quantifier, e.g. *Is John going to New York or Boston or Philadelphia?*: 'John is going to some city in the eastern United States.' The difference is that the range of the quantifier is more highly specified; here, not 'some place', or 'some one of an indefinite list of places including place x', but 'some one of a particular sort of place', cf. *Would you like tea or coffee?*: 'I assume you would like something hot and non-alcoholic to drink.'

List polars are probably best seen as non-polars with a limited, specified range of choice: *Which would you like: tea or coffee?/Where is he going: New York, Boston or Philadelphia?*, i.e. 'Which *which*/which *where*, etc. out of the following restricted and specified set of possibilities?' The shorter the list, the greater the degree of speaker–teller's knowledge conveyed.

Not all list polars give mutually exclusive possibilities, e.g. *Are you going to take time off, or relax for a while or something?* Here the alternative is a matter of phrasing, not content, and the questions may be answered 'yes/no'.

Diagram II treats second order (echo) non-polars as a grammatically distinguishable class. Halliday (1967a) identifies them on intonational criteria. I suggest that the important part played by intonation here supports the view, advanced in Chapter 5, that one of the primary functions of tone is to realise relationships of discourse linkage. Intonation in echo interrogatives would, for me, fall under realisations of that aspect of telling.

I omit the detailed SGSs of constructions given in Diagram II; they can be worked out on the same principles as those used in illustrating the imperative, above.

The principles given in §§43, 54 can be applied to interrogatives as to imperatives. Let us take the (non-predicated, non-list) polar interrogative, e.g. *Is it raining?* and exemplify it as follows: (I omit features of teller–role transference; performer role occupancy is freely variable).

$$\text{SGS}_{\text{INT}_1} \left\{ \text{polar : (non-predicated/non-list/positive)} \right\}$$

$$\text{LMMS}_{\text{INT}_1} \left\{ \begin{array}{l} [(\text{Teller : Speaker}) \neq (\text{Knower : Addressee})] \\[2ex] \left[\begin{array}{l} \text{Knowing}^{-} \\ \text{Performance}^{+} \end{array} \right] \end{array} \right\}$$

$(\text{SGS}_{\text{INT}_1} + \text{LMMS}_{\text{INT}_1}) = \text{X}_{\text{INT}_\alpha}$ in an FOS rule of the type 'X counts as Y in context C' (where 'Y' is a category of FOS).

Context C_a = 'Addressee can be conventionally assumed to know whether or not p.'

C_b = 'Addressee cannot be conventionally assumed to know whether or not p.'

Y_1 = open question
Y_2 = challenge

Then:

(1) '$\text{X}_{\text{INT}_\alpha}$ counts as Y_1 in context C_a'

I.e. '(plain, positive) polar interrogative counts as an open question in context:
Addressee can be conventionally assumed to know whether or not p.'

(2)   'X_{INT_α} counts as Y_2 in context C_b'

I.e. '(plain, positive) polar interrogative counts as challenge in context:
Addressee cannot be conventionally expected to know whether or not p.'

This appendix relates principally to Chapter 8, §§310–314 (deductive conditionals).

I take the examples,

(1)   *If she's got six children she must be busy.*
(2)   *If he knows about the old workings he must be a local man.*
(3)   *If she isn't busy she can't have six children.*
(3′) *If she isn't busy it must be that she hasn't got six children.*
(4)   *If he isn't a local man he can't know about the old workings.*
(4′) *If he isn't a local man it must be that he doesn't know about the old workings.*

In (1) the occurrence of the event in the dependent clause is a sufficient cause of that in the main clause. In (2) the occurrence of the event in the main clause is a necessary cause of that in the dependent clause ('only local men know'). In (3) and (3′) the Ov of the main clause event is a necessary condition of the Ov of that in the dependent clause (not having six children is a necessary cause of not being busy). In (4) and (4′) the Ov of the event in the dependent clause is a sufficient cause of the Ov of that in the main clause (not being a local man is enough to ensure the lack of knowledge).

In all cases, knowledge of the Ov of the event in the dependent clause is a sufficient condition of knowledge of the Ov of the event in the main clause.

The examples illustrate the four types of valid argument as follows:

(1)   From a sufficient cause to effect.
(2)   From effect to necessary cause.
(3)   From non-occurrence of effect to non-occurrence of sufficient cause.
(4)   From non-occurrence of necessary cause to non-occurrence of effect.

Let us relate these constructions to the logical calculus. I shall use 'p' and 'q' not as the names of propositions describing events, but as the names of propositions describing knowledge of the occurrence of cause and effect. That is, I introduce an intermediate level between the occurrence values of events and implication relations between propositions describing those events.

    Let 'p' be the name of the proposition 'a cause, x, is known to occur',
    and 'q' be the name of the proposition 'an effect, y, is known to occur'.

Then '~ p' us the name of the proposition 'a cause, x, is known not to
    occur'; (which is equivalent to a false value of 'p')
and   '~ q' is the name of the proposition 'an effect, y, is known not to
    occur'; (which is equivalent to a false value of 'q').

Let   'α' and 'β' be the names of events.
Let   '+' be a positive occurrence value for an event,
and   '–' be a negative occurrence value for an event.
Then 'x' may be specified either as '+ α' or '– α'
and   'y' may be specified either as '+ β' or '–β'.

Using these definitions,

    (i)   Where the occurrence of x is necessary to the occurrence of y
('x is a necessary cause of y'), then 'q implies p' is true; and '~ p implies
~ q' is also true.
    (ii)   Where the occurrence of x is a sufficient cause of the occurrence of
y ('x is a sufficient cause of y'), then 'p implies q' is true; and '~ q implies
~ p' is also true.

Taking (4') above,

Let α = *his being a local man,*
     β = *his knowing about the old workings.*
Then x = + α
     y = + β

(4') presents '+ α' as a necessary cause of '+ β'. But it also presents accepted
knowledge that 'he isn't a local man': that is, knowledge of '– α'.
    Now, if x = + α, and 'p' is defined as the proposition that 'a cause x is
known to occur', then a minus value for α means that x does not occur,
which means that 'p' is false. But this is equivalent to '~ p' being true.
    (4') tells that '~ p' is true. Where x is a necessary cause of y, '~ p implies
~ q' is true.
    (4') both tells that '~ p' is true, and asserts that the implication relation

between its dependent and main clauses is valid by virtue of using the 'if . . .
(then) . . .' construction (cf. §319). '∼ p' is presented in the dependent
clause: '∼ q' in the main clause.

Given that '∼ p' is true and '∼ p ⊃ ∼ q', then the truth of '∼ q' can be
derived from the truth table of '∼ p ⊃ ∼ q'. '∼ q' is defined as the proposition that 'an effect, y, is known not to occur'.

$$y = +\beta$$
$$\beta = \textit{his knowing about the old workings.}$$

Therefore, the deduction carried in (4′), that it must be the case that 'he
doesn't know about the old workings', is legitimately arrived at in terms of
the logic of implication.

In (3′)

let γ = *her having six children*
and δ = *her being busy*

(3′) presents *her having six children* as a sufficient cause of *her being busy.*

$$x = +\gamma$$
$$y = +\delta$$

But it also presents accepted knowledge that 'she isn't busy': that is, knowledge of '− δ'.

$$y = +\delta$$

'∼ q' is defined as the proposition that 'an effect, y, is known not to occur'.
Therefore (3′) tells that '∼ q' is true. Where x is a sufficient cause of y,
'∼ q ⊃ ∼ p' is true.

(3′) asserts that the implication relation between its dependent and main
clauses is valid. '∼ q' is presented in its dependent clause, '∼ p' in its main
clause.

Given that '∼ q' is true and '∼ q ⊃ ∼ p', then the truth of '∼ p' can be
derived from the truth table of '∼ q ⊃ ∼ p'.

'∼ p' is defined as the proposition that 'a cause, x, is known not to occur'.

$$x = +\gamma$$
$$\gamma = \textit{her having six children.}$$

Therefore the deduction carried in (3′) that it must be the case that 'she doesn't have six children' is legitimately arrived at in terms of the logic of implication.

The same approach, using the definitions for 'p' and 'q' on p. 190, may be used to show that (1) and (2) also realise valid exploitations of the truth tables for 'p ⊃ q' and 'q ⊃ p' respectively.

But, both 'p ⊃ q' and '~ q ⊃ ~ p' are said to be true for the case where x is a sufficient cause of y. Both (1) and (3) operate on the same underlying performance relation between the same two events.

Similarly, 'q ⊃ p' and '~ p ⊃ ~ q' are both said to be true where x is a necessary cause of y. Both (2) and (4) operate on the same underlying performance relation between the two events.

In the logical calculus,

'p implies q' is equivalent to '~ q implies ~ p'; and
'q implies p' is equivalent to '~ p implies ~ q':

1. (p ⊃ q) ≡ (~ q ⊃ ~ p)
2. (q ⊃ p) ≡ (~ p ⊃ ~ q)

Table A.1 gives the truth table showing the second equivalence (that for the first is strictly analogous).

Table A.1 '(~ p ⊃ ~ q) ≡ (q ⊃ p)'

	~p	~q	⊃	q	p	⊃	≡
1.	T	T	T	F	F	T	T
2.	T	F	F	T	F	F	T
3.	F	T	T	F	T	T	T
4.	F	F	T	T	T	T	T

This may be derived from Table 8.4 (§320) by (i) accepting the convention that, where p is false, not-p is true; and where p is true, not-p is false, and so, also, for q, and (ii) using the definition table for the equivalence sign '≡', in Table A.2.

Table A.2 'p ≡ q'

p	q	≡
T	T	T
T	F	F
F	T	F
F	F	T

That is, p is equivalent to q where they always have the same truth value, either true or false.

In Table A.1, '∼ p ⊃ ∼ q' is true in lines 1, 3 and 4; and 'q ⊃ p' is true in the same lines, that is, for the same value of 'p' and 'q'. Similarly, '∼ p ⊃ ∼ q' is false in line 2 of Table A.1 (where p is false and q is true) and so is 'q ⊃ p'. These two expressions have the same truth value as one another in every line of the table (for every combination of values for 'p' and 'q') and they are, therefore, fully equivalent.

The significance of the two equivalence relations above with respect to dedutive conditionals is that it explains the cognitive relationship between the members of such pairs of examples as (1) and (3), (2) and (4) above, which depends on them having the same performance relation in terms of cause and effect. If the proposition names in the calculus, 'p' and 'q', are taken as names for propositions describing the occurrence of a cause and of an effect respectively, and not as the names of propositions describing the occurrence of events, then a regular relationship may be recognised between the valid forms of inference realised in deductive conditionals, and the truth tables for 'p ⊃ q' and 'q ⊃ p' in the logical calculus.

However, it is not the underlying performance relations of cause and effect which are realised in the grammar of decutive conditionals, but the knowledge relation derived from them. The major syntactic difference between dependent and main clause realises, not 'what is known': occurrence value of cause as opposed to that of effect; but 'what that knowledge is worth': that is, its status as a necessary or sufficient condition of knowing the occurrence value of the other element (cause or effect) in the performance relationship. The sufficient condition of knowledge of the other is realised in the dependent clause, the necessary condition of knowing the other is realised in the main clause. That is, the grammatical distinction between dependent and main clause realises the logical status of the proposition realised there in terms of 'implying' and 'implied' (antecedent and consequent), and not the identity of the proposition: that is, not the status of the event referred to in that clause in terms of cause and effect.

Hence all four examples have in their dependent clause a description of the occurrence of an event, knowledge of which is sufficient to ensure knowledge of the occurrence value of the event in the main clause.

But 'what is known' differs in each case:

in (1) it is the occurrence of a sufficient cause;
in (2) it is the occurrence of an effect;
in (3) it is the non-occurrence of an effect;
in (4) it is the non-occurrence of a necessary cause.

(1) and (2) are, however, grouped together in the grammar, by having *must* in the main clause, and (3) and (4) by having *can't*.

In deductive conditionals of 'asymmetric polarity' (one clause positive, the other negative) the same possibilities exist for the performance relation to run parallel with, or counter to, that of knowledge. The principles are the same. We need only to note: '$\sim q \supset p \equiv \sim p \supset q$'.

We have seen that *can't* can be interpreted as 'must be that doesn't/isn't'. If we take (5) *If the bonfire didn't light it must have rained*, we are given 'its raining' as a necessary cause of 'the bonfire's not-lighting'. So, the non-occurrence of 'its raining' (failure to occur of a necessary cause) is a sufficient cause of the non-occurrence of the effect, 'the bonfire's not-lighting'; i.e. 'its not-raining' is a sufficient cause of 'the bonfire's lighting'. We can view (5) in this way as realising inference from the non-occurrence of an effect to the non-occurrence of a sufficient cause. If we do this, *must have rained* can be interpreted as 'can't have not-rained/can't not-have rained'. That is, *must* can be seen as 'can't be that didn't'.

The possibility of analysing *must* as 'can't be that isn't/doesn't', and *can't* as 'must be that isn't/doesn't' tends to support the analysis given in Chapter 6, §§266, 268.

Two main points arise from this analysis:

(i)   The dependent/main clause distinction in the grammar realises a relationship in terms of knowledge, and not of cause and effect (occurrence). The dependent clause carries a sufficient condition of knowing the event in the main clause, and this may be either a cause or an effect of its 'happening'.

(ii)   *Must* and *can't* in these constructions do not realise the analytic truth or falsehood of the proposition in which they occur: logical necessity or impossibility. They realise the status of the knowledge which is told of the event/state of affairs described in the proposition: 'necessarily known', not 'necessarily true'.

BIBLIOGRAPHY

Anderson, J.M. (1971). *The Grammar of Case*. London & New York: Cambridge University Press

Anscombe, G.E.M. (1957). *Intention*. Oxford: Blackwell (2nd edition, 1963)

Austin, J.L. (1961). *Philosophical Papers*. London: Oxford University Press (2nd edition, 1970)

Austin, J.L. (1962). *How to do Things with Words*. Oxford: Clarendon Press

Bach, E. & Harms, R.T. (eds) (1968). *Universals in Linguistic Theory*. New York: Holt, Rinehart & Winston

Bar-Hillel, Y. (ed.) (1971). *Pragmatics of Natural Languages*. Dordrecht—Holland: Reidel

Bazell, C.E., Catford, J., Halliday, M.A.K., Robins, R.H. (eds) (1966). *In Memory of J.R. Firth*. London: Longman

Bloomfield, L. (1935). *Language*. London: Allen & Unwin

Bolinger, D.L. (1967). 'Imperatives in English' in *To Honour Roman Jakobson*, I. The Hague: Mouton. 335-62

Boyd, J. & Thorne, J.P. (1969). 'The deep grammar of modal verbs'. *Journal of Linguistics* 5, 1. 57-74

Bühler, K. (1934). *Sprachtheorie*. Jena: Fischer

Burgess, E.W. & Locke, H.J. (1953). *The Family*. New York: American Book Company

Chomsky, N. (1965). *Aspects of the Theory of Syntax*. Cambridge, Mass.: MIT Press

Chomsky, N. (1976). *Reflections on Language*. London: Temple Smith

Cole, P. & Morgan, J.L. (1975). *Syntax and Semantics, Vol. 3: Speech Acts*. New York: Academic Press

Crystal, D. (1966). 'Specification and English tenses'. *Journal of Linguistics*, 2.1. 1-34

Curme, G.O. (1931). *A Grammar of the English Language, Vol. 3: Syntax*. Boston: Heath

Davidson, D. & Harman, G. (eds) (1972). *Semantics of Natural Language*. Dordrecht—Holland: Reidel (2nd edition, 1977)

Davies, E.C. (1967). 'Some notes on English clause types'. *Transactions of the Philological Society, 1967*. 1-31

Davies, E.C. (1968a). 'Aspects of general linguistics'. *Papers of the Programme in Linguistics and English Teaching*. Series I, 8. London: Longman

Davies, E.C. (1968b). 'Elements of English clause structure'. *Papers of the Programme in Linguistics and English Teaching*. Series I, 10. London: Longman

Davies, E.C. (1976). 'A study of conditional, causal and interrogative constructions in English, with reference to situational factors.' Unpublished Ph.D. dissertation. University of London

Dummett, M. (1973). *Frege: Philosophy of Language.* London: Duckworth

Ehrman, M. (1966). *The Meanings of the Modals in Present-day American English.* The Hague: Mouton

Ellis, J.O. (1966). 'On contextual meaning' in Bazell *et al.* (1966: 79-95)

Farber, B. (1962). 'Types of family organisation: child-oriented, home-oriented and parent-oriented' in A.R. Rose (ed.) (1962). *Human Behaviour and Social Processes.* London: Routledge & Kegan Paul. 285-306

Fillmore, C.J. (1968). 'The case for case.' in E. Bach & R.T. Harms (eds.) (1968: 1-88)

Fillmore, C.J. & Langendoen, D.T. (eds.) (1971). *Studies in Linguistic Semantics.* New York: Holt, Rinehart & Winston

Fillmore, C.J. (1972). 'Subjects, speakers and roles' in D. Davidson & G. Harman (eds) (1972: 1-24)

Firth, J.R. (1957). *Papers in Linguistic Analysis, 1934-51.* London: Oxford University Press

Firth, J.R. (1962). 'A synopsis of linguistic theory, 1930-55' in J.R. Firth (ed.) (1962). *Studies in Linguistic Analysis.* Oxford: Blackwell, 1-32

Frege, G. (1952). *Translations from the Philosophical Writings of Gottlob Frege.* P. Geach & M. Black (eds.) Oxford: Blackwell (2nd edition, 1960)

Gordon, D. & Lakoff, G. (1975). 'Conversational postulates' in P. Cole & J.L. Morgan (eds) (1975: 83-106)

Greenberg, J. (ed.) (1966). *Universals of Language.* Cambridge, Mass.: MIT Press

Grice, H.P. (1957). 'Meaning'. *Philosophical Review* 66. 377-88

Grice, H.P. (1968). 'Utterer's meaning, sentence-meaning, and word-meaning'. *Foundations of Language* 4. 225-42

Grice, H.P. (1969). 'Utterer's meaning and intentions'. *Philosophical Review* 78. 147-77

Grice, H.P. (1972). 'Intention and uncertainty'. *Proceedings of the British Academy* LVII. London: Oxford University Press

Grice, H.P. (1975). 'Logic and conversation' in P. Cole & J.L. Morgan (eds) (1975: 43-58)

Halliday, M.A.K. (1966a). 'Some notes on "deep" grammar'. *Journal of Linguistics* 2, 1. 57-67

Halliday, M.A.K. (1966b). *Grammar, Society and the Noun.* Inaugural lecture, University College, London. London: H.K. Lewis

Halliday, M.A.K. (1967a). *Intonation and Grammar in British English.*

The Hague: Mouton

Halliday, M.A.K. (1967b). 'Notes on transitivity and theme in English, Part 1'. *Journal of Linguistics* 3, 1. 37-81

Halliday, M.A.K. (1967c). 'Notes on transitivity and theme in English, Part 2'. *Journal of Linguistics*, 3, 2. 199-244

Halliday, M.A.K. (1967d). *Some Aspects of the Thematic Organisation of the English Clause.* Santa Monica, California: The Rand Corporation

Halliday, M.A.K. (1968). 'Notes on transitivity and theme in English, Part 3'. *Journal of Linguistics* 4, 2. 179-215

Halliday, M.A.K. (1969). 'Options and functions in the English clause'. *BRNO Studies in English* 8. 80-8

Halliday, M.A.K. (1970a). *Course in Spoken English: Intonation.* London: Oxford University Press

Halliday, M.A.K. (1970b). 'Language structure and language function' in J. Lyons (ed.), *New Horizons in Linguistics.* Harmondsworth: Penguin. 140-65

Halliday, M.A.K. (1970c). 'Functional diversity in language as seen from a consideration of modality and mood in English'. *Foundations of Language* 6. 322-61

Halliday, M.A.K. (1973). *Explorations in the Functions of Language.* London: Edward Arnold

Halliday, M.A.K. & Hasan, R. (1976). *Cohesion in English.* London: Longman

Hare, R.M. (1971). *Practical Inferences.* London: Macmillan

Hasan, R. (1968). 'Grammatical cohesion in spoken and written English; Part I'. *Papers of the Programme in Linguistics and English Teaching.* Series I, 7. London: Longman

Hilpinen, R. (ed.) (1971). *Deontic Logic: Introductory and Systematic Readings.* Dordrecht—Holland: Reidel

Hjelmslev, L. (1961). *Prolegomena to a Theory of Language.* Translated by F.J. Whitfield (2nd edition revised). Madison, Wisconsin: University of Wisconsin Press

Hockett, C.F. (1958). *A Course in Modern Linguistics.* New York: Macmillan

Hockett, C.F. (1966). 'The problem of universals in language' in J.H. Greenberg (ed.) (1966: 1-29)

Hodges, W. (1977). *Logic.* Harmondsworth: Penguin

Hook, S. (1969). *Language and Philosophy.* New York: New York University Press

Huddleston, R.D. (1971). *The Sentence in Written English.* London & New York: Cambridge University Press

Hughes, G.E. & Cresswell, M.J. (1968). *An Introduction to Modal Logic.* London: Methuen

Hymes, D. (1972). 'On communicative competence' in S. Diamond (ed.). *Anthropological Approaches to Education.* Ciba Foundation

Isačenko, A.V. (1964). 'On the conative function of language' in J. Vachek (ed.) (1964). *A Prague School Reader in Linguistics.* Bloomington: Indiana University Press. 88-97

Jacobs, R.A. & Rosenbaum, P.S. (eds) (1970). *Readings in English Transformational Grammar.* Waltham, Mass.: Ginn

Jakobson, R. & Halle, M. (1956). *Fundamentals of Language.* The Hague: Mouton

Jespersen, O. (1924). *The Philosophy of Grammar.* London: Allen & Unwin

Jespersen, O. (1931). *A Modern English Grammar* Part 4; (1940). *A Modern English Grammar* Part 5; (1949). *A Modern English Grammar* Part 7. Copenhagen: Munksgaard

Kamp, J.A.W. (1973). 'Free choice permission'. Paper given at a meeting of the Aristotelian Society, London. Nov. 1973

Kelvin, P. (1970). *The Bases of Social Behaviour.* London: Holt, Rinehart & Winston

Kenny, A.J. (1966). 'Practical inference'. *Analysis* 26, 3. 65-75

Klemke, E.D. (ed.) (1968). *Essays on Frege.* Urbana: University of Illinois Press

Kruisinga, E. (1932). *A Handbook of Present-day English* Part 2. English Accidence and Syntax 3. (5th edition). Groningen: Noordhoff

Lakoff, G. (1972). 'Linguistics and natural logic' in D. Davidson & G. Harman (eds.) (1972: 545-665)

Leech, G.N. (1971). *Meaning and the English Verb.* London: Longman

Lees, R.B. (1963). *The Grammar of English Nominalizations.* Bloomington: Indiana University Press

Lewis, D. (1969). *Convention: A Philosophical Study.* Cambridge, Mass.: Harvard University Press

Lewis, D. (1972). 'General semantics' in Davidson & Harman (eds) (1972: 169-218)

Linden, E. (1976). *Apes, Men, and Language.* New York: Penguin

Lindesmith, A.R. & Strauss, A.L. (1968). *Social Psychology.* New York: Holt, Rinehart & Winston. (3rd edition)

Linsky, L. (ed.) (1971). *Reference and Modality.* London: Oxford University Press

Lucas, J.R. (1970). *The Concept of Probability.* Oxford: Clarendon Press

Lyons, J. (1966). 'Firth's theory of "meaning"' in Bazell *et al.* (1966: 288-302)

Lyons, J. (1968). *Introduction to Theoretical Linguistics.* London & New York: Cambridge University Press

Lyons, J. (ed.) (1970). *New Horizons in Linguistics*. Harmondsworth: Penguin

Lyons, J. (1977). *Semantics I*. London & New York: Cambridge University Press

Malinowski, B. (1930). 'The problem of meaning in primitive languages'. Supplement I in second and later editions of Ogden & Richards, *The Meaning of Meaning*. 296-336

Malinowski, B. (1935). *Coral Gardens and their Magic*. London: Allen & Unwin

Mathesius, V. (1928). 'On linguistic characterology with illustrations from modern English' in *Actes du Premier Congrès International de Linguistes à la Haye*. (1928). 55-63. Reprinted in J. Vachek (ed.). *A Prague School Reader in Linguistics*. (1964). 59-67

Mathesius, V. (1936). 'On some problems of the systematic analysis of grammar'. *Travaux du Cercle Linguistique de Prague*. 6. 96-107. Reprinted in Vachek (ed.) (1964: 306-19)

Mead, G.H. (1934). *Mind, Self and Society*. C.W. Morris (ed.). Chicago: University of Chicago Press

Mead, G.H. (1936). *Movements of Thought in the Nineteenth Century*. M.H. Moore (ed.). Chicago: University of Chicago Press

Mead, G.H. (1938). *The Philosophy of the Act*. C.W. Morris (ed.). Chicago: University of Chicago Press

Mead, G.H. (1964). *On Social Psychology*. A. Strauss (ed.). Chicago: University of Chicago Press. (2nd edition revised)

Mitchell, D. (1962). *An Introduction to Logic*. London: Hutchinson

Mitchell, T.F. (1957). 'The language of buying and selling in Cyrenaica: a situational statement'. *Hesperis* 1957. 31-71

Montague, R. (1974). *Formal Philosophy*. Selected Papers. H. Thomason (ed.). New Haven: Yale University Press

Mustanoja, T. (1960). *A Middle English Syntax* Part I. Helsinki: Société Néophilologique

McCawley, J.D. (1968). 'The role of semantics in a grammar' in Bach & Harms (eds.) (1968: 124-69)

Ogden, C.K. & Richards, I.A. (1923). *The Meaning of Meaning*. London: Routledge & Kegan Paul (10th edition 1949)

Palmer, F.R. (1965). *A Linguistic Study of the English Verb*. London: Longman

Partee, B. (ed.) (1976). *Montague Grammar*. New York: Academic Press

Poldauf, I. (1966). 'The third syntactical plan'. *Travaux Linguistiques de Prague* (New Series I). 241-55

Poutsma, H. (1924). *A Grammar of Late Modern English* Part I. (2nd edition 1928). (1926). *A Grammar of Late Modern English* Part II. Section 2.

Groningen: Noordhoff

Quine, W.V.O. (1951). *Mathematical Logic.* (Revised edition). New York: Harper and Row

Quine, W.V.O. (1953). *From a Logical Point of View.* Cambridge, Mass.: Harvard University Press. (Harper Torchbook edition 1963. New York: Harper & Row)

Quirk, R., Greenbaum, S., Leech, G., Svartvik, J. (1972). *A Grammar of Contemporary English.* London: Longman

Rescher, N. (1966). *The Logic of Commands.* London: Routledge & Kegan Paul

Rose, A.R. (ed.) (1962). *Human Behavior and Social Processes.* New York: Houghton Mifflin

Ross, J.R. (1970). 'On declarative sentences'. Jacobs & Rosenbaum (eds) *Readings in English Transformational Grammar.* (1970: 222-72)

Russell, B. (1912). *The Problems of Philosophy.* Home University Library. (Reprinted in Oxford Paperback University Series, London: Oxford University Press, 1967)

Sadock, J.M. (1974). *Toward a Linguistic Theory of Speech Acts.* New York: Academic Press

Sadock, J.M. (1975). 'The soft, interpretive underbelly of generative semantics' in Cole & Morgan (eds) (1975: 383-96)

Salmon, V. (1963). 'Sentence-types in modern English'. *Anglia.* 81, 23-55

Saussure, F. de (1916). *Cours de Linguistique Générale.* Paris: Payot. (5th edition 1962)

Searle, J.R. (1969). *Speech Acts.* London & New York: Cambridge University Press

Searle, J.R. (ed.) (1971). *The Philosophy of Language.* London: Oxford University Press

Searle, J.R. (1975). 'Indirect speech acts' in Cole & Morgan (eds.) (1975: 59-82)

Seuren, P.A.M. (ed.) (1974). *Semantic Syntax.* London: Oxford University Press

Sinclair, J.McH. & Coulthard, R.M. (1975). *Towards an Analysis of Discourse.* London: Oxford University Press

Sinclair, W.A. (1937). *The Traditional Formal Logic.* London: Methuen. (5th edition 1951)

Skyrms, B. (1966). *Choice and Chance: An Introduction to Inductive Logic.* Belmont, California: Dickenson

Stalnaker, R.C. (1972). 'Pragmatics' in Davidson & Harman (eds) (1972: 380-97)

Steinberg, D.D. & Jakobovits, L.A. (eds) (1971). *Semantics.* London &

New York: Cambridge University Press

Stenius, E. (1972). *Critical Essays*. Amsterdam: North Holland Publishing Company

Strawson, P.F. (1952). *Introduction to Logical Theory*. London: Methuen

Strawson, P.F. (1967). *Philosophical Logic*. London: Oxford University Press

Strawson, P.F. (1971). *Logico-linguistic Papers*. London: Methuen

Stryker, S. (1962). 'Conditions of accurate role-taking: A test of Mead's theory' in A.R. Rose (ed). *Human Behavior and Social Processes*. (1962: 41-62)

Sweet, H. (1891). *New English Grammar* Part I; (1898). *New English Grammar* Part II. London: Oxford University Press

Thorne, J.P. (1966). 'English imperative sentences'. *Journal of Linguistics* 2.1. 69-78

Turner, R.H. (1962). 'Role-taking: process versus conformity' in A.R. Rose (ed.) (1962: 20-40)

Vachek, J. (ed.) (1964). *A Prague School Reader in Linguistics*. Bloomington: Indiana Univeraity Press

Vachek, J. (1966). *The Linguistic School of Prague*. Bloomington: Indiana University Press

Vendler, Z. (1967). *Linguistics in Philosophy*. New York: Cornell University Press

Vendler, Z. (1968). *Adjectives and Nominalizations*. The Hague: Mouton

Von Wright, G.H. (1951). *An Essay in Modal Logic*. Amsterdam: North Holland Publishing Company

Von Wright, G.H. (1957). *Logical Studies*. London: Routledge & Kegan Paul

Von Wright, G.H. (1968). *An Essay in Deontic Logic and the General Theory of Action*. Amsterdam: North Holland Publishing Company

Von Wright, G.H. (1971). 'Deontic logic and the theory of conditions' in R. Hilpinen (ed.). *Deontic Logic*. (1971: 159-77)

Wittgenstein, L. (1953). *Philosophical Investigations*. Oxford: Blackwell

Wunderlich, D. (1974). *Grundlagen der Linguistik*. Munich: Rowohlt

INDEX

(Abbreviations for some of the items in the Index are enclosed in square brackets.)

acceptance 33; of teller role 108-9
act 94-5; illocutionary 19, 21, 40;
  locutionary 66
addressee 46, 114 *et passim*
advice 24, 31, 38
affirmation 124, Chapter 6 *passim*
agreement 33, 105, 125
Anderson, J.M. 15, 57, 139
asking (undirected) 114
answer 34
area (of grammar) 77
as: as an alternative to *because* 168;
  in relation to *if* 148
aspect 61, 62-3
assertion 106, 113
assignment (of roles) 50-1. 63; static *v.*
  dyamic (of teller) 107-8
assumptions 19-22, 23, 39-40, 82; of
  item/statement 58-9; assumed
  knowledge 106
Austin, J.L. 15, 16, 18, 19, 31, 32, 41
  n.4, 66
authority: *see* roles

because (*/as*) 168; *because test 175*
belief 132; determinate *v.* indeterminate
  134, 137; *v.* doubt 132; explicit
  132-4, explicit *v.* implicit 132-3;
  implicit 134-7; modality 142-3;
  modals 134-6, 137-8; *v.* prediction
  143; believing 124
Bolinger, D.L. 17

can('t), (capability) 143-4; (decision)
  87-96, (92); (knowledge) 135, 138,
  194
capable performer 19, 21, 40, 42 n.5,
  143-4
cause 17-18, 152-4, 162-6, 172-3,
  189-94
challenge 33-4, 187-8
Chomsky, N. 16, 24, 35
cohesion (intonational utterance linkage)
  108-11; cohesive bonds (in non-polar
  interrogatives) 129; cohesive function

cohesion *continued*
  147, 170
command 24, 27, 30, 37, Chapter 2
  passim
commendation 30
comment adjuncts 106
compulsion 87
conclusion forms 168, 174
concord 64
conditional constructions 17-18, 114-15,
  146-68, 177-8, 189-94; contrary to
  fact 167-8; counterfactual 157-61;
  deductive 162-6. 189-94; double
  decision 147, 149-51; fulfilled: *see*
  reason, constructions of; inductive
  156-7; of decision 147-52; of open
  prediction 152-6, of performance
  152-61; of telling 114-15, 146-7,
  148, 170
congratulation 30
construction (aspect of telling): *see*
  telling
context 18, 37-8; of situation 58
contradiction 33, 105-6, 111, 123-4,
  125; weak *v.* strong 136-7
could(n't), (capability) 144; (knowledge)
  134, 135, 138

decider 40, 48-50, 91, Chapter 4 *passim*
decision Chapters 2, 4 *passim*, 147-52,
  170-2; direct *v.* indirect 82-3; double
  147, 149-51; modal verbs of 86-103;
  operation of 40, 65, 72, 82, 85; plane
  of 81; relayed 91-2
declarative 17, 39, 124, 126, 181, 182
deduction 131, 135, 136; deductive
  conditionals: *see* conditional
  constructions
deep grammar 17, 23-4, 177, 179
denial 124, Chapter 6 *passim*
description 64-7; description sign: *see*
  under sign
directness, levels of 77, 85-6
discourse 33-4, 67, 110-11, 115
displaced speech 60, 80 n.8

distancing: *see* placement
doubt 132-4; doubting 124
Dummett, M. 15, 64, 136

effect 152-3, 162-5, 166, 189-94
exclamation *v.* exclamative 68
exophoric pronouns 58, 59
explanation forms 168, 172, 174

features 39, 79, 179-80
Fillmore, C.J. 15, 57, 58, 139
Firth, J.R. 15, 58
force 15; assertoric 106; -indicating
    devices 64, 71; -indicator 79; sign 71;
    see also: illocutionary force
Frege, G. 15, 64

Grice, H.P. 16, 34, 37, 66, 112

Halliday, M.A.K. 15, 17, 57, 105-7,
    111-12, 139, 179
happening: *see* reason for occurrence
hortatory subjunctive 83-4, 86

if 114-15; closed 147; open 146; related
    to *as* 148, 149, 150; related to query
    148, 150; related to *when* 148
illocutionary force 15, 16, 18, 19, 20,
    25-7, 31, 35
immediate *v.* distanced: *see* telling
imperative 17, 19-25, 39, 40, 69-70,
    72, 83-6, 179-83; jussive *v.* joint *v.*
    fiat *v.* optative: 83-4; *v.* subjunctives
    84-6
implementation (of operations) 68-70
indicative 39, 60
inertia 19, 72, 81, 88, 89, 93
initiative 34, 105; conversational 48
initiator 110
instruction 24
intention 32, 33; relation to significance
    33; utterer's 34-7
interrogative 17, 39, 87, 112, 181,
    184-8; non-polar 55, 107, 128-30;
    polar 51, 108, 126, 130-1
invitation 25, 28

Jespersen, O. 15, 17, 18, 70, 120-1,
    160, 168
jussive: *see* imperative

knower 48-50; Chapter 6 *passim*
knowing, operation of 54, 65, 106,
    Chapter 6 *passim*; double 125-6;

knowing *continued*
    placement of 132; scope of 125;
    sign of 123-4
knowledge Chapter 6 *passim*, 162-8,
    174-5; direct *v.* indirect 123, 124;
    joint 128, 129; plane of 123

Lewis, D. 76, 82
Linden, 60, 178

may, (decision) 74-5, 94; (knowledge)
    134-8, 165-6; (performance) 139,
    141-3, 153-4, 157
Mead, G.H. 43, 45
meaning, interactional *v.* interpretational
    15; interactional 15, *et passim*;
    interpretational 31, 64; lexical *v.*
    grammatical 16; linguistic 15; literal
    mood meaning [LMM] 18, 38-41,
    77-9 *et passim*; literal *v.* non-literal
    (significance) 27; mood meaning
    [MM] 16, 17
might(n't) (belief) 134; (performance)
    144, 157
modality 74; modalities 177-8
modal verbs, of decision 86-103,
    (countermanding 87-96); of
    performance 139-41, 144 n.1, 145
    n.2, (capability) 143-4
mood 15-18, 60, 70, 71, 73, 139, 178
motive 170-2
must(n't), (decision) 87-96 *passim*,
    (92, 93); (knowledge) 134-8, 194

need(n't), (decision) 87-96 *passim*;
    (92-3); (knowledge) 135, 138, 166

obligation 94-5, 100-3, 103 n.3
occupancy: *see* role
occurrence value 67, *et passim*
offer 25
operands 70, 78
operations (*see also* decision, knowledge,
    performance, telling), 17, 54, 56, 65,
    177-8; alternating 125-7; double 55,
    125-6; neutrality to/relevance of 69;
    recursive 76, 117; recursive *v.* double
    125; repeated 125-6 (*see also*
    implementation, placement, sign)
optative subjunctive: 72-3, 83-6
order 25, 29, 40
ought(n't) to, (decision) 100-3;
    (prediction) 144 n.1
overlap of SU/SP 58, 60-3

performance Chapters 2-8 *passim*;
  achieved *v.* unachieved 69; operation
  of 54-5, 65; placement of operation
  of 85; plane of 139; *see also*
  conditionals, reason (for occurrence)
performatives 15, 16, 18, 19, 32, 41 n.4,
  76
performer 48-50, 55, 57-8, 80 n.4
  et passim
permission 24, 27, 87, 88, 89, 90, 94,
  95, 103 ns.1, 2, 3
person 47, 50, 125
placement (of operations) 57, 58, 59,
  69, 70, 82-3, 85, 86, 106-7, 113,
  115-16, 123
planes 76-7, 146, 168, 169, 177; *see
  also under* decision, knowledge,
  performance, telling
polarity (parallel *v.* contrastive in decl.
  + tag) 127
possibility 138
Poutsma, H. 15, 17, 62
prediction, Chapter 7 *passim*; indeterminate *v.* indeterminate belief 143;
  modals of 137, 139, 144 n.1 (core
  members: 139-41, 145 n.2)
  prediction modality 141-2, 144, 153,
  v. belief modality 141; prediction
  conditionals: *see* conditionals
presentation (aspect of telling: [Tp])
  65, 67, 69, 71, 79, Chapter 5, *passim*;
  full *v.* derived 67, 69, 113-5;
  immediate *v.* distanced 69, 70, 113,
  115-6, 120, 122 n.1; (non-
  presentation 70, 159)
primes 17, 18, 78, 178
probability 140-1, 144 n.1, 152-61
  passim
prohibition 87, 103 n.2
proposition, *v.* description 64;
  specification of 128-9
purpose 17-18, 150-1, 170-2, 176;
  v. motive 171-2

query 124-5; selective 128
question 27, 51, 110; open 187-8
Quirk, R. 61, 62, 83, 186

reason 17, 18, 168-9; for deciding 169,
  170-2; for knowing 169, 174-5; for
  occurrence 169, 172-4, 175; for
  telling 169-70
reasoning 60, 177-8
recollection forms 128-9, 184, 185

reference, generic *v.* specific 141, 142
relayed, speech 118-19; decision 91,
  150-1
repeated (quoted) speech 117-18
reply 34, 105, 110, 127
reported speech 116, 119-20
represented speech 120-1
request 19, 25; (polite request double
  decision 149-50, 151)
result 168-75 *passim*
role(s) 16, 17, 40, 42 n.5, 43-57, 177-8,
  passim; assignment of 50-1, 107-110;
  attributes on 40, 57, 78; authority
  55-7, 69-70, 78; combination of
  47, 52-3; family 43-4; institutional
  16, 43, 44, 80 n.3; occupancy of 47,
  50-1, 52-4, 56 *et passim*; occurrences
  of 53-4, 55-7; participant *v.* non-
  participant 46; primary (speech)
  45-7, 50, *v.* secondary 47; secondary
  (socio-linguistic) 17, 47-9, *et passim*;
  separation 55-6, 57; sharing 53-4;
  spread 55; transference of 51, 67,
  105, 107-9, 112-13, 127; universals
  179; *see also under* decider, knower,
  performer, teller
role theory 43-5

Sadock, J. 16, 24
Searle, J. 15, 16, 17, 19, 21, 23, 37,
  39-40
shall (/*shan't*) (decision) 97-9
should(n't) (decision) 100-3;
  (prediction) 144 n.1
sign 67; description 67, 68, 71, 73, 74,
  78-9, 90, *passim*; force sign 71;
  operation 67, 68-72, 73-4, 78-9, 123,
  passim
significance 18; first order [FOS] 26,
  27-8 *passim*, *v.* higher orders 31,
  37-8; higher order(s) 27, 30-1; *v.*
  intention 33; interactional 31, 32,
  37, discourse 34; intermediate level
  of 31; interpretational 31-2; mixed
  32, 34; types of 31-2
so 168
speaker 45-6, 47
speech function 53
stages 18, 78-9
statement 27, 32
subject-predicate bond 64, 68, 156;
  established 141, 144
subjunctive 39, 63-4, 69, 72-3, 74-6,
  83-6, 122 n.1, 160-1

surface grammar 17, 29, 39; 146, 168;
    specification [SGS] 39, 177, 179-80,
    Appendix 1 *passim*
Sweet, H. 15, 17
system network 39, 179, 182, 184

tags 54, 108-9, 125-8, 131
teller 48-50, 51, 91; *see also under*
    role assignment, transference)
telling 54, 65-7 *et passim*; construction
    [Tc] 65-7, 69, 79; distanced 144,
    159; dynamic aspect of 67, 107-9;
    full *v.* derived 67, 69, 113-15;
    immediate *v.* distanced 69, 70,
    106-7, 113, 115-6, 144; imple-
    mentation of 69, 70, 105; placement
    69, 105-7; plane of 105; presentation
    [Tp] 67, 69, 85, 105, Chapter 5
    passim, (non-presentation 70-1);
    recursive application of 117; retelling
    117-21; scope of 111; separate from
    knowing 106
tense, future 139-41; 'imaginative' 70;
    present *v.* past 60-3

therefore 168
third party 46 *et passim*
tonality 106, 111
tone 67, 107-11
tonicity 106, 111-12; marked 130
truncated forms 34, 125

universals 178
utterance linkage, direction of 109, 110

volition 171-2; volitional modals 87,
    96-9
Von Wright, G.H. 91, 94-5, 103 n.3

warning 26-7, 31-2
will/won't (decision) 28-9, 98-9;
    (prediction) 139-42, negation of *will*
    145 n.2, 154
wish (es) 24, 25, 28, 55-7, 81, 86, 88,
    89, 90, 93, 171-2
would(n't) (decision) 99; (prediction)
    144